FREE GIFT

Thank you for purchasing *Humanual.*

I'd like to offer you a free gift that will help you on your journey.
In times of doubt and fear, effectively utilizing your most basic human instincts can
deliver amazing results. I'm sharing with you my powerful breathing explorations to
bring you calm, peace, and insight in uncertain times.

Use the link below to get it now:

www.humanual.com/freegift

PRAISE FOR

HUMANUAL®

"Based on decades of clinical work and astute exploration, Betsy Polatin has, in this book, created a science-informed, concise, and elegantly practical step-wise guide to finding the space within our bodies for our true selves to exist and to expand. She brings us wisdom much needed in our times."

—**Gabor Maté, MD,** the author of *When the Body Says No: Exploring the Stress–Disease Connection* and *In the Realm of Hungry Ghosts: Close Encounters with Addiction*

"The author, Betsy Polatin, takes the reader on a journey of self-discovery, in which we learn how our body moves and relates to gravity. On this journey we uncover our historical choice of either welcoming ourselves into our body or functionally dissociating our sense of self from our physical structure. Humanual *teaches us, through processes focused on movement and awareness of our body, that we can reap the benefits of an embodiment celebrating the continuity among our physical structure, our feelings, our creativity, and our spirituality."*

—**Stephen Porges, PhD,** the author of *The Polyvagal Theory*

"Betsy Polatin has been studying bodies for 50 years—first her own as a dancer and then how people's bodies are affected by and affect their emotions and performance. In this intriguing new book, she integrates a wide range of approaches with her own wisdom and offers powerful, body-focused exercises to get to know and heal yourself. In doing so, you will experience and live more of your life from your expanded Self."

—**Richard Schwartz, PhD,** *developer of the Internal Family Systems model of psychotherapy*

"In Humanual, *Betsy Polatin invites us into a thrilling journey to living in a body. Her extraordinary understanding and training in multiple disciplines brings a unique integration of body therapy, psychology, trauma treatment, and spirituality. The beauty of Betsy's work is that rather than being an abstract expression, it is applicable in everyday life. It will be a book you turn to for thoughtful support and interventions for many years."*

—**Deirdre Fay, LICSW,** the author of *Becoming Safely Embodied Skills Manual* and *Attachment-Based Yoga & Meditation for Trauma Recovery*

"*In* Humanual, *Betsy Polatin provides us with a richly illustrated guided tour to help us connect deeply and consciously to our bodies, minds, souls, and spirits. A dancer by training; a student of movement, music, breath, and meditation; as well as an Alexander Technique Practitioner (among the many disciplines that she has mastered), Betsy in this volume passes on to us the vast wisdom and multiple skills that she acquired over many years working with artists, musicians, and other human beings who are stuck in dysfunctional habits.* Humanual *shows us how the body is organized to move, create, and adapt. However, sometimes our bodies create patterns that may momentarily allow us to cope, but that, in the long term, can transform into character traits that interfere with life's satisfaction. Angry people come to live in angry bodies; and frightened people carry their fears in their muscles, sinews, and bones. 'Every move you make, every thought, manifests as muscular reality.'* Humanual *shows us how to listen to the signals of our bodies, and guides us to shift out of habitual patterns that keep us stuck. This wonderful manual is a trustworthy guide to learn to feel at home within yourself.*"

—**Bessel A. van der Kolk, MD**, the author of the #1 *New York Times* bestseller
The Body Keeps the Score: Brain, Mind, and Body in the Healing of Trauma;
professor of psychiatry, Boston University School of Medicine

"*Enjoy this captivating, compelling book, the result of Betsy's lifetime of questioning, discovery, and pulling together information and knowing in a clear, unique, and practical way. Betsy guides us as grounded theory supports practice in the artistic work she does as a Master Teacher. The benefit to us all is this soulful offering encompassing neuroscience, mind, body, and spirit, with step-by-step counsel that works. Betsy's deep caring for the well-being of everyone on the planet shines through. This book is a gift to us all.*"

—**Ian Macnaughton, MBA, PhD, RCC, FEA, SEP**; the author of *Body, Breath, and Consciousness: A Somatics Anthology*

"*Every once in a while, you find that rare and wonderful book that can truly positively impact your life. This is it. Join Betsy Polatin on this practical and powerful journey to authentically and actively connect to your body, mind, and spirit-self. Her compelling* Humanual *provided the steps I needed to gracefully reclaim the energy and flexibility of my youth. Take a deep breath and welcome in a revitalized connection to the unity of your being. Fabulous and inspiring book!*"

—**Bishop Heather Shea**, CEO and Spiritual Director, United Palace of Spiritual Arts

"*I have seen my technique and sound change tremendously from the time I've been studying* Humanual *teachings with Betsy. I consider myself a completely different singer. I have much more confidence on stage and in myself while singing. Many of my fans and teachers have told me they have heard a huge growth as well. We have worked on tools for stage fright, anxiety, grounding one's self, fatigue, and on and on. As a performer who travels all around the world, these are 'tools' I use very frequently. I wonder how I got through my month-long tours before I studied with her! Before studying with Betsy I had no idea what I was doing to produce sound while playing saxophone or singing. Betsy has such an amazing way of explaining this work. I have been learning the importance of listening to my body. The potential of the* Humanual *teachings for me is endless.*"

—**Grace Kelly**, world-renowned saxophonist, singer, and composer

"In this masterful and encompassing work, Polatin draws on an unparalleled breadth and depth of experience—her work in somatic body practices and the Alexander Technique, yoga, meditation, trauma, breath work, and dance; her long history working with actors and musicians; and her knowledge of neuroscience, biology, physiology, and spiritual practices. Humanual is a remarkable synthesis of this master teacher and somatic body practitioner's life of inquiry and practice. Both an inspirational guide and a practical manual, it offers a clear pathway to genuine transformation, healing, living, and being."

—**Sarah Hickler, MFA,** the author of *In the Moment: A Practical Guide to Movement and Improvisation for Actors;* head of acting, Emerson College

"*Humanual* is a beautifully written masterwork, covering Betsy Polatin's 50 years of experience and knowledge as a dancer, seeker, artist, and teacher of somatic methods, blending the power of intuition, curiosity, creativity, and astute observation. In Humanual we have a wonderful encouraging, playful, confidante companion guide for learning the skills and practices that lead to deep understanding of the physical, emotional, mental, and spiritual point of balance that brings us to our essence, and our potential to live fully as expanded our selves."

—**Licia Sky, BFA, LMT,** artist, musician, bodyworker, and somatic educator

"*Humanual* stands out as one of the most unique and truly integrative books I've seen about discovering your authentic and embodied self. Supported by thorough research and cutting-edge science, Betsy Polatin's work as an international movement and trauma expert is evident in these pages, as she gently and carefully guides the reader through experiences and exercises designed to transform old wounds and pain into the gifts of embodiment, expression, spirit, and oneness. *Humanual* takes you on a heart-centered journey to understanding and utilizing your vast human endowment for love, healing, wholeness, and spiritual unity. This book is a compassionate offering to all of humanity at a time when we need it most."

—**Donald Altman,** the author of *Simply Mindful, Reflect, The Mindfulness Toolbox,* and *101 Mindful Ways to Build Resilience*

HUMANUAL®

(A Manual for Being Human)

HUMANUAL®

(A Manual for Being Human)

*an epic journey to your
expanded self*

BETSY POLATIN

Waterside Productions

ISBN-13: 978-1-949003-78-9 print edition
ISBN-13: 978-1-949003-79-6 ebook edition

Waterside Productions
2055 Oxford Avenue
Cardiff-by-the-Sea, CA 92007
www.waterside.com

Humanual is dedicated
to the continuation of the human race.
May health and well-being become more accessible to all.
Especially the children.

CONTENTS

PART I

EXPANDED SELF

Dynamic Unity of Self, Mind, Emotion, Body, and Spirit

PART II

EXPANDED SELF

Unity in Action

PART III

EXPANDED SELF
Undeniable Unity

FOREWORD

What it means to be a human being is a subject that has engaged, enraged, and perplexed psychologists, anthropologists, and philosophers—for thousands of years. So, what can anyone possibly add to this well-worn topic in a meaningful way? I believe that Betsy Polatin has given us a new lens into this subject. By exploring the tangible role of "embodied expansion," she shows how poorly most of us use our bodies and our being. Here I am referring not only to the physical, anatomical body, but to the living, sensing, and yes, knowing body.

This premise of an innate wisdom is explored in depth and with competence. Polatin draws on her decades-long work with actors, singers, musicians, and athletes—helping them (and all of us) achieve peak performance and realize our unique potential.

Moving the body properly carries multiple opportunities for how we feel, our levels of health and energy, and the equanimity of our emotions. Properly observing ourselves and moving our body efficiently has a bearing on everything we do. Read, experience, and learn what it means to be fully human.

—**Peter A. Levine, PhD,** author of *Waking the Tiger, Healing Trauma,* and *In an Unspoken Voice: How the Body Releases Trauma and Restores Goodness*

YOUR GUIDE

On any journey into unknown territory, it is prudent to have a guide. As a seeker, a teacher, and a healthcare provider, I have traveled many paved and unpaved roads. I also have had many coaches and guides. But, ultimately, I was usually guided by something inside me that knew what to do.

Therefore, I do not want to tell you how or where to find your answers, but rather help you find *your* something inside that guides you. Sure, I could help you shift that pain in your knee, diminish your stage fright, or view your sadness differently, but wouldn't it be better if you knew how to do this for yourself?

That's why I've created *Humanual*—to help you connect deeply and consciously to your body, mind, soul, and spirit. Then you will know what to do to discover and develop your sense of knowing and feeling—*your* something inside. This is the path to your expanded Self, which is about accessing more of your full potential.

I have coached thousands of people from all walks of life, helping them tap into and unleash their amazing potential. I've worked with John Denver, Rashida Jones, Christian Slater, Andre Gregory, Twiggy, LuLu, Jonathan Tucker, and many others who have stood in front of large crowds or a movie camera. I have also taught construction workers, accountants, service providers, doctors, lawyers, athletes, performers, students, teachers, and more. Throughout this time, I've discovered that most of us share a desire to feel better and live our best life.

Wanting to feel better came to me at a young age. In my early teens, I began to follow a macrobiotic diet, eating mainly whole grains and vegetables: I soon had more energy, and fewer mood swings. This improved balance led me to exploring deeper levels of consciousness. In 1966, I was initiated into transcendental meditation after seeing the Maharishi Mahesh Yogi at Harvard Divinity School. I have prayed and meditated with many traditions, studying the wisdom of ancient as well as modern spiritual masters, gaining valuable perspectives on human existence, in stillness and in motion.

As a young dancer in 1968, I took a choreography class with the late Albert Pesso. Al is known as the developer of psychomotor therapy, a body-mind approach to emotional well-being and peak performance. Back then, as a dance instructor, he was working out his technique—exploring on us. He would have us stand in a circle. One person would stand in the middle. Then the person in the middle turned to each of us in the outer circle, holding their arms open as an invitation. Each person in the circle said how this made them feel. Some people felt good, others cried.

I had thought the purpose of choreography classes was to learn how to put together interesting movements to create a dance piece. But instead, I remember understanding consciously for the first time just how much is "said" with body communication, and how powerful movement language is. It was amazing to me how emotions and feelings could be so influenced by the meeting of eyes and the opening of arms.

I will never forget that moment. Something clicked into place, with the body, mind, emotion, and spirit in me relating to those around me, vulnerable and exposed, and yet connected and held. The relationship seemed universal. Nothing was separate in that moment; the boundaries had disappeared. This was a taste of my expanded Self meeting the expanded Self in others. Now, fifty years later, this information is foundational to what I do.

I proceeded to dance, study, and teach movement techniques for many years in New York City. I learned how to listen to signals in my body and how to move most efficiently to feel better, prevent injury and/or recover from one, and I taught what I was learning to others. I often describe myself as a movement specialist, even though my definition of *movement* stretches far and wide.

My unstoppable interest in how we are structured to move in a healthy way led me to more. . . . As a yoga practitioner and teacher, I attended the International Conference of Yoga Teachers in Japan in 1978 and studied with Swami Satchidananda and B.K.S. Iyengar. Living in a yoga dojo, under the rule of a samurai, the training was intense—up early, challenging poses, and little food led to a surprisingly clear mind.

In that same year, I had my first lesson in the Alexander Technique, a body-mind educational process that leads to ease of movement. I have had many wonderful teachers and am now recognized as a master lecturer and teacher in this field, having practiced and instructed for more than forty years.

Through my work with musicians, actors, and performers, I became curious about how to breathe most efficiently. This eventually led me to the late Carl Stough and his breathing coordination principles. After studying with Carl directly for six years, I was named one of twelve people qualified to carry his legacy forward—an honor I shall always cherish. Carl was a true pioneer in the respiratory field who emphasized how work with sound and breath is critically relevant for those with respiratory illness. I also discovered that contrary to popular belief, all voices can learn to sing with the right training of breath. My work with Carl helped me find my natural frequency, and to this day, I help others find theirs.

Still wanting to help myself and others, I began wondering why some people were unable to shift certain habitual patterns. My inquiry into solutions for this led me to the world of trauma healing, where I began learning how to help people who have suffered from traumatic events return to a state of harmony. For the past twenty-five years, I've studied extensively with the world-class innovators in this field, including Dr. Bessel van der Kolk (international trauma expert) and Dr. Stephen Porges (neuroscientist and originator of the Polyvagal Theory).

I explored healing my own past while incorporating this work into mine. I've come to appreciate the principles and life-changing strategies that heal old wounds. I feel especially fortunate for the opportunity to study deeply and extensively, for twenty years, with my teacher, mentor, and colleague, Dr. Peter A. Levine, internationally renowned expert and founder of Somatic Experiencing®, a body-based approach to healing trauma.

At present, I co-teach "Trauma and the Performing Artist" and "Trauma in the Public Eye" with Dr. Levine in New York, Los Angeles, and London. They are thrilling and innovative classes that result in opening up new pathways for individuals to stand in front of someone else or an audience and tell their personal story with less anxiety. Imagine being able to speak your truth from a connected stance.

In summary, *I have spent the last fifty years of my life training, clearing, and exploring.* I now know a great deal about how the body is organized to move; how the mind forms patterns and functions as one with the body; and how spiritual practices affect our body, mind, heart, soul, and overall consciousness. I want to share it. This book is my unique approach—a summation of my observations and experiences, with one additional critical piece: I now emphasize our unity and oneness. I observe the unity, the oneness, that exists within us that no one can take away. Everybody has unity, no matter how challenged or unhealthy. Something in the life force is coordinated and coherent.

Like you, I have laughed, cried, wondered, suffered, and searched. *Over the years, I have concluded that each and every one of us has had to adapt to some kind of block or interference to our expanded potential—by the latter I mean the aspect of us that allows us to experience our freedom, moment to moment.* The most uplifting message I can share with you is this: Adaptive patterns that no longer serve us can be transformed, along with their lingering effects—I've seen it first-hand. The *Humanual* teachings in this book are one very real potential pathway to this end.

PREFACE

It is hard to succinctly define the expanded Self, but I can describe features: all-knowing, fully embodied, clear-thinking, authentic, aware, calm, attentive, rhythmic, and truthful, where every move is just the right effort, connected, coherent, and appropriate for the moment. The vast potential of being human is part of the force that motivates evolution and keeps us moving forward. This force can be tapped to enhance an individual life. The expanded Self, which is what I created *Humanual* to address, allows us to evolve consciously and in accord with our natural structure.

The good news is that since your expanded Self already exists within, you are in possession of a blueprint for organized movement. My job is not to fix you (there is nothing to be fixed) or take you out of your own experience. My job is to accompany you on your journey to rediscovering your essence, providing guidance for your inquiry into your own experiences and sensations. In this sense, *Humanual* is a guidebook for...becoming fully human.

Being fully human simply means that we are consciously allowing the innate, natural order of our particular body, mind, and spirit to be our primary interface with the world. This is in contrast to leading with our adapted, circumstance-made self, which is not the true reflection of who we are, or our potential.

Each of us is unique. In your quest to become and live from your expanded Self, it is crucial to discern and open up to what speaks to and works for you; this is why I'm offering numerous exercises, explorations, and journaling opportunities. The work of this book is your learning experience, with the potential to provide whatever you seek.

The work of *Humanual* is taught through the body-mind-spirit self. The journey to the expanded Self includes exploring many areas: awareness, consciousness, gravity, biology, psychology, evolution, physicality, and human-movement dynamics. I share currently accepted principles—including some resurgent ancient principles that offer great opportunity for expansion. Myths will be broken for you here, and some of the clichéd ideas about our natural design might be cracked wide open.

The *Humanual* way teaches that the body is not separate from the mind, and the body-mind-spirit is not separate from environments, near or far. All the bodily functions and systems—digestive, circulatory, respiratory, nervous, musculoskeletal, and so on—constitute one large network carrying out multiple individual roles to maintain balance and homeostasis, to keep the organism's life-force thriving and resilient. This one network—a microcosm—intertwines with the larger universal macrocosm. For as much as we might argue about our separation, it simply cannot be so; both science and spirituality now confirm this.

The more I work with these principles and their effects in our lives, the more certain I become of the pervasive unity of human functions and abilities, and their vast potential. Today, after teaching a lesson, I am ecstatic with the joy and fullness of doing what I feel I was made to do. Time and space seem to have expanded, my body feels light as a feather, my mind is free of triggers and heavy, negative thoughts. No one thought or feeling sticks to me. They pass into the next moment of consciousness. I am present and I feel part of and one with this amazing, large universe around me. I wish this expanded Self for every human being.

I describe this true moment knowing full well that I do not live in this state all the time, and I don't want readers to think I do. I say it because I want you to know it is possible to experience the unity and oneness of life. I doubt that any human dwells in this state constantly, though you can make that an ambition. The act of living from your expanded Self is something we must practice to recognize. Glimpses or moments of the expanded Self give us something to long for. Many people have fleeting experiences of it and practice to develop their awareness sufficiently to get a feeling of what is possible. So take it step by step, and don't give up! The efforts build upon themselves and bring you closer and closer, making moments of expansion more frequent and predictable.

It is precisely because the expanded Self is so unfamiliar to most of us that I wanted to write *Humanual*. My hope is that these descriptions, explorations, and reminders of the ever-present unity will trigger greater awareness and a desire to look more deeply into one's habitual and conditioned responses and thoughts. Simple changes of body position and use, made and maintained with awareness, can create big changes in a life. It can also profoundly alter the way we view and treat each other.

I focus on the practical effects and wonders of expansion, but I am not unaware of the egregious evil and wrongdoing that humans are capable of. Betrayal, deceit, and lying go on in the human mind and in societies throughout the world. When we face up to this fact and strive to understand our shadow, or nonvirtuous, side, we can become a force for powerful change, holding our shadow together with virtue.

Despite the civil rights movement and social changes gained in recent decades, humans remain pitted against other humans because of skin color, beliefs, gender, and so much more. These issues seem even more polarized today. If there was ever a time for us to explore our shared reality of being *human*, it is now. After all, we are human first...prior to creating the identities that compel us to see "others" as other.

I do not talk much in this book about the issues of discrimination, class inequality, and gender identification, which constitute significant challenges or even perceived obstacles to our full expansion of self. I am faced with these issues frequently in my work as a master lecturer in a major urban university. I believe, however, that as each individual connects to his or her expanded Self, they will find their chosen path to effectively address these challenges in their own lives and thrive nonetheless, whether it be fighting tooth and nail, or posting on social media, or taking a nonviolent but vocal stance, as Gandhi did. Perhaps yours is a completely private realization of the expanded Self that ushers in contentment and peace at last.

The journey to your expanded Self is the journey to *you*. It is your greatest potential, and it's already in you. If you want to know it, you absolutely can. All that is required is an open and willing mind and heart and a spirited exploration. Please join me.

INTRODUCTION

I was working with a singer at the Opera Institute one day when I noticed that her upper ribs were not moving. I said, "You know these ribs can move." She smiled, a little embarrassed, and replied, "I need a manual for this body."

She meant an instructional guide for moving the human body. And you have that here. But, as you will see, *Humanual* is so much more. Moving the body properly carries multiple ramifications for how we feel, our levels of health and energy, and the equanimity of our emotions. Properly observing ourselves and moving our body has bearing on everything we do.

Being human is more than just moving through a day, eating and surviving. Within us, there is a natural impulse to create, to expand, to be more. Humans are able to act on the desire to improve their lives, and to make hopes and dreams come true.

Humans fight for what they believe in. We've learned how to cooperate, to help, and to put up with one another; we've even learned to love one another. Is that what drove human evolution?

Humans are the ones who tell stories. We pass on traditions from generation to generation. We have the imagination to create the myths, the archetypes, and the language to talk about it. Psychiatrist and trauma expert Bessel van der Kolk says it well: "Despite our excitement about the linguistic feats of chimpanzees and rhesus monkeys, only human beings command the words and symbols necessary to create the communal, spiritual, and historical context that shapes our lives."[1]

But is that changing? Many lives now are disembodied and lived through technology. Devices dictate. As I teach any group of younger people, I see addictive symptoms. There is anxiousness and fidgeting and sometimes great struggle to wait for the end of class, when they can be reunited with their phone. For all the blessings that technologies bring, it remains to be seen if we can move into a technology-centered culture and still be able to embrace and expand our humanity.

Will people in younger generations live only in their heads and send brief text messages while ignoring bodily messages? Will face-to-face communication be a rarity instead of a human imperative? Being human includes being present, with organic consciousness, and being able to touch another heart with yours through in-person communication. It would be a shame to lose this. Some scientists believe that a robot will be developed in the near future that will be able to feel and express this communication and love.[2] Do you think true humanity can be manufactured? Time will tell if technology can improve upon the unity of body, mind, and spirit.

I find it very telling, and also very sad, that in our society and language we do not have one word for the collective expanse of this holistic trio. As a movement and breathing specialist, when I watch someone walking, I see the body moving, the mind thinking, and the spirit guiding. Although body-mind-spirit cannot be separated, you sometimes lead with one or another.

1. Emphasizing the physical body, this book offers awareness techniques, movement exercises, and tips on how you are designed to function and move. I have witnessed that the vast majority of people have no idea how the body functions optimally, even those who talk about the body. How do you stay upright within a gravitational field? How can you breathe to circulate and absorb the most oxygen?

   Humanual presents simple practices to help you comprehend that we are embodied beings, with a magnificent and very efficient, specific structure and organization. If your body has aches and pains after you walk your dog or perform your gym routine, you can be sure there is some kind of inappropriate movement, or over-efforting. We do not have discomforts for "no reason." In order to function as our best self, we must first learn how we function best.

2. For the mind and through the mind, you learn to watch habitual thinking patterns. With *Humanual*, you will have the opportunity to tap into and shift psychological behaviors developed in your past. The body reflects your patterned thoughts, and there is constant bidirectional communication between mind and body. Any patterns that you discover can be changed with a variety of methods and therapies, some simpler than others. Neuroscience has proven and wisdom traditions have long known that witnessing and watching yourself and your

thoughts can reveal a vast amount of inner sensations, self-knowledge, and intuitive insights. Just learning to train your mind to focus on one object or process, such as watching your breath, can be invaluable for restoring balance and guiding you on your journey through life.

3. When leading with the spiritual, the journey includes questions of human existence, mindfulness, and meaning. Exercises explore meditation, spiritual practices, generosity of heart, and delicate perceptions that grace the path. These practices reveal the soul, the persistent background support of the expanded Self that connects to all nature and beings. Part of human existence is the element of mystery; what is *it* all about? And do I do it, or does it do me? Both exist. Doesn't this say it all: *"Trust in God and tether your camel."*

Integral to using your body, mind, and spirit is the way you function under stress. Life has its difficult moments; no one is free from them. Relationships, both casual and intimate, can be challenging to navigate. There is loss, illness, and just plain miscommunication. And we tend to hold on to these negativities.

We also tend to be negatively affected by our traumas, our deeply distressing or disturbing experiences. Trauma can occur at any time in life, but because of our lack of self-sufficiency, we are greatly influenced by our childhood experiences. As babies and children, we needed food, love, and shelter, and we did what we needed to do to get that, and to survive.

Childhood trauma affects every part of one's self—mind, body, soul, and spirit—and brings about mental, emotional, and physiological patterns, called *adaptive patterns*. Employed successfully in the moment as a way to protect us from a distressing life experience, the patterns can turn out to be costly in the long term, from both a behavioral and health standpoint: they affect how we respond to everything in life.

To access and utilize our expansive, multifaceted self, we need to become aware of the patterns that are locked in the body, identifying the cause and where we are stuck. Then we must discover the key to turning it around. *Humanual* gives concrete instruction on both, facilitating change in habitual responses, *so that you do not have to continue to reinforce the patterns that bind you to repeating the physical, mental, and emotional responses based on a past experience.*

No matter what the adaptive presentation and how many layers cover it, the expanded Self is there—I know it is in everyone. This is the most radical aspect of my practice. When I work with people, I always recognize their expanded Self; I do not just address their aches, pains, and habits. I address the unity.

Most people have adapted to a limited version of themselves, through no fault of their own. Your task, if you choose it, is to find your way back, following the steps for unraveling these various contractions so that you can recognize and move with a more expanded version of yourself. Choosing to be free from habit is a human gift. Many of us need help with this, and professional guidance is recommended when patterns feel intransigent, and we are not able to see our potential.

There is an order to the universe. Similarly, the mind, the body, the emotions, and the spirit have specific evolutionary designs that allow ease: maximum function with minimum effort. When we don't follow our natural design, *dis*ease is the result; it's a warning signal that something is off.

In addition to the specific order, there is always the unknown, the mystery, and the chaos. In nonlinear science, there are too many variables and complexities for true predictability. However, when we access the built-in intelligence and order, we can meet the existing unpredictability with greater support, and we can arrive at being one with life and love, meeting them in each moment.

Every day, new pathways to salvation and healing are touted. What works? The question is, *what works for you?* How can you live a healthy, coherent, human life on your journey to your expanded Self? Those are questions I hope to help you answer with this book.

Start with this nugget of wisdom from movement pioneer F.M. Alexander: "Come to a full stop, and believe in the unity of all things."[3]

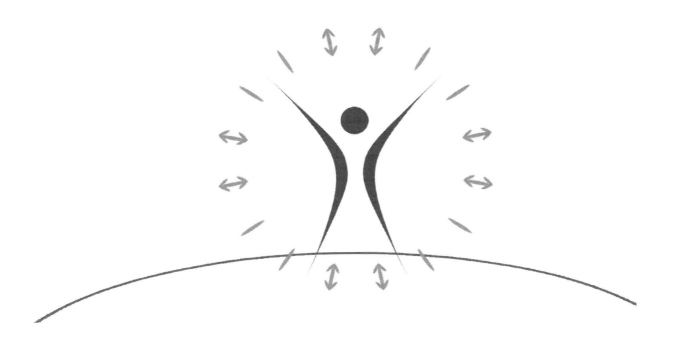

PART I

EXPANDED SELF

Dynamic Unity of Self, Mind,
Emotion, Body,
and Spirit

THE EXPANDED SELF ARISES FROM UNITY

In this chapter, I collect some key guiding principles and offer my vision and approach to the journey of human life and its expansive potential. The background on how I came to teach what I am teaching will illustrate and preview the exploratory synthesis you are undertaking.

1. YOUR EXPANDED SELF

Each of us has an everyday self that we assume our self to be. But what if there is more to us than meets the eye? What if there is an *expanded* version of our self that includes not only the habitual patterns, the lost parts, and the innate organization but also a connection to the grand, scintillating space of the universe and the possibilities it offers us?

One of the most frequent phrases I hear from clients after I have worked with them is, "I feel like I have more space inside." With that opening comes a look of wonder that sparkles—a taste of an expanded version of self. I find that with the right kind of knowledge and support, this expansive human experience can become more common.

A good deal of conversation today is focused on human potential. So far, such discussions center on the brain and have not prioritized our physicality, but it is essential to our humanness *and* the workings of the mind. There are two basic ways of "moving" through life: One way is through our innate, organized, primary design; the other is through the voluntary, created, efforted undertaking. Whichever way we move affects us physically, mentally, emotionally, and spiritually. Most people live in a mode of too much effort, stress, and strain, or too little effort, which is a form of collapse. There is a point of balance, and accessing it enables us to walk the line between over-efforting and under-efforting.

Then, with this harmony, you are so alive, vibrant, responsive, compassionate, and connected. When you speak from this place, you use the right words; and when you move, you move with just the right amount of energy and motion. All systems are synchronized. This innate organization can be tapped no matter what we do or where we are in life; and it is present in health, illness, or life challenges. I call this phenomenon the expanded Self, with a capital "S." When I use a small "s" for self, it is usually for one partial aspect of Self. The expansion can be spatial or an opening of possibilities.

The expanded Self is an innate internal organization—a profound yet ordinary unity of body, mind, soul, and spirit that is health and well-being, our birthright. To say it another way, the potential of the expanded Self is the *synchronized embodiment*, the full expression of your humanity. But access to it can become limited, blocked, or desynchronized through the accumulation of difficult experiences and our subsequent adaptations, which often include some form of bodily contraction.

When someone enters my studio, I see their potential and their wholeness. Yes, another person can look at you and see your expanded Self, even if you don't see it or feel it. When I look at the body in front of me, it's not just a body that I see. It is an evolved human being with a history, a host of life events, archetypes, and a story. It is both spiritual entity and biological being, embracing millions of years of evolutionary changes. And even though I am using the body as the "doorway" to a person's vast matrix of knowledge, gifts, memories, and experiences, what I do is not body work, and I am not a "body worker." In fact, in my world, there is no such thing since body, mind, and spirit are always connected.

It goes much deeper than this. Some of our greatest motivations, intuitions, and emotions move the body. The spirit moves the body. The mind moves the body. Every thought and experience manifests as a muscular reality. To move your arm, you need to think first, before the action can take place.

Most of us miss this level of detail in our busy, day-to-day experience. However, as you begin to practice looking around and sensing yourself in relation to your environment, you will discover more and more of these layers in yourself. *The body is the medium for the deepest knowing.*

Thirty-five years ago, one of my colleagues, a teacher at Berklee College of Music, asked me to substitute-teach for her Alexander Technique voice class. I was thrilled by the invitation, because I have always enjoyed and been involved with music in one way or another. Intrigued by the idea of exploring voice related to movement, I had the singer sing. Then I did some hands-on work with her to illustrate other possible ways to approach singing, an experience outside of her habitual breath and body pattern. This was all pretty routine, so far. Then something quite extraordinary happened. All of a sudden, I could hear the sound her voice was going to make before she opened her mouth to sing! Her whole-self emanated, or reverberated, this sound. The exact frequency and vibration radiated out of her in such a way that her body was no longer separate from the air around her that carried her sound. I was fascinated. Then she began to sing and there it was—her sound was exactly as I had perceived it. That moment revealed to me, in a very deep and visceral way, the unified interpersonal network in each of us, beyond everyday perception. I was able to expand my subjective experience of myself to include another person, sometimes called a *biofield*.[4]

How and where one acquires the ability to perceive this, I'm not sure. Perhaps I was born with ability in this direction; and many years of studying, training, and working with others helped to uncover this innate talent. Doing hands-on work with so many people, and correlating the bidirectional communication between body and mind, has certainly opened a channel to deeper perception in me and my clients and students, facilitating awareness of their expanded Self and greater embodiment of it.

I believe that everyone, including those who have had to ignore (disconnect from) their expanded Self to adapt to their environment to survive, can learn to put their attention within themselves in some (even small) way that connects to this unity of self and surroundings. These skills can be learned and practiced. It is not only possible to remove the cloud cover and recognize moments of oneness, or nonduality, in this everyday dualistic world, it is inevitable—if you open to it.

The unity that is our essence can be felt, perceived, or experienced, but it's not something you can make happen. You can't will or force the expanded Self because it is ever-present; it's always there. You simply need to tap into it. And when you get a glimpse of it, something miraculous happens: Every word, movement, and breath is purposeful, precise, and present with what is going on for you; your mind becomes clear with less anxiety, and your spirit feels alive, with no limiting boundaries. *Nothing is stiff, held, or fixed, unable to move in the next moment to respond to whatever life brings your way.*

2. LOSS OF UNITY AND HOW WE RECOVER IT

You can be sure that the departure from oneness, or unity, shows up in patterns formed in the brain, body, and psyche. Some of the body patterns you can see. They also show up in the mind, emotions, and spirit, which you can't see. This new, adaptive network then becomes your default and filters out so much of your experience. The dilemma is that we make ourselves small and then struggle to be part of the larger oneness that exists. By evolutionary design, however, the potential for freedom and ease is hidden underneath discomfort. In the work we are doing here with *Humanual*, we are bringing to light adaptive psychological and musculoskeletal patterns to reveal the connected unity and expansive nature that lies within.

One day, I sat in the Apple store with a malfunctioning computer. The young man at the "Genius Bar" was asking me about how much I use my computer, what I use it for, etc. I told him that I have been writing a lot. He asked, "What are you writing?" I told him about *Humanual*. The first thing he said was, "I have terrible posture," as he showed me his slumped-down stance. Given my work, this was not the first time I have heard this comment, or been given the opportunity to witness this type of gesture. Then I asked him what other options he had. He immediately stiffened up into a military-like upright posture. I asked him if that worked for him. He said, "No." I showed him the *Humanual* option of lengthening up with ease through his whole back. He was curious and interested, excited to learn a new perspective on what seemed to be an age-old problem for him.

I never tell anyone to go directly into a more upright stance because the response would be a forced manipulation, like the one performed by the young man in the Apple store. It led to further loss of unity. Instead, the process involves deep somatic inquiry, paying attention to your bodily rhythms and responses, including sensations and images. This naturally leads to the recognition of habits and patterns—emotional, physical, and otherwise. And it includes an aspect of "non-doing," which is stopping and observing how we express, or embody, our experience. The young man in the Apple store was collapsing down in his chest with his "terrible posture." He needs to be aware of that pattern and allow the collapse to change, before he is able to lengthen with ease. The order here is important.

I do want to be clear that the manipulation of the body that most people do to recover unity and correct themselves is not an efficient way to move through life, nor does it match our human design. Understanding the effects of these types of exaggerated corrections of posture and comprehending how form and function really meet are key objectives of mine. In a very basic sense, *Humanual* is a myth-breaker: The old "pull your shoulders back" or "chin up" idioms do not match how the body functions best. Nor is the oft-heard command "stand up straight" ever interpreted elegantly. Many of these idioms create a network of disunity. I offer a more integrated, organic approach.

Deep inside each of us is a voice, or consciousness, that can detect positive change. I have always found it interesting to watch students observe and know that a change is positive. How do they know? No one ever taught them this. One student, for example, was standing too far forward, leaning over her toes. When I showed her how to distribute her weight over her entire foot, she let out a huge sigh of relief. How did she know this was better for her? It is built in; it's our innate capacity to recognize and aim toward the direction of health and well-being—a truth-o-meter, so to speak. In any moment we experience this, we realize that the unity network is lasting, solid, and grounded in Truth and connection to ourselves, each other, and the universe at large. This anchors us in our own gifts and gives us agency to move forward in our lives.

To return to unity, try this: Notice the movement in your torso for your breathing, either by feeling it from inside or putting your hand on your chest to feel it.

Is there any movement at all? If so, where? Watch it.

Does it change as you observe it? If so, how?

Now recognize that as your lungs fill with air, they move, and that movement can spread. Can you feel that slight opening on each inhale? Try not to force, push, or pull.

Release fully on each exhale.

Stay with it. Your breath has the potential to feel like water moving through sand in your body. Notice changes, perhaps starting in your chest and radiating throughout, and moving the air around you.

Look around the room with this subtle but dynamic change. Notice shapes, colors, and objects. This simple exploration brings a possibility of presence, rhythm, and unity, and connection to the world around you.

Simple as it may be, you have just connected your inner world to the outer and begun the journey to your expanded Self. I hope this sparks your curiosity.

I know that for some people the idea of becoming aware and feeling inner embodied sensations seems strange and impossible. Your first response might be, "I don't feel anything. What is she talking about?" I will address this with a few different choices.

You can imagine what it would feel like, and explore that. Or you could behave like an actor and pretend you are another person who lives in these imaginary circumstances, and can feel inside. These are viable strategies for feeling your way into unfamiliar territory. Also, you could start very simply. Start to notice your breath. Can you notice any movement? If you are alive, there is movement! Then begin to notice: Is the movement fast or slow, easy or labored, soft or hard? All these observations bring you to notice what is happening inside, so you can eventually choose to change it, or allow it to change.

3. PREPARATION FOR THE JOURNEY

The journey to your expanded Self is no different from the journey of human life; you meet challenges, and life is full of them. However, there are some larger points of view and many helpful practices that you can learn in order to help alleviate the pressures associated with these challenges and, potentially, make the journey that much more enjoyable.

Perhaps the biggest challenge to consider as we begin is the brain's built-in bias toward negativity. It's actually not a bad thing. From an evolutionary perspective, we see that the brain is set up to operate this way, to look for what's wrong, *or different*. This is part of an elaborate, unified mechanism to ensure our survival.

In small, reasonable doses, this *negativity bias* is not a sign of mental instability or depression: We naturally jump to negative conclusions. And you do not have to feel bad about always thinking unpleasant events are going to happen, especially as you watch your teenage son drive off in the family car, right after receiving his driver's license. Of course, you might imagine the worst; we are vulnerable creatures.

But all of this is a result of what was important for human evolution as our brain developed. In evolutionary terms, it is more prudent to look out for something dangerous approaching, because if you don't, that might be the end of you. Your awareness, thoughts, senses, and body movement all tune in to the danger. Looking out for something good, on the other hand, is not a priority, as your life does not depend on it, and you can look at these things another time, after the "danger" has passed. That is why if ten good things happen and one bad thing happens, what do you remember? The bad thing.

This perspective was necessary for our ancestors, but how necessary is it for us today? Neuroscience tells us that, indeed, we can adapt our brain bias to suit modern life. Since we are no longer being tracked and hunted by tigers, there are practices that can help us adopt a more expanded view, including making more space for positive reflections and experiences.

Another sizable challenge (some would say "obstacle") impacting our journey to our expanded Self is the widespread lack of knowledge and proper education on how our body works. This particular issue has puzzled me for as long as I can remember. Childhood education includes cognition and emotion, but there is no training for motor development or the body in action. Our bodies are wholly fundamental to our enjoyment of life. Wouldn't it make sense, then, for all of us to learn more about them?

We need a change in mindset that can acknowledge the inherent wisdom and intelligence of these magnificent creations we call "body." Given the proper conditions, the body can heal itself. What are these conditions? That is the purpose of *Humanual*: to provide a guide for accessing the expanded Self, so that the potential of health becomes more available.

A few years ago, I watched Dr. Peter A. Levine, my mentor and colleague in trauma-resolution work, give a session to a woman who was depressed. Depression as a feeling state will show up in the body as some kind of compression, or shortening, typically in the midsection of the body. After one of the exercises he had her explore, her spine lengthened spontaneously. He noticed it and so did she. He then pointed out that the lift in her now-lengthened spine and the depression that was held within her torso could not coexist; it was a neurophysiological impossibility. In other words, since compression and expansion are reciprocal states, they cannot both be present at the same time.

Wouldn't anybody with depression or anxiety, or any other ailment, want to know this physiological reality? Of course, it matters how you get the length in your spine. If you just stiffen yourself up into "good posture," that will not relieve depression because it is not the genuine lengthening that Dr. Levine facilitated and witnessed in his client. *Humanual* will teach you how to get the spontaneous lengthening, and as you use the technique, you might find any number of pleasant results.

Another key challenge in maintaining our connection to our expanded Self is that most people are so out of touch with their body. When we tighten or constrict the body for a long enough time, we become unable to actually feel it (explained in detail in Chapter 7). As this occurs, the body becomes more of an object that we carry around, rather than a source of feedback and intelligent information. In this book, I use the word *tension* in its commonly applied context as a noun, but in reality, in reference to your physicality, it is only a verb, *tensing. Your body is not a static object that you feel. You don't feel your body. You feel your current state of organization.*

There is also a tendency in our culture to objectify the body, as if "it" is a separate thing from the rest of us: "This shoulder" or "the shoulder" hurts, instead of "my" shoulder hurts. It may seem like simple semantics to you, but the implications are much more widespread. Along the same lines, "I have a bad back" implies that the back is not a part of you and, as such, you only have a distant relationship with it and no authority over it. It's not even you. Is this thing you have, called a "back," really bad? You can see how thinking in this way could prevent you from addressing whatever bodily challenges you might have. (In *Humanual* work, it would be more accurate to say, "I did something today that strained my back." Or you might contemplate, "This is how I tensed my back when I was a child and the environment was challenging.")

When we speak about our body as if it is one with us, we empower ourselves to see and respond in a unified manner. When we objectify the body, we lose feeling, and when we lose feeling, we lose our ability to empathize with our self and others.

Early on in my teaching at Boston University, a young man registered for my class in the Alexander Technique. He was in ROTC, the Reserve Officers' Training Corps. After a few classes, he told me that he had to drop the course. He said that he wanted to focus on building muscle and firming up his body (so that he would not feel); this, of course, was to prepare him for battle. Because taking my class increased his capacity to feel what was going on inside him, it simply wouldn't work for his goal.

There is a dehumanization, or separation—a biological or musculoskeletal dissociation, a type of desynchronization—that happens when we view our bodies as being separate from the rest of us. Our various biological and muscular systems will not fully work in sync, as we lose balance and feeling.

4. PRINCIPLES AND THEMES TO GUIDE YOUR JOURNEY

A number of principles and themes guide my personal and professional life. I'm presenting them briefly here, so that they are in mind as we proceed. I will elaborate on each of these throughout the rest of the manual.

As a movement specialist, I observe cues that show up as Self, Movement, Mind, Emotion, Body, and Spirit responses. I pay attention to the raw footage, the state of the person I see in front of me, and give much less attention to the story he or she is telling me. Someone may say he feels calm, for example, but I can see his foot madly tapping away. This is his version of calm.

With this manual, you will access physical shifts through awareness of your own embodied sensations. These changes are stimulated by your own inquiry. What am I doing that is causing me to feel this way? I may prompt you, for example, to connect thoughts with what you notice in your body. Following those sensations will lead to the next step. Spend some time pondering the questions in the manual, rather than just reading them; this offers the best opportunity for insight.

Support, Suspension, Breath

Support, suspension, and multidimensional breath are three main principles or concepts woven throughout the book. I call them *Humanual* Basics™.

Support: Many people talk about support. That is because it is crucial on so many levels—physical, emotional, spiritual, and psychological. I include an even larger picture. *The Humanual version includes embodied tracking of your inner supportive sensations combined with universal forces of gravity and antigravity.* Our life is here on Earth in the physical plane, and we are connected physically to the planet for support. We receive support from planet Earth. We are also connected interpersonally to many others and receive support from them. Begin to observe the various sources of support in your life.

Suspension: There is always a slight expansion from the inside, no matter how your body is configured. *Suspension in Humanual is the concept that all the muscles are slightly lengthened for balance and efficient functioning, with a movable balance between expansion and contraction forces.* You expand and then you meet your own resistance. In the human body and experience, as in nature, there is a continuous play between these forces. We reach to expand and are held back by constriction. The tensegrity model explained in Chapter 9 exemplifies this perfectly—expansion with boundaries, in a web of suspension. Begin to wonder about your own suspension and your ability to expand within.

Breath: There are many varied approaches to breathing. Without breath, there is no human life. *Your breath reflects your every thought, emotion, and movement.* It connects you to the environment and every other living thing on planet Earth. Your breath is so close to you, intimately moving in all directions within you, echoing your state; this is the principle of "multidimensional breath." Begin to wonder about how you experience your own breath.

Additional Themes

The following themes (summarized in the phrases or words in italics) are interspersed throughout *Humanual*.

Unity of the expanded Self: Unity is the oneness within each person, and the Oneness that connects everything and everybody. Every individual's oneness encompasses *Self, Movement, Mind, Emotion, Body,* and *Spirit*. This biological *unity* is inherent and always available in your system.

Habits and *patterns* form as we adapt to our surroundings out of necessity. These adaptive patterns are shaped early in life and typically stay with us until we address them, forming much of our character. Many students talk to me about getting rid of their bad habits. I tell them, "There are no 'bad' habits. You did what you needed to do to survive. The habit or pattern is just outdated now and no longer serves you."

In this work, you observe how you find *balance* in your work life, your relationship life, and your physicality. Noticing aspects of yourself such as patterns and balance requires developing *conscious awareness*, which allows you to recognize your interpretation of what is going on in the moment; it is attention and presence, and involves the whole of one's being. Easy to say, but less easy to do. How much conscious awareness are you bringing to your day: How much are you thinking, feeling, or sensing?

This consciousness involves a good portion of *sensory awareness*. Sight, hearing, taste, touch, and smell (the five primary senses) tell us a lot about our world and our desires. Sensory awareness also encompasses other senses, including but not limited to: the kinesthetic sense, the awareness of our own muscle movement, and the proprioceptive sense, which is awareness of the movement of our joints and inner space.

Sensory awareness, like conscious awareness, is a whole-self experience. *Collective consciousness* expands awareness to other people, the environment, and the larger world around us; and it is a big influence, whether we acknowledge it or not. Everything is connected energetically, according to ancient wisdom as well as modern neuroscience and quantum physics research. *Connection* is real, and it is a theme of this book and work. You'll learn to use connection to your advantage.

To do or not to do? *Choice* is a big part of life. To not do something is as much of a choice as to do it, and sometimes the better choice. I've noticed that we overexert (push) ourselves as a regular course of action; this is against the nature of the expansion, which is all about flow. Do you exercise your right to choose? Do you exercise your right to say "No"? In terms of connection, what do you choose to filter out or push aside? Do you even notice?

Safety is essential to an expanding Self. No one is able to direct their life toward health and well-being unless they feel safe. If you are a teacher or therapist, create a safe, welcoming space for your student or client, so change can occur comfortably and naturally. If you are working through this book on your own, do the same thing for yourself. If you find yourself in a vulnerable or defensive mode, take time to restore safety in your body and environment. Begin to explore when you feel safe in life.

One of the key aspects of any journey is *inquiry*, and we may find ourselves frequently asking "Why?" or "What?" Always question and be curious about your own experience, as this will help you navigate your current path and discover new ones.

Stillness (non-doing) is a sublime state. Responding appropriately in the moment, in a nonreactive way, is an advanced skill that can be learned. Pausing in the moment between stimulus and response allows us to connect with our innate biological wisdom to formulate a suitable and even elevating response, rather than reacting from our adaptive self and our associated ego.

Sometimes a *miracle* occurs. If you put two ideas together, you get a third totally different idea. There is an element of alchemy to life: transmuting everyday experiences into something substantially more engaging and valuable. Do you see the tiny and not-so-tiny miracles in your own life?

5. *HUM JOURNAL*

I strongly recommend that you create a journal for this journey. Use paper or a computer. I am calling it a **HUM Journal**, short for *Humanual*, but also for that soft voice that is like a hum in the back of your mind, telling you what you are thinking and feeling. As you track your observations of Self, Movement, Mind, Emotion, Body, and Spirit, you will gain insights on how to better access your expanded Self. Notice energy, patterns, and relationships as well as beliefs, emotions, and thoughts.

Notice physical states and changes. You may write one day that your arm cannot move independent of your shoulder. In a few weeks' time, you may write that you have developed the skill to make space between your arm and shoulder, and that your arm is moving more freely and efficiently.

You can keep it simple, or you can explode with creativity and take photos of images of what you feel like one day, or how you feel after an exploration. Or you can write music or sing a song to convey your observations, and record them. A short theater piece, an art installation, or authentic movement are other creative ways to express your experience of the journey. "This is how I experience myself today." One day, the photo may be of the brightly shining sun; another day the photo may be a boxing match.

I suggest **HUM journal**ing in many places throughout this book, and it is your choice as to when and what to express. Most important, allow the artist in you to help create your experience.

EX-PLORATION: WAKING UP AND GETTING OUT OF BED

When you see "EX," I am presenting you with an EX-ploration or EX-ercise. Below is the first of the explorations or observations we will carry out to learn more about the body-mind-spirit. I share sample **HUM Journal** entries as guides for what you might consider noting or documenting. The exercises are not the sweaty "no pain, no gain" type. You will simply be paying attention to your thoughts, sensations, and movements, and being curious about the information.

A. Waking Up.

When you first wake up, lie in bed flat, or with your knees bent and your feet flat. Place both hands on your chest, your heart area, and lie there paying attention to your breathing for a few minutes. Notice any small changes.

SAMPLE *HUM JOURNAL* ENTRIES THAT I MAY WRITE:

I woke up and my muscles were tight, especially my leg muscles.
I felt a bit anxious about a conversation from the day before.
After a few minutes of breathing, my muscles released a little;
they just changed direction from constriction to expansion.
I felt a bit less anxious and some overall settling.
My mind seemed freer and more open to the day.
And it took only a few minutes.

OR

I took a photo of the tree outside my window to remind me of this settled state,
and I looked at it a couple of times in my day when I needed it.
Very simple, very practical, and it didn't take much time.

OR

I woke up, my muscles are tight and I'm in a rush, and late for work.
I'm going right into my day anyway, not doing breathing.
Leave me alone; I don't want to pay attention today.

B. Rolling Over.

Roll on your side to get out of bed. Listen to your breath for a moment. Feel the support of the bed. It does not take longer than popping up, just a change in attention.

> **Sample *HUM Journal* entry:**
> *It feels good to lie on my side. My head can rest.*

C. Getting Out of Bed.

As you get out of bed, take a moment to put your feet on the ground, and keep them planted there as you stand.

> **Sample *HUM Journal* entry:**
> *Usually when I get out of bed, my toes curl as I stand.*
> *I like this feeling of uncurled toes and want to explore it more.*

In closing this chapter, I want to note the following: Remember that just changing the direction of your muscles, your thoughts, your emotions, and your spirit from constriction to expansion can make a big difference in your day. When you greet your partner, your family, your friends, and then work colleagues with your expanded Self, it spreads to others. Yes, constrictions and discontented faces will be there at times, with good reason. However, some-times the simplest things, like a hug or a genuine smile, will be a reminder to yourself and others of the innate expansion that balances constriction and leaves us happily suspended in contentment.

HOW WE DEVELOP AS HUMANS

Ancient wisdom has myths and stories about human development, and modern science has theories and research. My curiosity about human development led me to study the work of anthropologists as well as movement specialists and development therapists, combining my findings into a comprehensive viewpoint that I offer you here. The *Humanual* exploration into humans' physical, mental, and emotional development is a platform for understanding your own evolutionary impulses.

1. YOUR PRECIOUS LIFE: EMBODIED SENSING AND MOVING

There is a story traditional to Buddhist teachings about the soul's decision to "take human birth"—we might say "to be born" or "to incarnate on planet Earth":

> *There is a giant ancient turtle swimming in the oceans of the world for countless eons.*
> *There is also a large, round wooden ring floating on the numberless ocean currents*
> *for just as long. Once every hundred years, the turtle surfaces. It is said that*
> *the odds of his head coming up exactly through the hole in the wooden ring when*
> *he surfaces are the same as the difficult odds of taking human birth.*

In traditional Buddhist cosmology, human birth is not an accident or a random event, but a precious opportunity. So many of us forget this, and what is supposed to be an opportunity becomes laden with earthly obligations and societal goals. My hope is that *Humanual* helps you reconnect to the precious opportunity of your life. Becoming more fully aware of your expanded Self will help you feel the possibilities.

As you think about the statement, "This life is a precious opportunity," what do you notice? Is there expansion or contraction in your chest? Does the thought stimulate you to move or be still?

Together with our precious opportunity, we have a finely tuned biological organism that we inhabit to live this life. It has developed over time in specific ways for specific purposes. Understanding physiology enables us to best use this body. I devote some chapters to discussing evolutionary biology and aspects of our structure in order to elucidate and illustrate the importance of moving in accord with our design. When I use the phrase "by design," I mean that in terms of evolution. When we use the body in any way that diminishes this evolutionary accomplishment, our design, we are not living up to our human potential.

All our physical actions, including thinking, involve the *sensorimotor system*, which enables motor activity caused by sensory stimuli. The two key components are the sensory aspect and the motor aspect. The motor system is stimulated by our intent, or will, which then creates the movement patterns carried out by the musculoskeletal system. The sensory system registers the action, providing feedback to regulate the muscle tone.

The will-directed motor system is involved with muscle speed, force, and power. The motor system receives its impulses directly from the higher cortex of the brain, through *alpha motor neurons*. This is how intent becomes action: we think about doing something and the body-mind-self is already working it out.

The sensory-directed system feels the pressure of the arousal (the movement or intention). The sensory system is independent from the motor system and ruled by a different part of the brain, which functions on impulses from the nervous system. The sensory system includes such human activities as tasting, discovering, balancing, and sending and receiving information. It can provide the experience of an expanded inner space by facilitating calmness in the nervous system. But the sensory system is overridden or left out when its function is overpowered by the motor system: the strong contraction of muscles limits effectiveness of the sensory feedback loop.

As you sit reading, stop for a moment, and do not consciously move your body. As you sense your inner landscape, the workings of your muscles, viscera, and tissue, what do you experience? Can you feel some pulsing, vibrating, or movement? Can you realize that this sensory system is distinct from your active motor system?

> **Write in your *HUM Journal* about how you experience your sensory and motor systems.**

We utilize the sensory and motor system together, and generally it acts as one, living up to its merged name, *sensorimotor*. I sense danger and move away, or I sense hunger and go get an apple. However, these sensorimotor pathways can become dulled with any type of *dysregulation*, which is an abnormality or impairment in the body's management of a metabolic, physiological, or psychological process. This causes us to miss safety or warning cues from our brain, which is otherwise occupied with stabilizing some aspect of our system related to the dysregulation. For example, you may have had an argument with your partner earlier in the day and are feeling the emotion of it, thinking about what to do, and feeling tension in your chest and back. Your attention is mostly on all these things, rather than where you are walking. Then you don't notice the crack in the sidewalk that you're about to trip over. It's a classic example of a dulled sensorimotor system.

2. HOW YOU USE YOURSELF TO DO WHATEVER YOU DO

As you are able to sense and move, no matter how limited you may be, you have some choice as to how you do it. In my work, many health-seeking people come into my studio for a session and ask: What kind of exercise should I do? Should I do yoga, Pilates, or swim? Or should I run, stretch, lift weights?

It may seem strange, but I give them all the same answer: *It is not what you do, but how you do it.*

One student came in after a yoga class and felt great; another student came in after a yoga class and complained of an aching back. This brings me to the concept of *use*. Take a moment now to notice how you are sitting. How comfortable are you? Do you know that some ways of sitting are more healthful than others (see Chapter 11)? Throughout *Humanual*, I suggest optimal approaches to everyday activities to facilitate your discovery of greater possibilities for both sensing and moving your body.

In general, when people look at human development, they focus on heredity/genetics and environment. I include "use" as another concept in this conversation, meaning how you use yourself to do whatever you do—whether it's picking up a pencil, fixing your hair, or walking across the room. There are many ways to move through any activity. The principle of "use" is about how your entire body moves, not one specific part. No matter what you might think, body parts do not move independently; the whole self is involved.

Use is an orchestrated activity of your whole self. The parts make up the whole, and each part reflects the whole. Another way to think of use is the body's form in the moment that it is carrying out a task, meaning: How is the body shaped while walking? How is it aligned in space while sitting at your computer? And how are the body parts relating to one another as you do fitness activities?

Use includes biology: if you sit hunched over, your inner viscera will be compressed and not function well, and digestion could be disturbed, thereby affecting the synchrony of other bodily systems. And use affects your biography—for example, if you are hunched over your whole life, this habit will influence your mental outlook and life outcomes. No matter how set your patterns of use might be, changing them can happen with a new decision in a moment of conscious awareness. When you choose to allow your spine to lengthen more often, or decide to let the sensations of happiness fill your body, mind, and spirit, you are consciously changing your makeup.

Some hereditary patterns of movement and disease are programmed in our genes, yet we understand from neuroscience that genes predispose but do not predetermine. What triggers a gene's activation? Or whether we develop a particular disease that has "run in our family" for generations? *Our environment.* It can be comfortable and nurturing, or unsupportive and hostile, and everything in between. Because we are biological beings, living organisms, we are compelled to respond to our environment. Bottom line: our heredity is affected by our environment, and our environment affects our use, which in turn affects our heredity. Studies today in epigenetics show that offspring are affected (heredity) by emotions and physical patterns of past generations (use).[5]

Years ago, I was teaching a group of MFA (master's in fine arts) visual artists a class on use, breath, support, and suspension, and how the body moves. I slowly realized that although these very talented artists were able to draw the body in exact proportion and detail, they had no idea how to use their own bodies to move! I found this incongruent, and puzzling. They understood how bodies were put together but could not apply that knowledge to their movement, or use. They all had aching backs from leaning over their projects all day, and looked to me for advice on how to sculpt and paint without pain. Applying what they saw in anatomy books would have helped their use.

> **Write in your *HUM Journal* about your everyday use.**
> **How could it improve?**

3. ADAPTIVE STATES CREATE CHARACTER TRAITS

Developmentally, each of us has a strong life-force guiding us through every stage of growth. But if there is trauma, that life-force is directed into managing the traumatic situation rather than attending to our growth. So, a stage of development gets hijacked and does not complete. Then some aspect of us is stuck in an earlier stage of life. It is not uncommon to see a very successful, grown adult behave emotionally like a five-year-old when certain triggers are present. The nervous system's development got interrupted, but the cognitive brain must push on. *Humanual* aims to shed light on some of these patterns.

In terms of development, let's not forget that we are greatly affected by what happens before birth, while in utero. The mother's state, stress levels, and overall condition influence the forming fetus. Blood, chemicals, and hormones flow through both their bodies. After birth, the child depends on the parent or caregiver for food, shelter, and nurturing within the household environment.

Let's take a look at how we developed, because this knowledge aids our understanding of use, form, and function, as well as our early dependency and adaptive processes. When human babies are born, they do not have fully formed brains. Why? The head is the largest part of the body at birth, and given the mother's narrow pelvis, the baby must come out at around nine months or it gets too large.

Compared to other mammals, human brains are considerably smaller and less developed at birth. The human baby, because of its undeveloped brain, is utterly helpless, thus requiring intensive caregiving and nurturing. Human babies are born with a cerebellum in the lower brain, which controls movement, and an auditory cortex. Most other circuits need to be formed. The remaining parts of our brain are developed over many years. During the first three years, the child's brain undergoes rapid growth, tripling in weight and establishing about 1,000 trillion nerve connections.[6]

When this developing brain is forming—including impulse and stress regulation, self-regulation, and sensory regulation—it requires certain input. For the eyes to see properly, for example, you need light. In an experimental setting, baby rats born with sight were put into a dark room with no light. After some time, they were blind.[7] It is the same with other parts of the developing brain; certain input is needed for proper development. If you are shown love and nurturing by caregivers, the love and nurturing circuits will be enlivened within you. If not, those circuits do not activate immediately, but can be awakened later.

The Developing Brain and Bonding

I want to spend a little more time on this subject because it is so important. All children need and long to be held and nurtured. In fact, *bonding*, which is the process of a baby connecting to his or her mother or caregiver, is one of the most critical factors for the development of the human brain and, therefore, healthy life experiences. It is a necessary and crucial part of our mammalian heritage.

There is a basic human need for connection, care, and love. Oxytocin, the "love hormone," ensures this connection. Not only is it present at birth, it plays a pivotal role in bond development throughout life. It is released when social bonding takes place. But stress hormones can slow down the secretion of oxytocin—for example, when children do not get the care they need.

Dr. Sue Carter, biologist and internationally recognized expert in behavioral neurobiology, tells us, "The most important things in a human life require oxytocin to be present. This includes birth, caring for offspring, finding a mate, creating a social bond with our partners, and restoration and healing in the face of stress."[8] From the moment we are born, positive social interaction is essential to health.

The baby's relationship with the caregiver is called *attachment, an early social interaction.* Simply put, this attachment can be secure and promote health, or insecure and not conducive to health. A healthy attachment meets a child's needs in terrific ways. They are picked up, soothed, and nurtured, and their emotions are tended to on a consistent basis, which provides a great sense of comfort, thereby reinforcing trust and attunement in the child's environment. Their optimally functioning muscular network continues to develop and expand with healthy skin tone, coloring, and breathing patterns. The child feels supported, loved, and confident.

On the other hand, let's look at what happens with an insecure attachment. Let's say the caregiver is angry, tired, depressed, or what we call stressed. Because of this, he or she doesn't have the time, energy, or available emotions for the child. The child is not being sufficiently nurtured or recognized and begins to feel sad, bad, and confused. The muscular networks tend to constrict and/or collapse. The young child's limited nervous system cannot handle the stress of the situation because there is no ability yet to regulate or calm his/her own nervous system.

Electrical wiring of the brain is deeply influenced by the quality of the attachment relationship between a child and the primary caregiver, which especially applies early in life because the brain is developing so rapidly. The self, mind, movement, emotions, body, and spirit are all forming patterns as these circuits are created. Therefore, how you move, how much energy you can handle, how much you dissociate or stay present, how resilient you are, and more are all set in motion during this critical time. If the environment is unpleasant, the child may dissociate and live in their own world.

If there were many joyful moments in our childhood, then our body and our character would reflect this; we might then develop the tendency to feel and see the upside of situations.

The opposite is also true. According to one researcher, experience and environment exert an influence comparable to genetics: "Genes determine the general form of the brain, and genes determine how the brain reacts to experience. Experience, however, is required to refine the matrix of synaptic connections, which in its developed form contains far more information than the genome does. In some respects, all that matters is the presence or absence of experience during critical periods of development."[9]

The confluence of environment, experience, genetics, and our responses creates adaptive states of body use and mental accommodation, leading to character traits with corresponding muscular patterns governing facial expressions, body positions, and use. In psychology and other areas of human development, *adaptive behavior* refers to when a person (typically a child) shifts their authentic behavior in order to get along in their environment with the greatest success and the least chance of conflict with others. After all, we want to remain alive and unharmed. As Gabor Maté, addiction specialist, put it, "Adaptive coping mechanisms go from an uncomfortable state the child is in to a character trait that guides their life."[10]

> **Write in your *HUM Journal* about your understanding of your own adaptive states.**

How Adaptations Translate to Movement Patterns

Let's take a closer look at how these developed patterns affect the musculoskeletal system.

When the environment invites it, children love to play and laugh, from early peek-a-boo to hide-and-seek to throwing kisses. Biologically from an early age, they love to make sounds in a singsongy manner. They enjoy moving their bodies and dancing when music is played. Rhythmic movements are the heart and soul of our bodily fabric. Children, uninhibited, allow sound and movement to burst their energy forward, as their muscles are developing.

Early muscular patterns become habits of motion for life. I see the quality of early attachments and other environmental influences reflected in a person's physical balance and movements, which can be secure or insecure. People with secure attachments tend to have more physical stability and more solid grounding than those with insecure early bonding. They also tend to move their bodies with greater assurance and confidence.

When you are born, you are not able to hold yourself up. Your head needs to be held and supported. If you do not receive this specific kind of support from your caregiver, you will likely feel that you need to hold yourself up in life. What that might look like is a kind of stiffness or what we call poor posture, or a lack of ease in movement. Over time, this holding-up action becomes a pattern, which can lead to stiff joints and rigid muscles. Most critically, the habit of holding yourself up prevents you from accessing the very beautiful freedom of support that is available through the reflex system and Earth's gravitational field.

You are born into and designed to live in a gravitational field. A set of muscles called flexors fold the body inward toward Earth's core from the force of outer space. Another set of muscles called extensors lift the body upward, away from the spinning centrifugal forces of Earth. This combination of musculature that supports the body in the gravitational field is organized by the dynamic relationship of the head, neck, and torso. When this system is working properly, with the head freely poised on top of the spine, the neck and back muscles are lengthened, widened, and supported. The entire torso has expansion with no unnecessary stiffness, and the muscular support network functions optimally, with maximum efficiency and minimum effort. We see this in healthy children.

Babies discover, explore, and stretch into this developing muscular system. If their head is not freely poised on top of the spine, as it's meant to be, the child (often uncomfortable or startled) will pull his head back and down. This action shortens the body and is meant to be a time-limited response. But if it lingers or becomes a pattern, then physical, emotional, and even mental patterns of tension begin to build, interfering with the child's natural expanded response. This has vast ramifications as the child matures.

4. OUR BODY TELLS US HOW WE FEEL: DEVELOPMENT OF EARLY EMOTIONS

The signaling and perception of internal bodily sensations is referred to as *interoception*. This sensory system has receptors located throughout the body to "tell" us how we feel. Uncomfortable feelings make us feel bad. To a child, "the body feels bad" equals "I feel bad" equals "I must be bad." They do not understand that the obscure shame and guilt they may feel at this stage have more to do with something inappropriate or missing in their environment than with their own personal failure. Their brains are simply not developed enough to understand this perspective.

Most child psychologists agree that young children are generally incapable of considering the caregiver as wrong or bad on some level (because that is their survival). Instead, they think, "I am the one who's wrong, unlovable, or bad." If this is happening while the delicate brain is developing and laying down circuits, the "I am bad" thought can become an imprint. This is quickly followed by shame and guilt, which can be the basis for crippling self-identifications and self-judgments that can last long into adulthood. This is an example of how these early states become character traits.

A child's view of the world is egocentric; children are the center of their universe. If good stuff happens, they think, "I must be good," and that little face just beams with joy at their success. Breath is full, while confidence and poise develop and emanate from their body and soul. However, if bad stuff happens, they think, "It must be my fault." Then their little body collapses in and breathing becomes shallow.

This body configuration is the essence of the shame posture. If these experiences are reinforced and the posture continues, the overall background muscular support system breaks down. Some muscles overtighten and some get flaccid. Meanwhile, the emotions go toward anxiety, fear, and anger at the loss of integrity of the system. Of course, children are not consciously aware that the boundary of their structure has been breached. They are simply doing what they need to do to protect themselves, as our bodies tell us how we feel. So, what is initially an instinctual protective response to their environment becomes a recurring pattern of use.

As children grow, they have an emotional "choice." One option is to keep their authenticity and autonomy, and listen to their gut feelings and behave from there. They can remain who they really are, in essence, whether anybody loves them or feeds them; meanwhile, their body remains upright and balanced with the capacity for full breath. Or, they can choose the behavior that secures the attachment, ensuring some amount of love and food—even if it means not listening to their own needs, not rocking the boat. In this choice, the body is either overly collapsed or held up rigidly, and the breathing is shallow.

Needless to say, a young child must keep the attachment for survival. This is why I wrote "choice" in quotation marks above; it is, essentially, not really a "choice"—until later in life when the choice to change is available.

It should be apparent that children need truly loving, attuned caregivers who are emotionally present. Newborn babies are not able to self-regulate; they cannot find their own way back to calmness. Upon being overwhelmed, the baby or child must have a caregiver to hold and calm them. This is called *co-regulation*, and it means the ability to calm oneself using the presence of another. Mammals are naturally co-regulating creatures, and healthy emotional development requires co-regulation from a loving, caring source.

Co-regulating with parent.

Co-regulating with friends.

"There is no such thing as a baby; there is a baby and someone."
—D.W. WINNICOTT[11]

How We Make Ourselves Smaller

Expansion and contraction are part of the movement of the universe. If you are alive, there is some movement somewhere inside you, even if your physicality is limited. Our life-force moves through expansion and contraction. The expanded Self has a component of physical expansion, but this is not a chronic state or always the best choice. If you lived in a household with a raging parent, you would try to make yourself smaller in order to not be seen. This, too, would be the wisdom of the expanded Self, in response to the needs of the moment.

Many people feel small in life and (somehow) separate from the great multidimensional universal oneness that exists. This typically stems from situations in our environment and experience where we did not get our needs met. When we don't get our basic needs met as a child or simply lack loving attention, we can interpret the encounter as "I don't matter" or "I'm not important enough." Then we contract, believing the story we tell our self. A child with a beaming face and puffed-up chest says, "Mommy, look at what I made!" But Mom is busy cooking dinner for the family, or getting a document ready for tomorrow's meeting, and says, without turning to her daughter, "I'm busy right now, Haley." Haley's face darkens and her chest collapses. She has the experience of being unimportant. *No* one is to blame. But is the expanded Self now less available under the pattern? Something to consider.

Write in your **HUM Journal** where you think you might be developmentally stuck in your thinking and in your body. What triggers you, and where do you feel it in your body?

EX-PLORATIONS FOR DEVELOPMENT

A. EX-ploration: Orienting

Orienting is something that all living creatures do. It involves looking around at your environment to see if you are safe or if there is danger lurking, and if there are objects to relate to or people to connect to. When you turn your head to investigate your surroundings and engage with others, the movement involves your sternocleidomastoid, the big muscle that you sometimes see protruding on the side of someone's neck. When people have experienced trauma, or a series of overwhelming emotions, they respond to their environment in one of two ways: they are either hypervigilant, looking around all the time, typically nervously, and the sternocleidomastoid muscle is overactive; or they are the opposite of this, not wanting to investigate their surroundings or engage with others because of the potential for danger—in which case the sternocleidomastoid is often stuck, limiting head movement. Practicing orienting can help both.

1. The first way to practice orienting is to consciously look around and see your environment as it is now. Notice what happens in your body. Your biological (nervous, respiratory, and musculoskeletal) systems synchronize and register, "This is what is happening now."

2. The second way is to allow your eyes to go where they want to go. What are you drawn to? You are not using your thinking brain to choose now. You are using your lower brain to be led to colors, and shapes. Notice what happens in your body.

3. The third practice for orienting is to allow your environment to come to you. As you look around, do not focus your eyes outward but instead allow your eyes to receive. Notice what happens in your body. Can you be the still point in a turning world, as T.S. Eliot wrote?

4. The final exploration for orienting is to "look with fresh eyes," as if you are seeing your environment for the first time. In this practice, you withhold your patterned assumptions. You may notice that the wall you always called yellow has a tint of gray in it.

In your *HUM Journal*, write about how much you enjoy or don't enjoy orienting to your surroundings.

> **DO** Every day, many times

B. EX-ploration: Arriving

Many different therapeutic models have named our various stages of development. One of the earliest human developmental phases is called the Existence Structure.[12] It is the period from six months in utero to three months after birth. During this time, we have the ability or consciousness to embrace, or not embrace, our birth into this life. Our decision depends on our sense of how we will be welcomed, held, treated, and understood, and also our experience of this after we are born.

Many people have difficult births (such as C-section), separation from their mother due to illness or prematurity, the experience of cold metallic hospitals, and more. When babies have a harsh and unwelcoming early experience, they can be unsure about whether they want to be here in the world and hesitate to put their feet on the ground. It is never too late to explore these feelings as you sit in a chair and focus on both feet together or one foot at a time:

1. Feel the parts of your feet that connect to the ground = you want to be here.

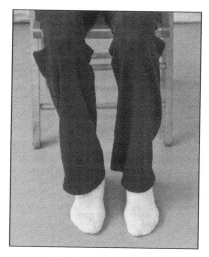

Feet resting down.

2. Feel the parts of your feet that pull up off the ground = you don't want to be here.

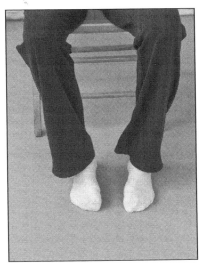

Feet pulling up.

3. Move back and forth between these two options. See where you land. This repetitive motion activates the spiral muscles in your legs that are the foundational support for your entire body on planet Earth. This exercise will help you arrive fully on the planet.

Write about your willingness to be here in your *HUM Journal*.

DO   **Every once in a while, especially when you feel disconnected or unsupported.**

CHAPTER

3

EMBODIED PATTERNS AND CHARACTER

Here you begin to look at your embodied patterns. Some you brag about, others you want to hide. By considering the different types of memory, you understand how these characterological patterns get formed. You will learn to distinguish two major choices for human development—innate reflex ease or voluntary labored effort—and to recognize these choices in your own life. We explore making different choices and the powerful self-discovery tool of micro-movements.

1. FEEDBACK LOOPS

Some small incident bothered you during the day—let's say your proposal was not chosen, or you lost the golf game. Thoughts begin: I am not clever enough; how did I miss that shot? You notice your neck is tense, and your head feels a bit heavy. In bed, you toss and turn. You can't sleep or don't get enough sleep. Then you're tired the next day, and it becomes difficult to accomplish anything because you're dragging. You start feeling bad about yourself for not getting enough done, now agreeing with your mind: I am not clever enough, not talented enough, etc. And so the cycle goes—that is, until you learn to intercept the pattern.

These adaptive patterns that are often formed early in life influence both your mental/emotional (psychological) self and your bodily (physiological) self, which are inseparable. As the thought/feeling patterns connect to the physical ones, they form a feedback and feed-forward loop, building on one another, creating an embodied pattern of character structure. I saw this in the young man in the Apple store, who likely had the unconscious experience of: I feel bad and I slump; I slump and I feel worse. With some real-life illustrations, this chapter addresses choosing new patterns to replace feedback loops that are less than optimal.

A journey back to an expanded voice

Here is a story from my teaching practice at the Opera Institute. It is about how the past influences singing in the present.

Thomas is a singer entering the professional opera world. He wants to be relaxed and engaged as he sings, but instead he feels constriction in his chest and the emotion of anxiety, especially when singing high notes. The feedback loop—he sings and constricts and then feels the emotion of anxiety—constricts him more because of the anxiety.

To begin the lesson, I had him sing. Afterward, Thomas talked about the anxiety he felt. As he spoke, we noticed that his hands were in the air in front of him, making the movement of pushing something away. We both observed the anxiety's physical pattern of pushing away.

I had him physically explore this pushing-away motion. I call this exploration "Be With." I urged Thomas to "Be With" the pushing action and do more with it. We touched it, felt it, played with the edges, and moved the energy back and forth, thinking maybe the pushing action of his hands might be some kind of incomplete defensive response that he needed to connect with and express. This can sometimes "complete" the action of an adaptive pattern from childhood that was in place to protect the person.

After we worked with the pushing action, Thomas sang again and his voice was much freer and more beautiful. We both noticed the patterns had changed somewhat. There was less anxiety and less constriction, even though these aspects were not completely gone.

It may have been fine to stop there, but something told me there was more. I wondered what else might be causing the pattern. I asked Thomas about when he started singing, and if he was young. He said, "Yes." In third grade, he was given a choice between gym class and music class. He chose the music class. After an audition, the music director told Thomas he was a boy soprano. I asked if that was okay for him. He said it was fine for him, and at the time he thought nothing of it.

But when he went home, it was a different story. He told his mom the news. She exclaimed, "A boy soprano! Don't tell anyone you're a soprano!" In that moment, as she spoke those words, she pushed her hands away, just like Thomas had pushed his hands away at the beginning of the session. The movement had the same direction, same speed, and same force. Wow, what a moment! We both realized the connection instantly. Because of his mother's reaction, Thomas made a choice—albeit an unconscious one—in that moment to hide his boy soprano voice.

"Don't tell anyone," she said. So he created the pattern of constricting himself in order to hold down his full voice—the voice of his expanded Self—and this is what made him feel anxious.

He became aware that he was still hiding his boy soprano nature, those high notes. When we went back to the musical passage, his anxiety was even more diminished—to the point that it was hardly noticeable. Deep inside, Thomas knew he could sing those high notes, but something had clearly been in the way. In our work together, he was willing to inquire into both the physical and psychological patterns of his character structure that were preventing him from realizing his full voice. Now his body, mind, and spirit understood why he had created the embodied pattern. This awareness allowed the process of beginning to undo it—from the body to the brain, bottom up, and from the brain to the body, top down. This is not trauma in the way we often think about it, such as a natural disaster or violent abuse at the hands of a caregiver, but to this singer, this lingering action of holding back was traumatic and carried long-term consequences.

Biting fingernails

Even though certain patterns are intergenerational, you are sometimes able to heal them.

Years after he had studied with me, one of my students wrote to me: "I have been biting my fingernails since I can remember. I saw my dad do it and his father did it, and I obviously wanted to be like them. [My interpretation of this: the psychological pattern was "I want to be like my dad"; the physical pattern was biting his nails.] However, this had been an undesirable habit of mine for years. I found it dirty, and I thought it made my hands look gross, but I was never aware of my hands consciously going to my mouth. I would only remember that I didn't want to bite my nails once I had started.

"So," he continued, "I was a student at London Academy of Music and Dramatic Arts. It was junior year, and I was reading *Richard III* in my bed for class when I started biting my nails. This was right after riding the subway. I was disgusted and wanted to stop, but I remember having this weird impulse, once I had started, that I needed to finish biting my nails so that they wouldn't be all lopsided and instead rounded. Then, two quotes from your class came into my mind. The first was, and still is, my favorite. 'It is better to do wrong knowingly because then you can make the choice to stop.' The other was, 'Inhibition is the cornerstone of the Alexander Technique.'" [My comment: inhibition in the Alexander Technique is non-doing of the habit.]

He then wrote, "I made a new rule that when I noticed I was biting my nails, I would inhibit that compulsion to bite that nail until it was complete. Also, I started carrying nail clippers in my backpack, so that I could clip them at an appropriate time rather than bite them. It didn't take very long, surprisingly! Sometimes I still catch myself biting my nails during tense sporting events, like my Dad may have done, or if I'm on my way to an audition, but then I feed myself my directions of support, suspension, and breath. I stop doing the undesired behavior of biting my nails and wanting to be like my dad, and the compulsion passes."

This student had a psychological pattern of wanting to be like his father and had developed the physical pattern of biting his nails. He was able to change the psychological pattern to "I want to feel good about myself" and then choose the new pattern of clipping his nails rather than biting them. We can change these longtime feedback loops of psychophysical patterns by sensing with awareness and making new choices.

2. IMPLICIT AND EXPLICIT MEMORY

We tend to form patterns of character based on memories from our past experiences of people and places. Relationships with family, friends, and others all provide experiences with associated emotions that are stored in various areas of our brain and body.

Explicit memory is the retaining of specific details, such as remembering where in the parking lot you left your car, or which items are on your shopping list. This can include some form of episodic memory, such as a special event in your life, like your wedding, or your dad taking you to your first baseball game.

Implicit memory, which is less conscious, is more deeply ingrained. These memories can be emotional in nature, such as the smell of an aftershave or cologne reminding you of a past love, or they can be *procedural*, like knowing how to ride a bike. Unlike explicit memories, we do not always recall the facts, but we "re-member": The members, or parts of your body, retain the information, and you bring them together again through awareness. Your body knows what happened in the past and stores that data, even though you don't think too much about the experiences. Implicit memories include the early patterns we developed as children and the before-language memories of being held and nurtured, or longing to be held and nurtured. These body memories are very deep and very potent. They are foundational to our sense of self.

Most of us are not able to recall many events that occurred before eighteen months of age, but the physiological imprint is there. This imprint plays a central role in human development because 80 percent of the brain develops in the first few years. The body holds so many implicit memories, and they are key for healing the deep wounds or adaptive patterns of childhood.

Dr. Diane Poole Heller, somatic attachment and trauma expert, and one of my extremely skilled trauma instructors, tells the story of a male client who had a panic attack every year on the same day and had no idea why. As it turned out, after some therapeutic investigation of his present symptoms, which reflect implicit memories, he recalled that he was involved in a serious car accident on that same day when he was younger—and he had forgotten. His panic, which was stuck in his body, was linked to his unconscious memory of the accident. The accident was not a conscious memory, but the timing of it triggered a bodily sense of danger.

Have you ever noticed a strangely familiar feeling or sensation and not known why you felt it? Your body may be remembering something, like my client Vern did. . . .

Prison revisited: Vern's revelation

Life often presents you with reminders of why and how you formed the memory patterns that you did. It is as if the universe is giving you a chance to heal your past physical and psychological patterns. Here is a true story from one of my clients who was able to sort out his mysterious pattern of body imagery in a real-life situation.

Vern had a pain in his right hip for many months and came to me for help. When he sensed inside his body, the image he saw in his hip was a "black baseball of goop" that hurt and would not move. Our work was improving the intense pain over time, but the pain still intermittently lingered.

Vern went to visit a friend in the hospital when he noticed a county van that brought inmates there for care. It caught his eye because he had been in that van when he was younger.

After the hospital visit, Vern got on the elevator to go home. There in the elevator was a man seated in a wheelchair with shackles on his arms and legs, big metal handcuffs, and chains on his legs, keeping him in place. The man was accompanied by three very attentive corrections officers carrying clubs and guns. Vern immediately recognized all of this; he had been in that same position many years ago.

When it was time to exit the elevator, Vern waited to let them leave first. But a corrections officer motioned for Vern to proceed. As he was walking away from the elevator, Vern noticed that he was not in that wheelchair with those metal chains holding him anymore, and he began to walk freely. The pain in his hip disappeared. The next time he came in to see me, we worked with the walking ability in his legs. His "black baseball of goop" was gone, and his hip felt better. In truth, so many of us live with these kinds of virtual chains.

Write in your _HUM Journal_ if something comes up for you.

3. EXPERIENCE OF SELF SHOWS UP IN THE BODY

We've been looking at how adaptive patterns create psychological and physiological loops. These embodied patterns influence both what we do and don't pay attention to, which further shapes our character.

Children lack the experience and awareness to consciously control physical patterns. It is important, then, as an adult, to be able to sense your embodied experience. Otherwise, how will you know what you are feeling, and when you are hungry or tired, relaxed or slumping?

To explore patterns of embodied self-experience with inquiry, pay attention to your movements, sensations, and emotions as you read the questions. Take note of your attention patterns and reflexes, which respond habitually. Take your time.

In order to observe, we need safety, which means an environment without pending threat or judgment. How do you know when you feel safe?

Please consider:

- Do you sense your body? Sometimes or never? Only when you have pain?

- Are you afraid to sense your body? Is there too much emotion, or feeling? Are sensations such as tingly, contracted, fuzzy, buzzy, metallic, trembling, or flowy familiar to you?

- When do you become aware of your embodied experience of self? While driving in your car? Alone, or with friends?

- Do you ever notice that you lost your support because you are ahead of yourself and tense? Or "trying" to get it right?

- How do you experience your expanded Self?

- Are you self-conscious, in an embarrassed kind of way, or conscious of self in a healthy way?

- As you read this book, do you feel the chair? Are you holding your breath? Is slowing down easy or anxiety-provoking?

Strong overwhelm or emotional disruption interferes with our ability to connect to our self-experience. Meaningful contact with our self and others becomes impossible, as the nervous system is so aroused. This is a logical response when danger is imminent. But when the danger is over, you want to be able to return to your self-awareness, and to care for yourself through rest and rejuvenation. Looking at these questions can help you understand how your experience of self shows up in your body. For example: Do you feel the chair? If you say "Yes," then you know that you tend to include your near environment in your experience. If you say "No," you would know the opposite, and then you can choose to alter your attention.

4. WHEN THE EXPANDED SELF CONTRACTS

What happens when you don't want to feel your expanded Self? That is part of being human. We can expect to have good days and not-so-good days. The problem arises when you never have an experience of your glorious expanded Self because your habitual embodied pattern has limited your character. Maybe you made yourself small as a child—as we described in the previous chapter—and it became an adult pattern. Or maybe you've just let yourself adopt habits as an adult that became rigid and opaque. Either way, contractive patterns need examining.

What is real comfort? Habits can be comfortable because they are familiar, not because they are actually comfortable. What can a practitioner do when a client says, "I feel more comfortable in my discomfort than I do in my expanded Self"? The character pattern is set up to avoid the expanded Self at all costs. Perhaps the last time she expanded she was ignored, or ridiculed, or hit, and left in a state of betrayal. So painful. Why would she ever expand again?

This was the story of one of my clients. To work together, I had her explore going back and forth between sensing—first her discomfort, what her body felt like (heavy)—and then her reluctance to expand (rigid). The question I wanted to answer was, "Is she really more comfortable in her discomfort, or is this an unhealed adaptive pattern from an earlier place and time?" After a few rounds, she said her discomfort "heavy place" had become less comfortable, and her reluctance to expand (the rigidity) had diminished. In this moment, we intercepted the pattern of always being more comfortable in the discomfort. The next week, she came in and told me that she had gotten very anxious and depressed one day during the week, but she had figured out on her own what to do about it from the work we had done. We celebrated her moment of success.

EX-ERCISE: MICRO-MOVEMENTS

Learn to make and/or notice small micro-movements, the tiniest motion possible, throughout your whole body. These can disrupt embodied patterns, awaken old memories, enliven physicality, and enhance your tracking skills. This is not meditation. It is a tracking exercise. Eyes can be open or closed.

START
Notice your whole body.

LEGS

Notice sensations in your legs. Start with your foot. (1) First just notice.
Any tingling, numbness, or holding? (2) Then move your foot with tiny movements.
Voluntary movement can challenge the autonomic nervous system to budge
from its fixed patterns. Continue with steps (1) and (2) to the lower leg and thigh.
Repeat with other foot, lower leg, and thigh.

Movement gives the brain new data to intercept the patterns.
Tingling, warmth, shaking, trembling, flow, or breath changes can
show up as you make micro-movements.

LOWER TORSO

Notice the movement of the muscles in your pelvis.

MIDDLE TORSO

Notice visceral response.

UPPER TORSO

Notice your chest, heart, and shoulders.

ARMS
Sense and then initiate micro-movements in your upper arm, lower arm, and hand.
Repeat with the other arm.

NECK, HEAD, and FACE
Be sure to explore the range of micro-movements in your face. If your neck is tight,
you may want to practice the Orienting exercises (see end of Chapter 2).

WHOLE BODY
To feel your whole body working together, allow your arms and legs
to make small micro-movements as you think about swimming,
crawling, running, fighting, or hugging.

Do you feel any flow or pleasure from these voluntary acts?

Write in your **HUM Journal**.

DO To awaken yourself before working out, doing yoga, or giving a presentation.

5. THE TWO BASIC CHOICES FOR HUMAN DEVELOPMENT: EASE OR EFFORT?

As a longtime observer of people's patterns, I have noticed options or paths for human development. Humans can follow their built-in, primary reflex system pattern (an expanded version of self), thereby creating authentic character and a body of lightness, ease, and rhythmic coherence; or they may follow a secondary, compensatory, voluntary system pattern (a contracted version of self) as a default, due to upbringing, injury, illness, or even lack of education about the body and mind, thereby creating inauthentic character and a body that is heavy, incoherent, and labored. Many people flip between these two choices and experience being either harmonious and resonant, or dissonant and constricted. What do you do?

With the primary system, there is an innate hierarchical pattern on all levels that seems to make life more manageable. This system also makes space to invite the expanded Self. Healthy babies and vertebrate animals in the wild do not deviate from the primary reflex system and total pattern, and its rhythm. In the physical realm, the primary reflex pattern facilitates movement that is light, rhythmic, and efficient. That is why a healthy child moves with ease, flow, and grace and why a two thousand-pound horse can jump over a fence so effortlessly.

When the primary system is not engaged, the secondary system is operative. In this case, the body is often collapsed, without tone, or rigidly held, which results in awkward or defensive movements. Activities require more effort in this mode and can feel labored and lethargic, affecting the mental and emotional aspects of life as well.

In the spiritual realm, the philosophy of the primary system can be expressed as "Let go and let God," and simply being. You go with the flow. With the secondary system activated, the ego is in charge, and it seeks to control and micromanage every one of your actions and the actions of those around you.

In the emotional realm, the primary system seems most effective when you practice what I call "Be With," allowing emotions to move through you with awareness: E-motion means to "move through" in the present moment. With the secondary system, there is a tendency to deny or repress emotions and feelings, and the associated preferences. The deviation from being in the present moment and expressing our needs seems to throw off the natural flow or rhythm.

One of my clients is a trumpet player, and I noticed that she was working with all her surface voluntary muscles to push the sound out. Her whole body was tense, rigid, and armored. She was exhausted after playing and felt pain in her upper, middle, and lower back. As we worked together, I taught her how to connect with the movement of her breath inside. When we started, it was tiny, but she was able to stay with it, track it, and sense it growing.

Eventually, it grew into the force that would play the trumpet. As she was able to contact the innate primary system that could also play the trumpet, she could allow the surface muscles to release and not work so hard. Of course, there is some effort required to do this. Now as she played, her sound was more focused and resonant; there was also more ease, and her back did not hurt. This is an example of how the two different modes affect people in real-life applications. I've seen this same situation play out for athletes, dancers, construction workers, bakers, you name it—basically anyone who uses their body for anything. You can either engage the secondary, voluntary, labored system or the primary reflex system, with its inherently organized and rhythmically pulsing movements.

Because most of us fluctuate between the two, depending on life circumstances and situations, the more awareness you have, the greater your ability to choose. Staying present, alert, and conscious of the primary reflex system will lead to better health and well-being. On the other hand, lack of attention to your physical use and denial of your emotional states can lead to disease and illness, in many forms.

In today's world, there seems to be a third path. Primary is natural, as intended: if you are hungry, you eat. Secondary is adaptive to outside forces: your family sits down together to eat and you're not hungry, but you are "forced" to eat. The third, I would say, is rejection of self and natural patterns by self itself. You were hungry, so you ate, and then decided you did not want that food in you, as it might cause you to have a belly, or look heavy, so you expel it. Modern culture shames and often does not welcome a person with a fuller body. Though maybe that is slowly changing.

The third category neglects many previously accepted human attributes. What is wrong with wrinkles and gray hair as a sign of growing old? Are Botox injections really necessary to prevent feelings and age from showing? New studies reveal that mothers who have had Botox facial treatments have less exuberance and less ability to communicate emotion to their babies.[13] Meanwhile, millions of people take antidepressant medications either instead of or in addition to confronting and working through feelings, exercising, and making other changes that could improve mood and outlook. One study showed that walking around the block could prevent a panic attack.[14]

The ongoing efforts to find an external "fix" for what we don't like about our bodies and minds demonstrates to me that there is a need for broader education about the human body for our entire community, including parents, teachers, and health professionals. Childhood education focuses mostly on cognitive development and emotional behavior, with insufficient proper education on ease or effort in all realms. Wouldn't it be great if children were taught how to bend, run, and move efficiently, and to cherish and care for their bodies and to celebrate life cycles rather than fight against them?

MOVEMENT AND IMMOBILITY FOR DEFENSE AND CONNECTION

This chapter briefly summarizes the primitive stages of movement and some of the reasons for movement or nonmovement. It is important to understand the historical development of our responses to danger. The self-protective states of fight, flight, freeze are not random—they follow a hierarchical pattern from an evolutionary perspective.

Safety, health, recovery and restoration, and the expanded states of creativity and growth are our normal biological default states. The fight, flight, freeze response is recruited only when we feel threatened, which includes being evaluated or judged. When our defense system relaxes, we are better able to be engaged, prosocial, creative, and wise. The feeling of safety or being welcomed can turn the fight, flight, freeze circuits off when they are not needed.

Dr. Stephen Porges's Polyvagal Theory is introduced in this chapter. It traces the evolutionary relationship of the autonomic nervous system with instinctual and social behavior. Considering the far-reaching roles of the vagus nerve helps us visualize or "map" how the nervous system responds when one of the three states of safety, danger, or life-threat occurs.

1. MOVEMENT FOR SURVIVAL

You might wonder what survival has to do with someone who complains of a sore neck, or with an athlete who's suffering from anxiety, or with a singer who needs to expand her range and tone. All these symptoms could be the result of some type of thwarted and ongoing survival response. Any holding in the body can be an adaptive response to perceived danger, as illustrated by the example below.

Wilhelm Reich was a psychiatrist and a scientist, performing many experiments in his quest to better understand the human psyche. One experiment involved an amoeba, a primitive organism consisting of a single cell and a membrane. It moves by extending its pseudopods, which resemble arms, and making basic swimming movements to engulf food particles. This organism is constantly in motion, and as long as it moves, it is alive.

Observing with a microscope, Reich lightly pricked the amoeba once, without damaging its membrane, to see its reaction. It seemed to contract then freeze and stop moving. After a while, the amoeba recovered. Its behavior showed nothing to indicate it had been pricked. But when the amoeba was pricked several times, although the membrane wasn't damaged, it remained clenched and didn't resume movement. Finally, because it was no longer moving, it could not engulf food and died. The most primitive form of defense from danger (or perceived danger) is *tonic immobility*, a natural state of paralysis.

What happened when you read the last sentence? Did your body's sensation change? Did you feel sorry for the amoeba? Do you see yourself doing the same behavior to a lesser degree? Why did the clenching response continue when the threat (being pricked) was over? How could we let the amoeba know it was okay to move forward? We can extend this question to human behavior: *How can we be free from our past experiences and habitual behaviors and respond appropriately in the present moment?* This is an important question to ask on the journey to your expanded Self.

Let's start with a basic understanding of why we move. From an evolutionary perspective, we can observe that all living creatures—a single-celled animal, a plant, or a complex human being—are organized to use themselves as one complete, efficiently operating organism. The whole of the amoeba is involved in moving toward the food, just like the whole of you is involved in going into the kitchen to put a meal together. The original reasons for movement are to get food, connect, or respond to threats. Everything is coordinated to get food efficiently and to maintain safety. Creatures move or don't move to survive.

From the moment we are conceived, we need to eat. We require nutrients for growth, development, and survival. How we are fed, or not fed, influences our every move and thought. How, what, and when we eat are complex issues. Suffice it to say that food impacts every area of our life and culture. More needs to be said about food and eating than there is room for here.

Historically, many animals find food by sensing or smelling with their nose, strategically located in the middle of the face. The nose is right in front of the atlanto-occipital joint, where the head balances on top of the spine. If a creature does not like a food, it pulls its head back onto the spine, as in the startle reflex. This stops the forward motion. When it wants to move on, the head resumes this forward direction and engages with the environment. As we saw with the amoeba, when there is danger or perceived danger, the picture changes, and the head or creature no longer moves forward freely, if at all.

The movement dynamic of safety and threat corresponds to the theory of approach and avoid, or attract and repel: we go toward what we want and away from what we don't want. This action is physical as well as psychological and emotional. It is also frequently discussed in spiritual teachings, where equanimity is advised.

2. POLYVAGAL THEORY AND HOW WE DEFEND OURSELVES

Let's look at the differences in how a mammal and a reptile respond to danger. My three-year-old grandson, Axel, and I (mammals) were at the beach in the tall grass. We met a lizard (a reptile), and the lizard froze. We walked toward the lizard, and then it ran. As mammals, we have evolved to respond to danger with a different hierarchical system than a reptile. If Axel and I were in the position of the lizard, we would not freeze the moment someone approached. We would attempt to talk and engage to see if the person was friendly or not. We are constantly scanning for threat or connection, welcome or warning. For a mammal, when cues of trust and safety occur, the nervous system can relax and shift out of the fight-or-flight defense mode and into social engagement.

We are all always on the alert to detect danger in our environment. As mentioned earlier, the brain has evolved to do this. When you walk into a social gathering or a meeting at your office or place of work, do you feel safe, the possibility of danger, or a life threat? These three states have a biological, emotional, and physical expression. When you feel safe, your voice is melodic, your gaze is soft, and your body moves fluidly, like when you are in the company of good friends and there is joy in the air. When you detect possible danger, your eyes fix on the problem and you get ready to defend yourself by taking action—possibly fighting or fleeing—even when you are merely arguing about who has the politically correct point of view. When you feel your life is being threatened, your eyes stare and disappear off into space, and your body might collapse or freeze into tonic immobility, as with the amoeba. This can occur on a smaller scale (not life-threatening) when, for example, you try to explain your point of view but nobody seems to get it. You just give up.

To better understand this essential process, I spent a week at the Cape Cod Institute, learning from well-known neuroscientist Dr. Stephen Porges. His cutting-edge research and discovery, summarized in what he named the Polyvagal Theory, links the evolution of the vertebrate autonomic nervous system to the emergence of social behavior.[15] The term *poly-vagal* refers to the relatively recent discovery that the *vagus nerve* (cranial nerve X or 10, the longest nerve in the body) has more than one main branch. It was long considered to be just one rambling nerve extending from the head (cranium) to the abdomen. There are in fact two definable and recognizable branches (ventral and dorsal). The polyvagal theory updates our understanding of the functional and adaptive nature of the vagus nerve in response to the environment, and particularly to danger.

As a species, we have hierarchical evolutionary patterns, meaning that there are primary responses and alternate responses with a descending order of importance for survival. Dr. Porges's theory proposes that we mammals have three adaptive autonomic nervous system responses to the environment, which we see as safe, dangerous, or life-threatening, with bodily responses to accompany each state. The threat can be located inside the body, as in the case of food poisoning, or outside, in the environment, like an active shooter or viral pandemic. Or it may be that we perceive these conditions when they are not present, and our body and mind react as if there is danger.

Historically, these three systems are orchestrated by the primitive structures in our upper brainstem. They're instinctive and nearly reflexive in all of us. The defense responses are intended to be time-limited. They appear, do the job, and turn off. The problem is that in humans they often get stuck and linger in the "on" position. An in-the-moment defense response is desirable, but a lingering defense response is not.

3. HOW WE MOVE OR DON'T MOVE IN RESPONSE TO DANGER

Over five hundred million years ago, many of Earth's living creatures were jawless fish, with skeletons composed entirely or mainly of cartilage. When danger appeared, they froze. This is called a *dorsal vagal response*. This primary defensive response is tonic immobility, manifested by freezing and/or collapsing. In freeze, some muscles seize up simultaneously; it's a height-ened contraction of opposing agonist and antagonist muscle groups, like having the gas and the brakes on together. The collapse is similar to feigning death or playing possum, which reflects a hypotonic or flaccid state. Either way there is no movement, and the creature is left without any energy. This is the response to what is perceived as a life-threatening situation.

The original function of the immobility response was to conserve energy. If there were a danger of not getting food or oxygen, the creature would need to save its energy by not exerting energy to move. Also, it was sometimes advantageous for the creature to be still, so it would not be seen or it would be perceived as dead; somehow creatures know that dead or nonmoving prey is not inviting to certain predators.

Then, three hundred million years ago, creatures began to develop striated muscles—voluntary muscles arranged in parallel bundles—that enabled them to move more. When danger appeared, the creatures were now able to fight with limbs or take flight with legs; in other words, they could respond to danger with movement. In evolutionary development, this is the *sympathetic nervous system*, the fight-or-flight response. The sympathetic response has the function of enhanced action—for example, energizing nerves coming out of the spine and going to the muscles.

The third and most recently evolved (about sixty-six million years ago) defense system for primates and other mammals is the *social engagement system*, and it is related to feeling safe. It is now an initial response to uncertain danger—we first engage in social behavior to check things out: we try to make friends, speak sensibly, and request to "talk about it" in order to defuse potential aggression or tension. Looking at this system from an embryological standpoint, we learn that some cells from the primitive brain migrated forward to an area that regulates the striated muscles of the face and head. This became part of the *ventral vagal complex*, a.k.a. the social engagement system, and it allows us to communicate using facial movements, breath, voice, and sensory awareness. The initial function of the system was to coordinate sucking, swallowing, breathing, and vocalizing. Later in evolution (and in an individual life), it facilitates human cultural accomplishments.

Human babies go through these stages of evolutionary development and adaptation to danger, starting with the immobility response throughout their entire body. Then sympathetic and muscular systems become more responsive, and finally the ventral vagal system is activated and facial communication develops.

Human Connection, or "Let's Talk about It"

The ventral vagal system is intimately related to heart, lungs, facial expression, intonation, vocalization, and even the muscles in your middle ear that enable hearing. These elements of the social engagement system are utilized as the first line of defense for modern humans, involving the sensory apparatus and vagal connections above the main muscle-organ for breathing, the diaphragm. Your voice can convey intonations of interest, or prosody—the patterns of rhythm and sound. Your ears can hear human voices with midrange frequencies or detect danger from low-range frequencies (as in horror-movie soundtracks). The area around your eyes animates your face for communication. Facial expression conveys your state and your desire to connect, or not. Is it safe?

Our distant ancestors created groups for trust and relationships in order to safely sleep and turn their backs. This led to shelters, houses with rooms, and places to socialize. Humans excel at creating places where we can give up the vigilance, so that our bodies can relax and we are free to engage socially. When we are comfortable in social situations, we can regulate to a calm nervous system without fight or flight.

> **HUM Journal.**
> **When do you feel safe or allow yourself to relax?**
> **Do you recognize and pay sufficient attention to cues of safety?**
> **Such cues can come from inside or outside the body.**
> **Many of us will not feel safe alone on a dark street.**
> **On the other hand, we usually feel safe when surrounded**
> **by friendly faces that emanate joy and laughter.**

Going to the Gym or Running for Your Life

As animals evolved, they became more proactive in the environment. The sympathetic nervous system enabled exquisite levels of mobilization. Not limited to being our fight-or-flight response, the sympathetic nervous system is part of our optimistic and energetic nature—it is the motivation for why we exercise and move into activity. It's our energizing system. But as we've seen, it can be diverted to fight or flight.

When social engagement does not work in the face of potential danger, and there is actual danger instead, the sympathetic nervous system engages. We then experience a more rapid heartbeat and faster breathing; blood flows to where it is needed in the outer muscles; and there is less energy for digestion, which causes "butterflies in the stomach." As confirmed by research from Dr. Bessel van der Kolk, international trauma expert, we also know that our thinking brain is less active.[16] We try to fight with arms, and if that does not work, we flee with legs, running for our lives.

Regardless of the origin of an overly contracted muscular response, with tightening comes a message of danger, and our unified structure reacts accordingly with an adaptive response of fight or flight. When you are in fight-or-flight mode, you will see others as the enemy.

There was a study done to demonstrate this. The researcher showed healthy subjects photos of friendly faces, eliciting brain activity in the medial prefrontal cortex—the part of the brain that facilitates communication. The same photos shown to traumatized subjects caused increased activity in the periaqueductal gray (PAG) in the mid brainstem, while the prefrontal cortex closed down. The PAG has a major role in behavioral responses to external threat, fear, and stressors. The traumatized subjects saw friendly faces as a threat, which indicates a chronic defensive response.[17]

> **HUM Journal.**
> Any thoughts on your tendency to respond with fighting or fleeing?
> How frequently does it show up? Remember that "fleeing"
> in today's world might be simply disengaging and absorbing yourself
> in the computer or your work.

Rest and Digest, or Tonic Immobility

The dorsal vagal system is a nerve pathway to organs below the diaphragm; its default mode is rest and digest, as it is part of the *parasympathetic nervous system* (PNS; responsible for conserving energy and stimulating automatic activities when the body is at rest). You feel and hear gurgling in your stomach and/or feel calm and relaxed. In defense mode, this system is shut down or immobilized. The early vertebrates' autonomic nervous system was basically a chemical system, and the first vagal pathway associated with this system was, in general, an inhibitory one: if oxygen wasn't available, the animal could go into a state of conserving limited resources. It is a type of shutdown (like shutting down your computer to save it from expending energy).

Our body needs to shut down because the fighting or fleeing can only go on for so long before the organism is exhausted of energy. So if the fight-or-flight response was unsuccessful, and there is ongoing stress or danger, the system collapses or freezes into helplessness or tonic immobility, as we saw with the amoeba. Since the vagal communication pathway is 80 percent from gut to brain, and only 20 percent from brain to body, if the gut system shuts down, the message that goes to the brain is that something is wrong; there is danger. So, the heart rate slows down, breath is shallow, and affect (expression of emotion) is flat; there is not much movement and the person often becomes dissociated, appearing not to be "here." But note that the dorsal vagal system has a continuum with comfortable resting and digesting at one end, and an emergency shutdown response at the other end.

4. HIERARCHICAL PATTERNS IN EVERYDAY LIFE: EXPLORING SOCIAL ENGAGEMENT, FIGHT, FLIGHT, AND FREEZE

In addition to different physiological propensities, each person is conditioned to behave in a certain way. I notice this immediately when someone arrives at my studio. It could be their sweet smile, their aggressive walk, or their nonexpressive face that catches my attention. What is your program? Do you react with fighting or argumentative behavior? Do you run and hide to escape the situation? Or do you freeze and hold your breath, hoping that nobody will notice you?

"Freezing or collapsing" is not a conscious choice, it is a predetermined program, reflexive and not intentional. So, if you had an episode where you needed to fight, flee, or collapse, your body made that decision for you, and there is no need for shame. However, we tend to create a narrative of shame about what happened, as the following story illustrates.

Helen was in a grocery store when suddenly there was an incident with a masked gunman threatening and hitting the cashier, then taking money from the register. Helen froze. After the gunman fled, Helen felt terrible that she had not helped the cashier. This guilt haunted her.

But let's look closer. Helen grew up in a household with an alcoholic father. When he returned home drunk, Helen never knew if he was going to beat her or her mother or siblings. She would freeze and sit as quietly as possible, in order to not draw his attention. Helen's adaptive pattern from childhood was to freeze. This is what her nervous system had learned as a response to danger of any type. When the grocery store incident occurred, Helen's familiar pattern of "freezing" came up. It was not that she was a coward, it was simply her programmed pattern; it was Helen's nervous system that made that decision, not her cognitive mind. You cannot say, "Oh, I would have helped the cashier," because you don't really know that. The nervous system aspect of the expanded Self decides in the moment.

This pattern of helplessness can also show up in small incidents, such as when you read a job performance letter with a list of people receiving a promotion. If your name is not on the list, the helplessness response might kick in. Another example might be finding out that everybody is invited to the party but you.

Someone with a strongly conditioned fight response is likely to automatically attack a gunman in a store—or anyone else, whether the situation is highly dangerous or just a mild threat. As far as not getting a party invite, this person may go as far as to insult the host.

Many useful therapies that fully address mind, body, and spirit can help to restore healthy defensive patterns that may have been lost due to traumatic circumstances in the past, so that when new danger appears you can defend yourself. You can learn to separate the old reaction, to recognize in the body and emotions, "that was then and this is now." For teaching, therapy, and/or coaching to be effective, the first step is to establish safety and trust. Biologically, safety is the beginning point for the nervous system to be able to shift out of its defensive mode. Then a person's muscles can become more pliable and flexible, the voice friendly and nonthreatening, and autonomic balance restored, in breath and heartbeat.

EX-PLORATIONS OF SOCIAL ENGAGEMENT, FIGHT, FLIGHT, AND FREEZE

These EX-plorations can help your body and mind to effectively distinguish the three states of safety, danger, and life-threat and the appropriate responses to safe and unsafe conditions.

A. Freeze.

Imagine yourself at your job. You have tried to do your best work, in every way possible, for months, but then you got that letter listing all the promotions and your name was not on it. Feel what happens in your body—perhaps your body feels collapsed, and drained of energy. Feel what it is like to walk around the room with this pattern of dragging energy. How freely do your arms and legs move? Do you move with constriction or flow? Slowly, after you have fully explored the feelings, continue to walk and release the collapsed pattern by gradually moving more actively. Notice the transition.

Stuck in a freeze state.

B. Fight/Flight.

Imagine a loud noise goes off nearby, a door slamming or an alarm sounding. Feel your body go into your version of a startle pattern, perhaps tightened shoulders, or a tense neck or limbs. Feel what it is like to walk around the room with this pattern. How freely do your arms and legs move? Do you move with constriction or flow? Slowly, as you walk and after you have fully explored it, release the startle pattern. Notice the transition.

Startled before fight or flight.

Enjoying social engagement.

Enjoying more social engagement.

C. Social Engagement.

Imagine you are with good friends. There is laughter in the air, smiling faces, and plenty of room to breathe with a long, slow exhale. Your eyes are taking in the pleasant atmosphere as you mill about the space, and you have a small smile on your lips. Feel what it is like to walk around the room. How freely do your arms and legs move? Do you move with constriction or flow? Can you stay with this pattern?

D. Do you feel safety, danger, or life-threat when . . .

You are in the arms of a loved one.

You walk onto a stage to perform or give a talk.

You want to tell your partner your relationship is not working.

You are opening the college acceptance letter.

You are waiting for that medical diagnosis.

OR

When you win the lottery!

CHAPTER

5

NERVOUS SYSTEMS AND RESILIENCE: THE ABILITY TO BOUNCE BACK

The different nervous systems run programs that govern so much of our lives. Understanding how they work can help to regulate *homeostasis*, our natural state of stable equilibrium. We have these multiple systems in place to ensure our well-being and to help us recover from difficult situations. The better our understanding of how these systems work, the more effectively we can access the possibility of our own health, which invites the expanded Self.

1. AUTONOMIC NERVOUS SYSTEM: ALL THE THINGS YOU DON'T HAVE TO THINK ABOUT

Jump up and down for three to five minutes. Feel your breath and heart rate speed up. Then stop, and feel your breath and heart rate slow down. You have just witnessed your autonomic nervous system in action.

The nervous system has two primary branches—the central nervous system and the peripheral nervous system. The autonomic nervous system (ANS) is a division of the peripheral nervous system, and it influences the internal organs. The ANS controls functions that happen automatically, such as heartbeat, breathing, digestion, sexual arousal, and more, in response to your life activities.

As presented in Chapter 2, your nervous system is shaped by your early childhood experiences. The good news is that your nervous system is also shaped by your present experiences. If your childhood was laden with developmental mis-attunements, it is possible to have better experiences now to change that wiring. Today, professionals commonly say, "Nerves that fire together, wire together," which means that when you repeat any experience over and over, the brain learns to activate the same neurons each time. So, focusing on positive experiences creates new and positive neuro-networks and pathways. Thus, "It is never too late to have a happy childhood."

All the nervous system functions are greatly affected by different parts of the brain. Simply put, we have a three-part brain. The lowest in placement and evolution is the reptilian or primitive brain; it is concerned with survival and basic needs (vital functions), and it communicates with sensation. Above it is the limbic brain, which manages our emotions and communicates through feelings; above that is the neocortex, or executive, logical brain, which communicates by thinking. Because some of the ANS is housed in the reptilian brain, sharing that space with the survival centers, if a person's survival has been threatened at any time in life, then most likely there is some autonomic dysregulation affecting one or more of the ANS functions. More on what to do about this in the next chapter ("Trauma").

The areas in the brain that regulate the autonomic system also influence immune and endocrine function. We can't think of these three systems as independent, as they are all closely related via feedback loops. For example, the emotion of fear triggers the fight-flight response in the autonomic nervous system, which causes the endocrine system to release hormones such as cortisol and epinephrine that support the fight-flight actions. Similarly, if these "stress hormones" remain elevated over time, they compromise our immune system, and disease is certain to follow.

One way to calm your dysregulated nervous system is to learn to "pendulate" (a usage coined by Dr. Peter Levine). You recognize the stress or contraction; and you also find something that is positive, expansive, or a resource in your life. Then you go back and forth or pendulate between the two. A rhythm is created. This often brings the nervous system into a less stressed, more regulated state.

The autonomic nervous system is not a motor system; it is a feedback system that monitors and regulates organs. If the feedback system is disrupted for any reason, then the organ(s) will not function fully or optimally. Thus, ANS function is always a factor in disease. In times of stress, the body's energy goes to protection, not to restoring organ function, and this leaves us vulnerable to illness.

If you think of the ANS as a surveillance system that regulates the organs, then you can consciously work to improve the safety of your environment. Dr. Stephen Porges uses the metaphor of the body as an automobile: If your car overheats, you can fill it with water (comparable to giving medication). Or, you can replace parts or valves (comparable to organ surgery). But if the problem is that the regulator, the thermostat (comparable to the ANS), is not working properly, nothing will solve the problem except fixing the thermostat.[18] Cues of safety in the body let the ANS regulator work in a more optimal way.

Often what seems, on the surface, to be the problem is not the actual problem. Just because a pain shows up in the physical realm, like in your heart, does not mean that the solution is a physical one, although it could be. Patching the symptoms may alleviate pain in the short term, but for long-term relief, you need to be willing to look deeper. Pain in your heart could be emotional in nature, such as with a relationship breakup or job loss; it also could be physical, as in the case of an arterial blockage. The pain you might experience in organs or other parts of the body due to ANS dysregulation follows this same line of thinking; the cause can either be emotional or physical, or both.

The heart is, of course, one of the main branches of the ANS. Prior to his death in 2008, Dr. Michael DeBakey, the famous heart surgeon, received the Presidential Medal of Freedom, the National Medal of Science, and the Congressional Gold Medal for his contributions to public health. At the ceremony, a humorous medical anecdote told by a speaker reflected Dr. DeBakey's worldwide fame:

> Joe was removing some engine valves from a car on the lift when he spotted Dr. DeBakey, who was standing off to the side, waiting for the service manager. Joe, somewhat of a loud mouth, shouted across the garage, "Hey DeBakey—is that you? Come over here a minute."
>
> The famous surgeon, a bit surprised, walked over to where Joe was working. In a loud voice, so all could hear, Joe said argumentatively, "So Mr. Fancy Doctor, look at this work. I also take valves out, grind them, put in new parts, and when I finish this baby will purr like a kitten. So how come you get the big bucks, when you and I are doing basically the same work?" According to the tale, DeBakey, very embarrassed, walked away, but first he said softly to the man, "While the engine is still running?"

2. ENTERIC NERVOUS SYSTEM: THE GUT LEADS AND THE HEAD FOLLOWS—SOMETIMES

Everyone knows about the brain in your head, but few people know about the second brain in your gut. It's called your "gut-brain," or the *enteric nervous system*, and it is in constant communication with the brain in your head. The gut-brain is often called the "primitive brain," since it responds to subtle cues in the environment. The common saying, "I know it in my gut," is a testimony to its informative powers.

The enteric nervous system is embedded in the lining of the organs of the gastrointestinal system—the esophagus, stomach, small intestine, and colon. It spreads its fibers out like an anemone. As a subdivision of the peripheral nervous system, the gut-brain directly controls the gastrointestinal system.

There are several reasons why the enteric nervous system is regarded as a second brain. First, it can operate autonomously and receives considerable energy input from the autonomic nervous system. In healthy bodies, the enteric nervous system communicates with the central nervous system through the parasympathetic and sympathetic nervous systems. However, vertebrate studies show that when the vagus nerve is severed, the enteric nervous system continues to function. This means that the gut is the only part of our body that does not need the spinal cord, or the brain in our head, to operate. The head's brain is not the enteric system's boss.

The gut derives its power from its many nerve endings—more than in the entire head-brain. To give you an idea of its "pull," the enteric nervous system contains one billion neurons, more than in the spinal cord. One of the interesting roles of these nerve endings is that they read the gut microbe activity and initiate a response to modulate inflammation, based on whether or not they detect pathogenic versus nonpathogenic organisms. In this way, the gut can have an effect on your mood, stress levels, and overall inflammation. Sometimes you may wonder why you feel blah for no apparent reason; it could be your gut.

Another reason the enteric nervous system is likened to a brain is that it makes use of the same neurotransmitters (such as acetylcholine, dopamine, and serotonin) as the central nervous system. Serotonin, in particular, is crucial for feelings of well-being; around 90 percent of the body's supply is made in the gut, operating as a signaling mechanism to begin the flow of digestive enzymes for foods moving through. This is why diet is key to mental health: a healthy gut-brain boosts serotonin levels and your mood.

Serotonin also acts as a go-between, keeping the brain in the head informed about what is happening in the gut. This communication exchange, however, is mostly one-way, with more of the information traveling from the gut to the head. This tells us that information from the gut-brain is more relevant than information in the head-brain: if the gut says there is reason to be alarmed, the central nervous system will not be able to calm down and the body will remain in danger mode. You know what it is like when you are agitated and someone says to you, "Calm down." You can't! If you could, you would.

The head-brain deals with thinking, reasoning, and logic, and the gut-brain deals with digestion and "gut feelings." When you have a gut feeling, it is a message about the environment—your inner environment, your thoughts or needs, or your outer environment, your surroundings. In our society, we often discount or dismiss these messages. This is a mistake. Gut feelings do matter, and they have a scientific and evolutionary basis; *they are part of your expanded Self.* I strongly suggest you pay attention to them if you don't already. The gut-brain and the head-brain work together to integrate and bring coherence and congruence to our social and neurological systems. We are wise to foster a healthy connection to both, so we can be resilient and bounce back from overwhelming incidents.

> **HUM Journal.**
> **Write about your gut feelings.**
> **What leads for you—your head-brain or gut-brain?**
> **When you were a child, were you able to follow your authentic gut feelings?**
> **If no one listened to or responded to your gut feelings,**
> **you had to hold them down—the painful feelings had to be shut**
> **off because they were too hard to hold alone.**
> **Now most people don't listen to these messages from the**
> **gut and wonder if they even exist.**

3. VAGAL TONE: A SENSE OF WELL-BEING

The nervous system is resilient: it goes up when excited, and down when dejected. A healthy ANS vacillates between up and down but readily returns to an even, calm flow. Dr. Dan Siegel coined the term *window of tolerance* for the even flow.[19] It refers to the space within which we can manage our lives and the events that happen to us. You can exceed your window of tolerance on the high side and explode with anger and rage, or go below it and experience helplessness and collapse.

We pick up nuances—interesting, intuitive, or important information—through the sensors in the ventral upper branch in the face and dorsal lower branch in the gut. When a potential danger is detected, the ventral vagus will engage and hold down the sympathetic nervous system's high-stress response until one can be sure of the degree of danger. Thus, keeping in touch with a person using eye contact, a gentle touch to the arm, or a prosodic voice, can prevent someone from entering the activated state. I am sure you have calmed a friend or loved one by speaking in a soothing voice, or in some other way.

In turn, if there is much danger in a high-stress situation, and you are operating in a sympathetic response (the heart is beating wildly, etc.) for too long, the older, more primitive dorsal branch will engage and squash the action of the newer sympathetic system. It is simply too dangerous to continue to live with that high level of sympathetic activation. This is one of the safety functions of the dorsal vagus nerve.

A safety function of the ventral vagus nerve is to act as a braking system and gently slow down the pacemaker of the heart. It is responsible for either increasing or decreasing the heartbeat in relation to what is going on around us. In its natural state, the heart has a pace-maker that keeps it beating more than one hundred times per minute, which is quite fast. But under normal conditions, the ventral vagus comes online to perform its function as a brake, to slow it down. That's why most of us have a nice, calm, regular slower beat of 60–80 beats per minute. In unusual or extreme conditions, where danger or threat may be present, the brake comes off. We then experience more energy and life-force, including a full blast of oxygen and increased blood flow and heart rate, in order to handle the situation.

Simply put, if you take the vagal brake off, there will be more energy and flow. If you put the vagal brake on, there will be more settling as the heart rate decreases. Balance is crucial: the expanded Self includes balance. Try it. Imagine bicycle hand brakes. When you need a bit more energy, picture the brakes coming off. When you want to calm down a bit, put the brakes on.

4. VAGAL TONE AND BREATH

An easy, flowing breath is deeply connected to heart rate and vagal tone. The social engage-ment complex includes breathing and heart rate. When your vagus nerve is toned, as you inhale, your heart rate goes slightly up; and when you exhale, your heart rate goes down. The difference between the inhale and exhale is called respiratory sinus arrhythmia, a sensitive index of cardiac vagal tone, which is a component of your heart rate variability (HRV). The measure of HRV (the variance in time between the beats of your heart) is being increasingly linked to a number of physical conditions. It is good to have a noticeable difference between the two, which indicates a healthy vagus nerve, or high vagal tone.

High vagal tone improves the function of many body systems: it causes better blood sugar regulation, reduces the risk of stroke and cardiovascular disease, lowers blood pressure, and improves digestion. Higher vagal tone is also associated with better mood, less anxiety, quicker thinking, and more stress resilience. Low vagal tone is associated with cardiovascular condi-tions and strokes, depression, diabetes, chronic fatigue syndrome, cognitive impairment, and higher rates of inflammatory conditions, including all autoimmune diseases.

EX-ERCISE: TONE VOO TO TUNE THE VAGUS

This EX-ercise is intended to help you learn more about vagal tone, nervous system flexibility, and "settling" or calming down.

1. Place your hand on your belly, two inches below your belly button. There is an energy center there. Feel your belly move as you breathe. On your exhale, give a slight push in toward your spine. Repeat four or five times. Take your hand off and rest. Notice. Joe Gifford, a wonderful performance coach who taught until he was ninety-seven years of age, often had his students put their hand on this energy spot to improve their performance with centering.

2. With your hand on that spot, notice your breath, in and out. As you exhale, allow your breath to continue to its uninterrupted conclusion. Then add a low-pitched vowel sound on the exhale: "oo." Repeat four or five times. Rest. Notice.

3. Many teachers over the years have had me put my hand on this part of my belly, which is also called the *hara* or energy center, to help me feel centered. And many teachers have had me make a low-tone "oo" sound to vibrate the belly and calm or integrate the nervous system. Both practices are valuable on their own. But it wasn't until I saw and heard Dr. Peter Levine demonstrating them together that things made more sense for me. Peter Levine teaches "voo" and explains why it works. The vagus nerve has many fibers in your belly. At least 80 percent of the fibers are afferent; they go from the body to the brain. This information tells your brain how you feel. As your belly vibrates with the sound, the nerve endings can release a bit, which allows the messages to be transported to your brain. And you can feel a change.

4. Tone the word *voo* and direct the low sound to your belly. Allow an easy, full breath in and exhale with a *voo*. Notice what happens.

If you are shut down, this exercise will bring you up and give you more energy to be present. If you are activated and anxious, it will calm you down. If for any reason you cannot make the *voo* sound, you can imagine it and get similar results.

> **DO** Practice the *voo* sound whenever you want to self-regulate your nervous system. It can settle you down or give you energy.

TRAUMA AND OVERWHELM: FINDING EASE UNDERNEATH PAIN

You have arrived at the chapter on trauma . . . . If you feel comfortable reading it now, that is fine. If you prefer to read it later, that is also fine. But do read it because your expanded Self includes everything—all aspects of human life. How can you have a manual for being human and not talk about trauma? Especially today, when people are recognizing a type of collective trauma that we are all born into.

Trauma is a fact of life: something occurs that is scary, awful, or overwhelming and no one was there to help. It happens to everybody at one time or another, occurring in one shocking moment or over a series of continuing events, such as chronic misattunement, neglect, or abuse (which is known as *developmental trauma* when it happens at a young age). With trauma, it is difficult to be fully present to life, as part of us is living in the past moment of the traumatic event. Understanding the underpinning biological sequences that require resolution can be instrumental for survival and well-being. Healing requires managing overwhelming and unbearable moments, transforming sensations, and finding rhythmic balance and safety in the present moment. This may be part of your work on the journey to your expanded Self—it seems to be for all of us, to one degree or another. Sometimes seemingly minor events or necessary medical interventions have long-running effects. It's important to look closely at your thoughts, bodily symptoms, and sensations to make connections and fresh choices at the right junctures.

1. "TOO MUCH, TOO FAST, TOO SOON"

Life, with its usual highs and lows, ideally flows along seamlessly with minor disruptions. When a major disruption or difficult situation comes along, we adjust, adapt, or regroup to try to resolve the problem and keep the flow going. Sometimes time stops. There is a realization that we don't have the resources to handle what is coming up. In the stress of the moment, a new sensory snapshot is taken, creating a two-channel reality for our lives moving forward—one channel where life moves on as best it can and the other one where we are stuck in the snapshot and the trauma.

With trauma, our sense of unity gets fragmented; parts of us split off, and behavior may subsequently ping-pong between rational thinking with presence and inappropriate reactions to everyday simple moments, due to subconscious or unconscious flashbacks.

It's important to remember that trauma is a personalized reaction to the event; it is not the event itself. Sometimes an event seems overwhelming and out of your control; you cannot adjust or adapt. It's as if the rug has been pulled out from under you. We experience trauma on all levels of self—mentally, physically, emotionally, and spiritually. The event is too much, too soon, or too fast: one insult might be okay, but constant putting down is…too much. A ten-year-old is placed on the fourteen-year-olds' baseball team and gets injured, because he cannot keep up; it was…too soon. Or, you needed to stop the car, but it was moving…too fast. In your attempt to try and save yourself, the situation becomes uncontrollable. At that point, the system fights, flees, or shuts down altogether. You have entered the world of trauma.

When our system is overwhelmed, fast-circuit learning takes place. The information bypasses the hippocampus, where normal memory is integrated, and goes directly to the lower reptilian brain, becoming lodged in implicit memory. The memory is then encoded in the body and later shows up as symptoms like aches and pains, stomach upset, or tension. Even if you edit information in your conscious awareness, the patterns of the traumatic response might continue to reside in your musculature and implicit memory and can emerge at inopportune times.

As many life stories and a great deal of research show, the adaptive patterns and pathways in your brain get carved out early in life. Not only must trauma's effects in the body be understood, but new neural pathways must be created. This is an important step on the road to healing and greater access to your expanded Self.

With trauma, we need completion; the defensive responses that became active in our effort to save or protect our self must be resolved, which we will examine next.

2. THE BIOLOGICAL MECHANISM: WHAT TRAUMA LOOKS LIKE

From the work of Dr. Peter Levine, we know what trauma looks like in the animal world.[20] The deer are grazing in the grass and nurturing their young. Then there is a sound nearby; perhaps a twig snaps. The deer become instantly poised and alert, defensive responses intact (muscles taut, ears perked up, noses sniffing), ready to spring in haste if necessary. They look around for the confirmation of danger. If there is none, the deer relax. Let's look at what needs to happen in a deer's physiology as it returns to grazing.

In the moment that there seems to be danger, the biology says, "Go for it. It is life or death." Tremendous energy arises, and all biological systems are prepared to work for survival. There is no second-place winner in the wild.

When the danger is a false alarm, a change takes place. At the peak of alertness, when the animal realizes there is no immediate danger, ripples of energy in the neck travel down the body, through to the deer's legs. The body experiences rhythmic undulations such as trembling or shaking, which transform the energy that would have been used to fight or flee. The energy gets discharged, as the nervous system resolves from high to low tension. When the trembling movements cease, the deer often takes a rather large spontaneous breath to signify its relief. It is over…for now.

As humans, we have the same mechanisms at play. And while genetic programs have not changed, modern society has—it causes many of us to suppress and repress our responses. As such, we tend not to complete all the biological steps that the deer went through. Shaking and trembling is not embraced or encouraged in our modern society, and crying is considered weak; this prevents the discharge. So, we don't shake and cry. We are also afraid to feel the strong energies that have been generated, and we have a drink or take a tranquilizer instead. Because the steps do not get completed, our human systems continue to operate as if they are still in danger. Our autonomic nervous system has become dysregulated; if we cannot restore balance, we can lose our sense of range of appropriate responses, perhaps finding ourselves not excited or aroused by life anymore. Behaviors are out of sync with the body.

For example, if a man is driving his car and out of the corner of his eye he sees another car coming toward him, his survival brain generates a tremendous amount of energy to save him. His sympathetic nervous system sends energy to his muscles, and his arms move to turn the wheel to avoid being hit. Even if he does not get hit, he is shaken up. All that energy that was generated is coursing through his body; meanwhile, mental images of what could have happened flash through his mind. Part of him wants to sit or lie down and rest a moment, to recover from the near hit. Another part of him remembers his meeting and his need to rush off and not be late. A process called *executive cortical suppression* takes over, and he overrides his need for rest—the biological imperative to "shake it off" and catch his breath.

The overridden instinct to rest and regroup needs to be acted upon for balance to be restored. The body's instinctive need to discharge was interrupted. The incredible amount of energy that was mobilized in his arms to turn the wheel remains in his body. The biological action plan, therefore, is still in action and wanting to do something. At a future time, that undischarged energy may show up as a physical symptom, like an eye twitch, digestive problems, or a mysterious ache in the rotator cuff of his shoulder. Or, it could appear as an emotional symptom, such as irritability or emotional outbursts.

Why do the symptoms show up as they do? As you've read, the reptilian part of your brain handles your survival mechanisms; it also handles your autonomic nervous system. If your survival responses have been disturbed and not restored, as in the case we just examined, then the ANS will begin to show dysregulation. Symptoms can show up in respiratory, cardiac, and digestive systems, and your sleep. If not addressed, the symptoms can turn into syndromes like asthma, fibromyalgia, irritable bowel syndrome, chronic fatigue, and more. Any kind of trauma resolution must include addressing the everyday functions of the ANS: getting enough sleep, digesting well, etc.

Resolving trauma, therefore, is critical for health, but that may be easier said than done. When the trauma response is not completed or resolved, it may become habitual and turn into post-traumatic stress disorder, or PTSD. Many people, both children and adults, suffer deeply from this condition.

3. RESPONSES TO TRAUMA

After a traumatic incident, there are two common modes of response: reenactment or avoidance. In the reenactment pattern, you get yourself into similar situations because the system is hoping to work through it—to complete it, once and for all—in a more constructive way. An example is the person who sprains the same ankle repeatedly. In the avoidance mode, you never want to go near the situation again. So, a person who got hit by a red car will more than likely not ever buy a red car.

I think the most helpful thing to remember is that when you have an accident or traumatic experience, allow yourself to stay in the moment afterward and feel the bodily sensations. This might include trembling, shaking, numbness, or crying. Just lie still and listen to your body's needs, and be grateful that you survived. You often do not like to experience these helpless feelings. Instead, you say, "I am fine," and try to act normally. But it is better to admit the truth: "I am not fine, and I need a little time to recover." This can save you from the possibility of ongoing physical, emotional, and psychological impairment.

Once when I was hired to work on a film set, the leading actress hit her head on the floor. She was ready to get up and continue the scene. I stepped in and made sure she stayed on the ground. She kept saying she was fine, but I could see that she was not. After a while, the director came over, as if to say "time is money." But I insisted she continue to lie on the floor. It took another minute or so and her head trembled a bit and she took a deep, spontaneous breath. Then, she was ready to return to the scene. She thanked me for showing her what needed to happen.

These steps work for single incidents. The beauty of our biology is that there are mechanisms in place that generate recovery—when we let them function. However, people exposed to chronic stress, particularly young children, experience more difficulty with resiliency and have to create stronger adaptive patterns. If the foundation is off balance from the stress of trying to survive, then stress becomes incorporated in the nervous system. Infants who are put to sleep in a room by themselves feel such terror at being abandoned that they cry and cry until they can no longer cry. Their system is so overwhelmed that they cannot bear the pain, and usually fall asleep out of exhaustion. They need to dissociate to survive the pain. Some parents see the child as peacefully sleeping. But this is not so, and it creates a mis-attunement between caregiver and child.

Or, going farther back, stress can come from the mother during the birth process. With fear or stress, the nerves in a mother's pelvis that sympathetically control blood flow to the placenta will diminish blood flow to the fetus, resulting in more carbon dioxide and less oxygen. In turn, the muscles in her thighs tighten, thereby passing this tension to the fetus.

An emergency response is needed. Thus, the baby's nervous system, trying to survive, adapts to the stress. The fetus learns to be anxious and depressed. The underlying foundation and problem are created by the body. Later, however, professionals will say the child has a tendency toward being stressed, or is hyperactive. But the mind and body grow together; motor behaviors inform mind development. "The fabric of your mind is woven by your body."[21]

Let it be clear that no one is to blame in this scenario. This is how modern life is: there is often too much stress for most people to handle efficiently, and it is hard to escape that fact.

"If evolution really works, how come mothers only have two hands?"
— MILTON BERLE

The Adverse Childhood Experiences (ACE) Study, a long-term, in-depth analysis of more than seventeen thousand adults enrolled in Kaiser Permanente's San Diego care program, revealed that children who experience multiple traumas are more likely to have illnesses as adults.[22] The study, headed by renowned physician and researcher Dr. Vincent J. Felitti, came about "by accident." Dr. Felitti was working with overweight patients in his obesity clinic. And although many lost large amounts of weight, when the patients were interviewed months later, they had regained the weight. Felitti wondered why, which led to the ACE study. His conclusion? If there was abuse, neglect, or household dysfunction (divorce, substance abuse, incarceration, mental illness, etc.) in childhood, those people were susceptible to early illness and disease.

I had one overweight client who tried everything to lose weight, unsuccessfully. As we started working together and she began paying closer attention to her body, she had a fleeting implicit memory of visits to her grandmother's house in the summers. The memory was an image of the refrigerator with a lock on it that her grandmother put there to prevent her from eating. So when she had access to food, she ate mounds of it. She had totally forgotten that memory. But once she recalled the denial and desperation, and began to work through the associated trauma, she began to lose weight.

Overwhelming events create what we call a *trauma vortex*, defined as the whirlpool of chaos in trauma's aftermath—a downward spiral that traps the traumatized. But nature tends toward balance, and its inherent spiralic quality is a built-in resource. In the world of trauma, the balance to the trauma vortex is called the *healing vortex*. It refers to humankind's innate resiliency—our capacity to manage tragedy and to heal on our own. Awareness and resources engage the healing vortex. But we often miss it.

When I was young, I had my tonsils out because my brother was having his out. In the following years and in my trauma training, I always looked at it as a painful, lonely experience. Fifty years later, I was complaining to my brother how that incident was so traumatic for me, painful and alone. He looked at me in wonder and said, "But I was there with you." I felt a wash of softness come over my whole body. I almost cried. The healing vortex was there.

What I know from years of training and experience is that a child undergoing difficulty, from mis-attunement to abuse, is trying—and forced—to adapt to his or her outer environment. Since the environment is unhealthy, the child needs to compromise his or her physical, psychological, emotional, and musculoskeletal integrity and well-being. I see examples of these compromises every day in my work. I also see the amazing changes that can occur with the right kind of somatic processing, which incorporates the inherent biological quest for well-being. *The key to this process is recognizing and holding the trauma vortex and healing vortex together.*

Personally, I find this to be one of the most amazing aspects of *Humanual* work. After so many years of treating trauma, I know, and I know this deep within, that there is something there in the moment of overwhelm that allows access to a kind of resource, or strength, on some very deep level, and that healing is possible. That is…finding the ease underneath the pain.

4. CORTISOL: WHEN IT HELPS, WHEN IT HURTS

Let's look at the adverse effects of toxic stress. Prolonged stress equals *cortisol* secretion equals mobilization equals fight-flight.

Stress can be external or internal, good or bad, perceived or real. Your body contains thousands of nerve cells, receptors, and neurotransmitters that respond to stress and keep you safe. During short-term stress reactions, the body secretes many hormones, including adrenaline (epinephrine) and noradrenaline (norepinephrine). If the danger passes, the chemical reaction will be over quickly and the system returns to a state of equilibrium.

Often the stress is not short term, but a chronic low-grade stress that can impact health in the long term. Whether the stress is a family dispute, financial debt, or an abusive boss (for example), if you have to be with it daily, the constant threat can make you feel helpless. The system needs a more lasting hormone—like cortisol—to combat the ongoing stressful dilemma.

Endocrinologist Hans Selye, a pioneer in the study of the stress response, writes, "Chronic stress, or threat, no longer demands the immediate and maximal cardiac and muscular response that is associated with an imminent life threat. It basically requires that the animal's body be prepared for a period of chronic readiness for danger and potentially higher demands of energy."[23]

Cortisol is a steroid produced by the adrenal glands that prevents the release of substances in the body that cause inflammation. Normally, cortisol is secreted in small doses and functions to keep us alert during the day, but it wears off by night. Many people have cortisol imbalances; they have a difficult time getting going in the morning, or getting to sleep at night without pills or some other kind of substance.

When secreted over the long term, cortisol interferes with our immune system. It can also lead to increased blood sugar levels, belly fat, and memory loss related to the hippocampus.[24] The Mayo Clinic corroborates this research.[25]

But remember, the instinctive body is always working to secure our health. The collected belly fat is a good example of our exquisite design. If you are under constant low-grade stress, the body is keeping fat for you to have energy to fight with. Of course, that would be helpful if you were fighting in the jungle. But if you are sitting at a desk fighting off unsatisfied customers all day, that fat just accumulates as a chubby belly. According to a book on this subject, *Fat Around the Middle*, "In a stressful situation, the adrenaline that is released helps you get alert and focused, whilst the cortisol increases levels of fat and sugar in the bloodstream. However, unless you do something physical (as your body is expecting you to), all that extra energy in the form of fat and glucose has nowhere to go and must simply be re-deposited as fat."[26]

5. RESTORING EQUILIBRIUM: HEALING SYMPTOMS OF OVERWHELM

The body-mind-spirit can heal itself back to unity from the fragments of trauma. Healing can most easily occur when you feel welcomed and safe. This sense of safety can help your body utilize homeostatic functions to rejuvenate and create health. Healing also involves finding the impulses that were lost in the midst of the difficult moment.

Self-regulation and Co-regulation

You know when you feel regulated, or synchronized—you sleep well, digest well, and breathe comfortably, and really don't need to think about it much. Because the ANS becomes dysregulated in trauma, its systems (sleep, respiration, digestion, etc.) can also be out of sync. This can be accompanied by pain and/or discomfort in the body, and you do start to think about it. And when your body is uncomfortable, you do not want to feel it.

The process called *interoception* is both the conscious action of paying attention to what is happening in your body and the unconscious monitoring of your body by the nervous system. Interoceptive feedback loops in the nervous system send messages regarding the status of your body. What happens with overwhelm and trauma is that these feedback loops are turned off, or at least dampened. That's why learning to pay attention to your inner bodily sensations is a crucial part of healing the body's systems and regaining health. The process may be slow, but you can begin reacquainting yourself with your body in very small increments.

EX-PLORATION: SELF-REGULATION, PART 1

Find one small, pleasant sensation in your body. It might be warmth, expansion, or waves. As you pay attention to it, allow it to move, or spread, or change, and then settle. Notice what happens in your whole body, your breath, and your emotions. Is your system more able to calm, or regulate? Note that I am not asking you to get rid of uncomfortable sensations or parts; just find a pleasant one, and see what happens when you work with it.

In interoception, signals from the body travel to the insula and cingulate in the brain, which have the capacity to calm, or down-regulate, the amygdala. The amygdala is the smoke alarm for the body, which goes off when there is real or perceived danger. But it is often stuck in the "on" position because of unfinished defensive responses or some kind of emotional turmoil. Once the danger signal has been turned off, the impulses for healthy responses are available. Sometimes simply placing your hands on your middle back (the kidney/adrenal area) can help calm the amygdala.

DO | When you feel mildly agitated.

If your parents were tuned to your needs and you got proper co-regulation as a young child, then you have a greater capacity to self-regulate. A healthy nervous system craves interactions that bring about health and well-being and allow creative thought processes. If you see someone as a threat, then there is no co-regulation.

Recovery from trauma involves learning to self-regulate your system, and to co-regulate with others. This means that you can recognize and change your arousal system as it becomes activated. A few minutes of watching your breath and extending your exhale, going for a walk, taking a warm bath, tapping some acupressure points, finding your support, meditating, or engaging in body awareness techniques (such as yoga, Pilates, Alexander Technique, Feldenkrais, qigong, tai chi, martial arts, defense training, or music and art therapy) all can be helpful for self-regulation and decreasing arousal from small overwhelming incidents. Orienting and finding pleasure in your surroundings can also be helpful. To learn to self-regulate from bigger events, more therapeutic approaches are advised.[27]

"The issue of self-regulation needs to become front and center in the treatment of trauma."
— DR. BESSEL VAN DER KOLK[28]

EX-PLORATION: SELF-REGULATION, PART 2

Some simple questions to ask when you feel constriction and want to self-regulate:

- Where is it in my body?
- Does it increase, decrease, or stay the same, as I am aware of it?
- What happens next?
- What else is there?
- How am I relating to my environment?
- Am I curious about what I am actually doing?

DO   Anytime you feel stuck or a sense of constriction.

A story of self-regulation

My client Sally felt frumpy and heavy all over, as if she weighed a thousand pounds. She began to work with herself in a *Humanual* way, which she learned in sessions with me. She started to wonder if any spot was not heavy. She noted that her hair was not heavy, but that was all, nothing else. She continued doing the "Be With" exploration (see Chapter 13, first section) and found that her pinkie finger was also not heavy. She said that this didn't seem like much, but it became an important player because it was not heavy. Soon her nose was added, and then eyelashes and brows, more fingers, toes, legs, and in very little time her entire body felt less heavy. She told me later, "When you pay attention, the system self-regulates. Usually when I feel grumpy, it stays on. I typically eat three ice creams, go to the gym and work out like crazy, or yell at someone. Who actually thinks to stay with what is happening on the inside in a curious and nonjudgmental way?"

> **HUM Journal.**
> Can you find your nonheavy places? Oddly, when you shift all the heavy bits of yourself, the whole of you releases in a way that lets you become heavy to connect to the ground, to receive support. I call it "good heavy."

Movement

People of all cultures have traditional movements that help to regulate and calm them. In Asian countries, you see thousands of people in the parks doing tai chi. Irish people do Irish stepdance. Africans have drumming circles. Argentinians do tango. Indians do yoga. Why do people do that? They've discovered that there's something they can do to regulate their internal systems. What do you do?

When you do any of these movements, you begin to realize that you can change yourself. You can find some self-empowerment—your feet on the ground supported by the earth, your breath flowing as your chest and belly move, and your head suspended and held high. You are not a victim. You can change your body and your thinking. This is a different approach from self-medicating with alcohol or drugs and lying around—or enrolling in the modern medical system where, if you can't stand something, you can take a pill or have surgery to change the symptoms.

Humans are social beings; we interact and communicate with words. Mammals are able to share their internal feelings and states. Sometimes talking to a friend or therapist about an overwhelming event helps you feel better. Expressing your inner experience can normalize it for you. Many trauma talk-therapists these days realize that including a physical approach is not really optional but necessary, as trauma lives on in the body, mind, and spirit even when the event is over.

Coherent activity can be a resource for recovery: survival responses need to be awakened with internal sensory integration and movement. Rhythmic movement, like rocking, or swaying, performed alone or within a safe community, helps people feel how their bodies move and relate in the environment. Jumping on a bellicon (a trampoline with bungee cords instead of wire springs) or throwing a ball can also help bring back a sense of inner and outer movement. Arm swinging, body rocking, or weight shifting all have a place here. Freedom of movement, in particular, is lost in trauma, neglect, and abuse, especially in kids. Rhythmical interaction can restore this, and is crucial to our well-being. Rhythm and synchrony are what we are made of—the very fabric of being.

Dancing, drumming, singing, and touching can allow you to feel your own sensations; and when undertaken in a group setting, one organism is placed in rhythm with other organisms. It's a way of overcoming the deep, frozen sense of separation that traumatized people have with others. Playing games or noncompetitive sports engages our body and nervous system to move back and forth in healthy, friendly, and appealing ways. Acting in Shakespearean plays has also been found to be helpful in recovering from trauma; getting in touch with the rage in you by killing the king or finding your true love (a Romeo or Juliet) can be highly therapeutic.

> **HUM Journal.**
> **Write about your rhythmic movement.**

Not only is movement necessary to heal, but *how you move* is crucial to healing and to not having to repeat the same pattern(s). If you continue to neglect connecting your feet to the ground, you will continue to feel like you need to hold yourself up. As you hold yourself up, you will feel like you need to do it all. Instead, realize that you are held by the earth and that the life-force is coursing within and around you, to help you feel supported as you relate to others and your own expanded Self.

EX-PLORE: DIFFICULT SITUATIONS

When there is some kind of difficulty, either an emotional or physical pain, here are two options:

1. Where do you notice it in your body? Sense it. Explore the sensations. Get to know them. Explore the parts of you that are involved, possibly with pendulation (Chapter 5). Allow the sensations to shift. This might include bringing the system to the level of energy charge that existed when the moment first occurred, and completing the action plan or contacting the deep emotion. Find what was there but did not get to be spoken or executed. Remember, it was already there; you just did not or could not see it or respond to it. It may also be helpful to explore making

up a new ending to the story—how you would have wanted the story to end. One client imagined what it would be like to fall on pillows instead of concrete.

2. Recognize the difficulty, or the habit. Stay with it. Be honest with yourself about what you are actually doing (trying to impress, hide, grab, or protect, etc.). At the same time, know that there is a larger reality or consciousness that is not the habit, but your *potential*. Remember who you were before the trauma occurred, or imagine what your life could be in the future. Feel the presence of the larger reality in your Self and in your use. Stay with both—the difficult moment and the potential. As you bring both perspectives, the difficulty will not be taking up all the real estate, or attention, in your brain.

> **DO**   When you notice something difficult in yourself.

6. UNITY OF NERVOUS AND MUSCULOSKELETAL SYSTEMS FOR HEALING TRAUMA

Improved use of yourself brings more mobility and less pain. With mobility you have more flow: Flow and bracing cannot coexist, like depression and a lengthened spine cannot coexist. They are mutually exclusive.

But can this small change in use—from bracing to flow—affect the nervous-system regulation of a traumatized person? Can improved use stop or inhibit the unnecessary or inaccurate firing of the nervous system? Taking this a step further, does practicing non-doing of the habitual pattern in the musculoskeletal system help non-doing in the nervous system? I believe it does. Humans have this choice. The work of Nina Bull, a somatic pioneer in body-mind relationships, is an inspiring example of this. She proved that if you stood in such a way that your body language said you were angry, you could not be "not angry" until this bodily position changed to a less angry posture.[29]

A person may not be able to immediately confront sensations in their nervous system that include sympathetic arousal or dorsal vagal shutdown, but they may be able to pay attention to how they meet the present moment and interpret it correctly. For example, when you learn to bend properly with support, you are meeting the present moment fully (see Chapter 10). With this conscious action, you are meeting reality exactly as it is right now, with new impulses. Instead of being occupied with the trauma from the past, you are fully embodied in yourself.

More practice of meeting the present moment fully with the flow and rhythm of the musculoskeletal system can help the nervous system meet the present moment. Thus, a person with PTSD will have fewer flashbacks. The rekindling of the nervous system that causes the fight, flight, or freeze cannot occur, because their musculoskeletal system is keeping them present to the reality of moving easefully in any number of activities.

One very anxious actor told me that she practiced picking up a pencil from the floor with good use and flowing movements to calm her nerves before a performance. She told me that she often arrived at the theater a "bundle of nerves, and bracing like crazy, trying to prepare." This did not serve her, so she began finding her feet and her support with the ground, and then suspension, which invited a sweeping breath. With that she said, "I knew I was on my way, a better preparation." Then she continued to bend and pick up the pencil with flow, and she was "good to go."

Animals in the wild cannot misuse themselves in the same way we humans do; the function of their nervous and musculoskeletal systems is hard-wired. Is this related to their ability to recover from trauma? Nonhuman animals complete the biological process to discharge the excess energy. Is this related to the fact that their nervous system operates optimally because they naturally maintain good use? I believe a well-functioning expanded structure helps all the body's systems, including the nervous system, to regulate better. If we do not naturally maintain good use of ourselves, for any number of reasons or circumstances in our past, we can certainly relearn this use and choose an expanded version of ourselves.

Good use with an animal and a child.

W.C. Fields is said to have told actors, "Never work with children or animals, they steal the scene." Is this because they naturally maintain good use and we are drawn to that?

PART II

EXPANDED SELF

Unity in Action

THE UNITY PRINCIPLE: PSYCHOLOGY, BIOLOGY, AND MUSCLES— HOW THEY WORK AS ONE

The more complex the organism, the more systems there are to coordinate. This chapter reviews basics of sensory guidance and the stretch reflex, and how the nervous system communicates with psychological and biological systems. The larger picture includes how we see ourselves.

1. SENSORY GUIDANCE, OR "THE PROBLEM"

I was teaching a group of musicians at the Tanglewood Music Festival in the Berkshire Mountains of Massachusetts about using their body and breath properly when performing. When I asked them, "How many of you have some kind of physical problem related to playing music?" almost every one of the seventy attendees put their hand up. The problems were varied—shoulder, knee, tongue, foot, and more. Common remedies are stretching and/or strengthening. What else might be involved? F.M. Alexander, developer of the Alexander Technique, offers us this keen observation.

I have shown that if there is something wrong with a person's physical development, it can be demonstrated that this wrongness is caused chiefly by his wrong manner of use of himself, and that this wrong manner of use is really what he is doing himself, *as a result of depending upon unreliable sensory guidance* in carrying out his daily activities, including, of course, any exercises he may perform.[30]

F.M. Alexander is saying that the senses are not always reliable and may not be reporting the problem or situation clearly to the rest of the organism. Or the senses are accurately reporting what you are doing but you are not interpreting the information accurately. You may feel tense while rushing, and try to get rid of the tension. But in reality, part of rushing is tensing and your senses are telling you that. You can't rush and not be tensing. He referred to the phenomenon of misinformation or misinterpretation from the senses as *faulty sensory perception* or *debauched kinesthesia*. In essence, this is "the problem." As far back as 1890, Alexander was using the word *psychophysical* to describe the mind-body connection.

As an example from my work, I often show students that they were not positioned where they thought they were, or not doing what they thought they were doing. A mirror can show some surprising results.

A common habit is standing forward on the balls of the feet, usually some form of getting ahead of yourself. When I guide people to stand over their whole foot, they feel awkward, like their weight is too far back. When they look in the mirror, however, they can see that they are not leaning back at all. *The senses are providing incorrect information and need to be reeducated by paying attention to the signals from your embodied experience of yourself, such as feeling off balance, constriction, lack of breath, etc.*

Have you ever intended a specific outcome but then discovered that a totally different outcome is occurring? I was coaching a group of therapists in a mock office setup. One therapist kept leaning forward; she did this to make the client more comfortable, thinking she was connecting and relating better this way. Meanwhile, the client said that she felt the therapist was leaning in on her (the client's) space, which was making her more uncomfortable. The therapist's intention did not match her desired outcome, but if we had not told her, she would not have known. In our *Humanual* work, the therapist would learn to detect the signals of her own leaning forward, such as a tightening in her legs, or a heaviness in her chest, or an unresponsive client.

"No matter how many specific ends you may gain, you are worse off than before if in the process of gaining them you have destroyed the integrity of the organism."
— F.M. ALEXANDER[31]

2. "EVERY MOVE YOU MAKE": EVERY THOUGHT MANIFESTS AS A MUSCULAR REALITY

Muscles perform a dual function. First, they maintain postural support in the gravitational field to keep you upright; second, they produce movement and allow you to be active.

After studying with me for many years, one of my students said, "I don't even think about it that much anymore, and I feel such changes in the way I am able to stand and move." I explained to her that the muscle lengths can change. Made up of small links called *sarcomeres*, muscles can lose or drop links depending on your intentions. In essence, how you use yourself tells your body what to do. If you stand slouched, for any number of reasons or thoughts (conscious or unconscious), then your body interprets that as "Oh, she wants to slouch and have her chest muscles shorter." The muscles then lose some of their sarcomere lengths and actually become shorter, by the sarcomeres being reabsorbed on the ends of the myofibrils (muscle cells).

The reverse is also true. If you start to use yourself in a more open and upright way, your muscles will interpret this movement as "Oh, she wants to live in a more expanded state, so I will add length to the muscles to give her what she wants." More sarcomeres will be added to the ends of the myofibrils to make the muscle fiber longer. Your consciousness and thoughts will change to match your expanded state. You will stand more open and upright without even trying to because it will be who you are. You won't have to think about it.

When you stand a certain way, or use or inhabit yourself a certain way, you embody a particular consciousness, with particular thoughts.

HUM Journal.
Are you aware of the link between your thoughts and your actions?

In truth, *every thought manifests as a muscular reality*. Sir Charles Sherrington, a world-renowned nineteenth-century physiologist, said, "I may seem to stress the preoccupation of the brain with muscle. Can we stress too much that preoccupation when any path we trace in the brain leads directly or indirectly to muscle?"[32]

If you think there is danger, your muscles will tense. Attempting to release these muscles is almost futile while you have this thought. You need to address the thoughts and feelings that are producing that muscular sensation in order to activate a different outcome.

When something uncomfortable happens, you think it in your mind, and you feel it in your body. If someone implies that you're "incompetent," you can feel that in the pit of your stomach. Enough of this happens and you do not want to feel this any longer. One solution is to stop feeling your stomach; you can do this by tightening the area around it. We tighten using muscles, and then the areas of tension create areas of not feeling. These adaptive patterns limit one's ease and fluidity.

Why is this tension a limitation to your expanded Self and even dangerous to your health? As we stated in Chapter 1, the expanded Self uses only the amount of muscular effort needed to accomplish the task.

The muscles have a small information center called a *muscle spindle*, which detects movement in the muscle and sends the information to the brain for decision-making. If the spindle says the muscle is stretching, the brain will check to see if that is matching your intentions. This information is crucial for linking up what you want and intend to do with what you are actually doing. But if the muscle is overly contracted because of an adaptive pattern or for any other reason, then the spindle is also contracted and cannot send or receive information. You won't know what you're doing if your sensory information is incorrect or incomplete. Like Alexander said—the real problem.

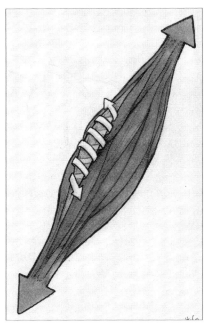

A muscle spindle.

When all muscles and bones work together, they form an expanded container that responds to one's thoughts and feelings. When there is a break or a breach in this container, we say the system has been overwhelmed or traumatized. Sigmund Freud said, "Trauma is the breach in the protective barrier against stimuli that leads to an overwhelming sense of helplessness."[33] The musculoskeletal framework has now collapsed in some way. To deal with the event, some muscles are overworking and others are underworking.

Let's say you are a happy-go-lucky young child, skipping through life. But because of your exuberance, you are scolded continually for making too much noise. You shrink in shame and become compressed, and your happy-go-lucky self is less available to you. Some children are resilient; they bounce back. But other children do not.

One of my trauma colleagues tells a story of watching a news clip of a war zone. A woman is walking across the street. A bomb goes off in the distance and her shoulders go up and then come down. She walks across the street again, and a second bomb goes off in the distance. Her shoulders go up and then down. After five or six repetitions of the same event, her shoulders stay up. Does this remind you of the amoeba story—or a story of your own? The tightness in her shoulders will now block the spindles that send information to the brain. After a while, she won't be able to tell that her shoulders are stuck in the up position. In other words, her sensory guidance will be off, and this new position will feel "normal" to her. Yet, I would call it "habitual."

Let's take a look at physical problems like backaches, which occur for many reasons, not the least of which is that incorrect or no information is being conveyed. When your back hurts, there is a tendency to think you need to fix or strengthen some of your muscles. But in truth, you often need to improve your sensory guidance. You need first to bring your senses back to your body, and the area, so you can accurately detect what is going on. You may be contracting muscles in your back more than you need to.

But if you have an adaptive pattern in place and don't want to sense the feelings in your body, then it will be difficult for you to detect what is going on. It is way too uncomfortable. So, instead, you do surface exercises at the gym to build muscle to relieve pain. Meanwhile, the real problem is not addressed.

But no partial cure will get to the heart of the issue. You need to look at the raw footage that is here now. What are you doing? And what do you think you are doing? Do they match up? The healing, or solution, is in the matching up. Then you can feel the sensations, which allows the muscle spindles to respond, and the muscles can reshape. *Being connected to the truth in this way creates a kind of calmness, even if the truth is unpleasant, because now you can do something to change.* This calmness creates safety in this moment. And where there is safety, health and well-being can follow.

You are a whole, unified being. Your body and muscles are what you think, feel, and sense; it is a bidirectional communication system. There are no exceptions.

I saw a YouTube video of a man giving a very interesting talk. But he was pacing back and forth and looking down at the floor most of the time. It was hard for me to watch. His ideas were all in his head and not in his body. I could appreciate some of his ideas, but he would never be a long-term teacher for me.

As a dancer, I watched different teachers move. If I liked how they moved, I studied with them. My daughter took piano lessons when she was about eight years old. One day, her teacher came in with a cast on her wrist for repetitive strain injury from playing. After the lesson was over and the teacher left, my daughter said to me, "If I learn from her, will I have a cast also?" Ah, the wisdom of children.

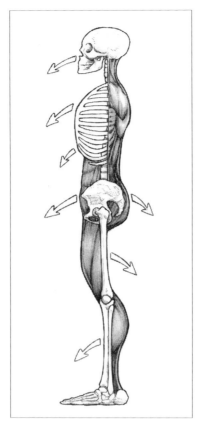

How we got our muscular shape.

Muscles form, not randomly, but to balance the instability of the skeletal system. The muscular connective-tissue system is one large web of suspension and support.[34]

3. STRETCH REFLEX

The nineteenth-century experiments of Sir Charles Sherrington, British physiologist and neuroscientist, demonstrated that extension (the expanded tone) of our limbs is not caused by the voluntary part of the brain but rather is automatic: our arms and legs receive constant signals from the brainstem that maintain their tone. Sherrington called this phenomenon *tonic activity*, which he defined as a continuous, low-level toning or enlivening in the muscles. This is different from more active contraction of muscles.

Most people know the familiar job of muscles—they move the bones around so we can do what we need to do to get through life. A lesser-known job of muscles is to keep us from "coming apart." In other words, muscles have an elastic quality and can stretch. But if they stretch too much, the tonic tone is disrupted. There is a built-in mechanism within our musculature called the *stretch reflex*, first described by Sherrington, who determined that when any muscle tone is stretched beyond its resting length tone, the stretch reflex kicks in to provide automatic regulation of skeletal muscle length.[35] In other words, the muscle begins to contract to maintain the integrity of the organism.

In an average physical exam, the doctor typically checks your reflexes. She stretches your thigh muscle by tapping your knee. A message is sent to the receptors in the thigh muscles to contract just enough to counteract the stretch. The stretch reflex has kicked in and contracts. This prevents us from stretching too much and keeps us from coming apart.

The stretch reflex can also be seen in the head–neck balance. The head is not centered exactly on top of the spine. The skull has more weight in front. If you're riding on the train and fall asleep, your head will drop forward. The forward weight puts a slight stretch on the extensor muscles of the back of the neck, the uppermost muscles in the spine. The stretch receptor or spindle senses this, and the stretch reflex kicks in and contracts the muscles in the back of the head to keep the head up. These types of reflexes combine with vestibular (inner ear) and visual (eye) information to be part of the righting reflex: they "right us up against" or "support us in" the gravitational field.

When the head is freely moving upward, away from the spine, and the neck muscles are lengthened, there is a sense of lightness and buoyancy. Then you get the feeling that you're supported in gravity without any sense of effort. Can you feel this? Or at least imagine it?

Most people, however, tend to chronically shorten the muscles of their neck and back of the head. In this case, there is no stretch, and the rest of their muscular system is overworking because the postural muscles can't lengthen properly. Also, since the muscles around the stretch receptor are contracted, important messages cannot get through.

Many people complain of "knots" in their shoulders. In this instance the shoulders are drooped forward and stretching too much, so the stretch reflex kicks in to contract the muscles, thereby producing small "knots." No amount of massage will permanently eliminate this.

A benefit of the stretch reflex is that a slight stretching of the muscle creates a rebound potential, resulting in stored kinetic energy. This rebound potential helps the muscle to contract, so that some of the muscle's ability to perform work requires no expenditure of energy. Think of a baseball pitcher as he stretches his arm back to get ready to throw the ball; there is kinetic energy stored through the stretching action so that the arm isn't working so hard to complete the throw. If, on the other hand, the muscle is already shortened and contracted, it has no elastic rebound, or stored energy, and the muscle has to work harder to contract in order to complete the throw.

In short, the stretch-reflex system cannot work properly if the muscular system is not working efficiently.

4. OTHER REFLEXES: THE DRIVE FOR SURVIVAL

A cornerstone of human existence is survival. How do we deal with and survive stressful events? What are the inherent mechanisms enabling this? The answer is that we have all kinds of reflexes and systems in place to "save" us.

You know by now how quickly your hand pops back if you touch a hot stove. Reflexes are linked to the autonomic nervous system, which means that they happen automatically. The functions of reflexes are to protect, to cleanse, to balance, and to nurture or feed.

In our mouth area alone, we have suck, swallow, salivate, yawn, and eject reflexes. In our ears, we have pressure balance reflexes; in our face, we have a blushing reflex; and in the eyes, we have blinking, pupil dilation and contraction, and tear flow. Farther down the body, in the larynx, we have cough, throat clearing, whimper, laugh, sob, and scream reflexes. Reflexes that influence the entire body are goose bumps, fight-flight, and freeze, as well as breathing, standing, and sweating. Some reflexes are contagious, like a yawn.

Reflexes are meant to work only when you need them. But some reflexes can become conditioned to work all the time, like the clearing of a throat or nervous laughter. These reflexes-turned-habits are often attempting to hide our real feelings in the moment.

Also worth noting are the many postural reflexes designed to keep us upright and prevent us from falling over. We don't usually think of it this way, but one of our greatest fears, on an unconscious level, is our fear of falling. The system has many detectors for this throughout the body. When you start to fall, a muscle becomes stretched too much, and a message is relayed back to the brain, "Do something, I'm falling!" Our system then kicks in with a healthy impulse, a compensation to keep us upright. The system works as one unified response.

These reflexes work very well for the small, albeit infinite, adjustments in daily life. But when the disturbing events that come our way grow larger, the everyday mechanisms are not enough to save us, and we find ourselves consciously trying to survive or just get through an experience. Our nervous system kicks into high gear and other systems follow. You read about that in the last chapter on trauma.

5. BODY IMAGE IN THE MIRROR VERSUS BODY IMAGE IN THE BRAIN

A tree is twisted because it looks for the sun and responds to the wind. Is that a problem? Our bodies twist, turn, dodge, advance, and retreat. I have had my hands on thousands of people over the years, and no one is symmetrical (or equal) on both sides. Yet many people think they should be, or try to be. We have this picture of a perfectly balanced body. But what is really going on?

In your brain resides a three-dimensional holograph avatar of yourself. It is different from the body image you see when you look in the mirror. In your brain is an image called your body *schema*, which is the picture of what you *think* you look like. So, we have a body image and a body schema.

Body schema can change, but it is not conscious action. We create our body schema from a combination of sensory information, primarily tactile. The body schema represents both position and configuration of our body as a three-dimensional object in space. Schema relates to *proprioception*, which is our sense of the relative position of our own body parts and the strength of effort being employed in movement, and schema is updated with movement.

Body image, on the other hand, is conscious and visual. When you look in the mirror you see your body image exactly as you appear.

Most people rely on body image and do not realize the power of body schema. The neuroscience literature tells us that when you think of lengthening your back, your back changes more than when you look in the mirror and actively lengthen.[36] An experiment was done with basketball players. One group practiced shooting the ball into the basket. The other group imagined themselves shooting the ball in the basket. When they all came on the court to play as a test of the two groups, the group that had imagined the shots did better.

Spiritual teachings tell us about being unaware of certain aspects of our self—a tiny kernel of our essence or awareness that is not seen or recognized. Other people in our life

Body image and body schema.

may see it, but we don't. Might this account for the discrepancy or difference between body image and body schema? The following story of my client Julian gives a vivid example of how we set up schema and image.

Julian's childhood idol

Julian told me that when he sits to meditate, after fifteen minutes he gets a pain in his back and tilts to one side. I asked him to watch the pain. He was able to stay with the pain, saying it felt like a tight spot in his right shoulder. After a few minutes, as he stayed with that spot, the pain began to move, and there was more movement in his back. We then added a little voluntary movement to break up his brain's fixation. The spot began to loosen, and he felt less pain.

At a certain point when the spot was loosening, Julian had the sense that his entire being and awareness expanded into the room and beyond, to become one with the larger environment. He related to me that it was a very pleasant and beautiful state to experience. He felt himself naturally expand, and there was less pain.

He suddenly remembered how, as a child, he idolized the Six Million Dollar Man. Julian later shared that he had often imitated his hero's body positions and his eye position—one eye rose a little bit, which of course raised one shoulder.

Before we worked together, Julian saw his body image in the mirror, but his body schema was that of the Six Million Dollar Man. Now, Julian put together that his idealization of the Six Million Dollar Man was actually a spiritual quest: he wanted to be as powerful a human as possible, from way back then. When we were working together, Julian had a real-life experience of *his own* mental, physical, and spiritual expansion—unity—revealing his expanded Self.

> **HUM Journal.**
> **Somewhere in your past, was there someone whom you idealized,**
> **internalized, and somaticized in your body schema?**

6. RED FIBERS, WHITE FIBERS: WHY WE CAN'T STAND STILL

Whether they are waiting in a checkout line or standing around the coffee machine at work, I see that most folks are fidgeting, shifting from foot to foot, or leaning into one hip or the other. Why can't we stand still? Let's look at the muscles that are responding to how we think and how we move in the world—the embodied messages.

There are two kinds of muscle fibers: red and white.

Red fibers, called *slow twitch*, are made for rhythmic movement and continuous support. They tend to be close to the bone. These small postural muscles are designed for sustained muscle activity, such as prolonged sitting or standing. The red fibers do not tire easily, as they are well supplied with oxygen. This means that if we are using our whole expanded system optimally, we can stand or sit for long periods of time with minimum effort. The white fibers, called *fast twitch*, are made for activities requiring immediate action or strength, such as lifting a child or catching the cup before it falls. These fibers "fire" quickly and are used for short, powerful muscle activity. The white fibers are usually closer to the skin surface of our body, and they tire easily. Therefore, a person who is a good long-distance runner has more red fibers, and a person who is a good sprinter has more white fibers.

From an evolutionary standpoint, we can understand that creatures who lived in water did not need red-fiber support; they only used fast-twitch muscles to go here and there. The change came when creatures arrived on land, where the red slow-twitch muscles are needed for constant support.

Most modern humans have lost the efficiency of their red-fiber network because they use their white fibers to hold or pull themselves up when sitting or standing. Because the red fibers that are made for sustained prolonged activity aren't used enough, they atrophy or weaken, and standing still becomes impossible for more than a few moments. The white fibers engage and try to hold you up, but they do not last long before tiring. It's one of those feedback loops (see Chapter 3).

To keep a good balance, it is wise to change one's use to include red-fiber activities such as walking, sitting, or standing with support, and without over-efforting, as red fibers are more "energy-efficient." Remember also that atrophied red fibers means there is less potential for rhythmic movements, which are basic to health and well-being and are often lost in overwhelming experiences and trauma. Healing these constrictive states will, therefore, help you in your development of red fibers and vice versa.

When astronauts are in space, even though they exercise regularly, they experience some atrophy in their red fibers. This leads some researchers to believe that our bodies need the constant force of gravity for stimulation of certain systems. It is a tonic activity—in other words, a persistent firing of the nerves from sensory mechanisms to keep systems active and healthy, similar to the stretch receptors that keep the muscles working properly. As a final note, there is controversy and ongoing discussion about how many red and white fibers we are born with and how much they can change.[37] The most current research at the time of this writing says that white fibers can change to red fibers when the muscles are both active and stretched—or in my words, when the muscles engage in support and suspension. We often see this in children.

For most children, muscles are lengthened, fluid, and flexible. Even when there is difficulty early in life, children still often exhibit an overall ease that is indicative of ready support from red fibers and a lack of accumulated shortening and constriction patterns. Children move effortlessly and sit for hours on the floor with no additional support and no complaining.

CHAPTER

8

SPIRALS: OUR DEEP SUPPORT

Throughout creation, we see many different manifestations of spiral-type movements and forms. Our bodies too have a spiral design of support. We are wrapped in an expandable web of spiral musculature and connective tissue. All our movements, including walking, are supported by a double set of spiral muscles.

1. THE MAIN WAY WE MOVE

Each time you turn to talk to your friend, you engage your spiral muscles. You rotate and turn in every movement you make—from picking a flower, to throwing a baseball, to rolling over in bed. All organic growth is created by two sets of spirals that move in opposite directions—one clockwise and one counterclockwise.

This illustration shows the cross-section of the core of an axoneme (minute elements within living cell structure), enlarged 90,000 diameters. A double-spiral arrangement is clear.

Raymond Dart, noted anthropologist, wrote a treatise on the double-helix spiral arrangement, demonstrating the two

The core of an axoneme.

sets of spiral muscles in humans.[38] These spirals are your deep support. When you can connect with them in a balanced way, they provide a foundation for both movement and stillness. Note that most everyday activities are carried out in an arc or a spiral, and not with right angles.

The broken lines in the illustrations show the opposite side of the body.

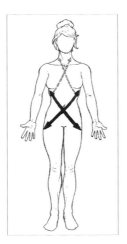

Simple muscular spirals, front view.

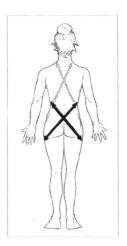

Simple muscular spirals, back view.

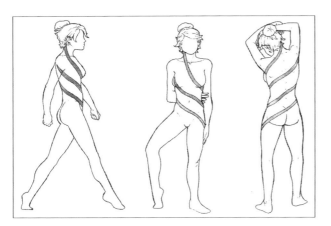

One side (right) of the muscular double spirals.

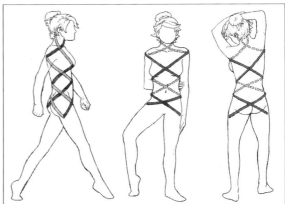

The muscular double spirals.

These spiral patterns occur in flowers, plants, animals, and humans. Many are fractals in which similar complex patterns repeat in different sizes. Since ancient times, harmonious proportions in humans, nature, and buildings have been observed and written about (e.g., the golden mean and the Fibonacci sequence). They are the cornerstone of our human design.

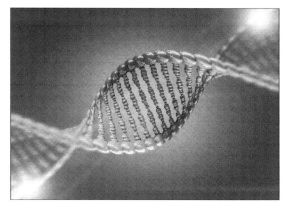

The double-helix spiral of DNA.

The head spiral.

The flower spiral.

The Romanesque cauliflower
is an example of spirals in fractals.

When you look at the photo of Romanesque cauliflower, can you feel a sense of the harmonious proportions? The unity? How much spiral activity can you detect in yourself? Your answer could be written in your *HUM Journal*.

The double spiral muscles support the spine. The flexible primitive spine that was just a cartilaginous cord in the early creatures evolved into a backbone in reptiles and vertebrate animals. Feel the strength of your own backbone. This solid vertebral column has bony protrusions on the sides that serve as attachments for muscles. Feel the muscles that move on both sides of your vertebral column. Can you sense the rotation as you turn side to side?

The spine houses key parts of the nervous system. The nerves branch out to give you feelings, sensations, and impulses. Sense how synchronized and connected these systems are—bones, muscles, and nerves—and how they seamlessly coordinate with any action, like lifting your spoon to eat or texting on your phone.

Although solid, the spinal column is built to be flexible. Its four curves give it movement, and intervertebral discs form cushions between vertebrae for shock absorption. Yet many people feel stiff and sore in their upper, middle, or lower back from misuse. Move your spine to lengthen then shorten, and notice your thoughts and feelings.

As spines evolved, the bones and muscles began to work together in new ways. Fish move forward by leveraging the spine's coordinated side-to-side movement. The fish swings from head to tail, producing the lateral undulations we call swimming—providing forward locomotion. This spiral-like nature of lateral flexion, or side-to-side bending motion of the spine, is foundational in all vertebrate movement. Explore bending side to side as you picture our ancestors, the fish, swimming through water—the rhythm propelling you forward.

Spirals in action.

While fish move from side to side to propel themselves forward, mammals generally move from front to back; think of apes knuckle-walking on all fours, or cheetahs running. During our evolution, the flexor muscles of the trunk divided into layers, with both abdominal and thoracic muscles wrapping around the trunk at oblique angles. Combined with the rotational muscles of the neck and spine, the entire torso (the double-helix spiral musculature) could now allow greater rotation for movement. Twist as far as you can to each side.

As humans and other creatures became more upright, the spirals allowed the spine to become weight-bearing and stable. The lumbar curve was last to develop; it facilitates our ability to stand upright on two legs without falling forward. Take a moment to appreciate your human uprightness and the stability your evolutionary form made possible.

Humans have a double-spiral rotational movement of the double helix to move forward; one spiral expands while the other contracts, producing the forward motion. Picture yourself as a four-limbed creature as you walk, so that it is not just your legs that move you—your arms swing in opposition to your legs. For locomotion, humans are able to engage both sets of torso spirals, which are directed by movements of the head. As you walk, feel your steadiness, supported by the spiral muscles and not just vertical muscles. What do you notice? Write about it in your **HUM Journal**.

Twisting Toward and Twisting Away

In the earliest movements of infants, you can observe spiral twisting. The motions can be avoidance patterns, turning away to escape or reject, or inviting patterns, moving toward an object of desire. You also do this all the time to express your needs. Can you imagine how you would have to turn your body constantly if you did not have spiral musculature? Just putting on a seat belt would be a real challenge, wouldn't it?

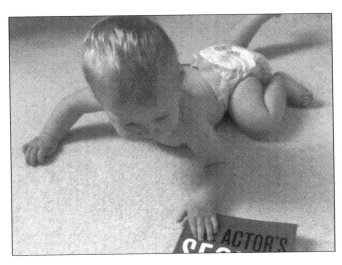

Human child spiraling in motion.

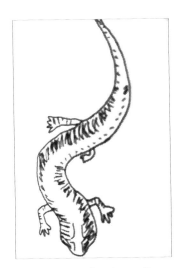

Reptile spiraling in motion.

When the human body compresses from the top down as if a heavy weight (emotional or physical) is on the head or shoulders, the body buckles. Since there is no extra room inside, the system needs to collapse to one side or the other, creating a rotation or twist. Most people twist more easily to one side or the other. When you rotate, which direction do you gravitate toward: right or left, or away from right or left? You can explore this by standing and turning your head to the right and then walking in that direction. Try the left. Which is more comfortable?

Evolution continues to unfold—the fluid movement of life contracting and then expanding, with so many moving parts. All facets are in their right place and developing naturally, each in its own way, generating the appearance of the next physical reality. We fluctuate between contraction and expansion, stillness and motion: the stillness of the ongoing present evolving into the next perfect moment.

2. THE HEAD LEADS AND THE BODY FOLLOWS—SOMETIMES

In all creatures, the relationship of the head to the trunk is the primary organizing principle for movement, scanning for threat, and connection. On land or water and relating to the environment, the head–spine pathway has remained a central organizing factor for millions of years.

As sensory connections developed in the brain, they were able to get information from their environment that directs the appropriate motor activity, from brain to body. All movement was organized and coordinated by the relationship between head and body in reference to the environment.

Our head and face have neural connections and the sensory apparatus to detect food, and our body takes action by bringing food to our mouth to ingest. Our head and face also detect connection and safety, danger, and threat, and organize the body to take necessary action or nonaction. The area around the mouth and face, in particular, has to be able to perceive and find food. Some creatures sense vibrations, some hear sounds, some see different light images, and some smell the presence of food. From an evolutionary perspective, as the face and front-end became more sensitive to the presence of food, the brain needed to rewire and increase in size. The brain formed to process this sensory information and further direct the body to move toward food. The outward senses in the head are directly connected to the spine, which sends messages to muscles to move to get the food. Feel the area around your mouth as you look at food. Does your body go toward or away from it?

The mouth then developed into a movable joint—the jaw. Open and close your jaw as you note that it was the first movable hinge joint to evolve, allowing the capture of food in the front part of the face. The head with its mobile jaw had now become a bony structure related to the spine but different from it. This is an important distinction, as the head and spine continue to function in dynamic opposition but also in synchrony. The head leads and the body follows—sometimes.

Based on input from the environment to the brain, the entire length of the spine moves a fish or reptile. This is no different for vertebrate mammals, including humans: the movements of the body and actions of the limbs and spinal muscles are all organized and initiated in relation and service to the head. The double-helix spiral muscles support this. It is the blueprint from which all subsequent vertebrate life developed. No matter what we are doing, the head and neck reflexes are designed to integrate and coordinate the total pattern of neuromuscular, skeletal, and connective tissue movement.

As you move your head, sense its relationship to your spine and the rest of your body.

3. A BRIEF LOOK AT EVOLUTION OF MOVEMENT

If you consider that most or all evolution is in service to efficiency, connection, and survival, how the remaining parts of our body developed makes good sense. Certain fish developed fins for moving about in shallow water, which then enabled them to crawl onto land. The fins had muscular attachments to the body. These creatures evolved into terrestrial animals, including small reptiles and large dinosaurs. Our limbs are simply highly evolved fins and flippers. Move your arms and legs as if you are a four-legged reptile, a turtle creeping along the ground with your head leading. Feel the spiralic coordination of arms and legs.

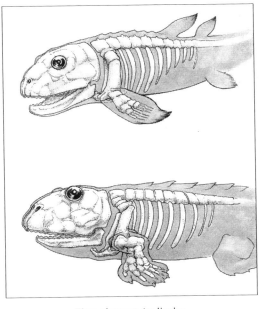

Fins change to limbs.

The pelvis is attached to the bottom of the spine, enabling force from the hind legs in four-footed animals to be transmitted to the trunk. The powerful thrust of the legs is now able to propel the body forward. The pelvis, as part of the back, provides sockets for the leg bones. The iliopsoas muscle plays a crucial role in stabilizing the pelvis. The release of the psoas muscle allows the lower back to lengthen, which helps to prevent lower-back compression. The evolved spine in four-legged creatures became a kind of backbone, or a bridge, for supporting the body with the head leading.

As creatures came up off the ground, the musculature of terrestrial animals was also forced to evolve. *Today this musculature has a dual function: it produces movement by acting on the bones to propel the creature in space, and the muscles continuously support the body, counteracting the tendency for it to buckle.* In essence, there is a "background" of muscular tone always in place; it supports the limbs in a stable but spirally suspended relationship during active movement in space. This dual capacity for the muscular system was established very early in evolution and still holds today. Explore both aspects of

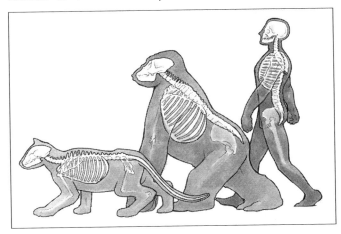

Transition from four legs to two.

musculature: first, as you stand still, recognize the core double-helix stability, and then see how that core stability needs to be there as you move for activity.

After many generations, some animals settled on their hind legs, with arms and hands free for gathering food and defending themselves. The shoulder girdle, which is made up of the clavicle and scapula, is the set of bones on each side of our upper back that moves the hand around. The scapulae are not attached to our back, or to the ribs on the front of our body; instead, they are suspended within a network of muscles. This way the whole body doesn't thrust forward every time you reach for something or do anything else with your arms. The shoulder girdle, in essence, is a mobile support structure for our arms, allowing them to bring food to our mouth, lift objects, touch things, climb, fight, and even stop a fall if we lose our balance. Explore how much range of motion you have in your shoulders and arms, even as you sit and read.

Muscles cover our entire back, giving us the ability to move our scapulae and arms. The shoulder girdle is mobile, but it also sometimes requires stabilization, or anchoring of our body weight, such as when mammals hung from trees. Picture yourself swinging from branch to branch, feeling the rotations in your shoulder joint.

Then you land on the ground. The thighs release out of the hip to allow the legs to move freely or to help you stand your ground on your feet. The foot has an arched structure with three points of contact creating a stable connection to the ground—the ball of the big toe, the ball of the little toe, and the heel, forming three arches. The strongest push-off point is from the ball of the big toe, and it is very helpful to runners. Many martial arts emphasize the big-toe connection to the ground. Feel your feet connecting to the ground, especially the big toe and heel. What do you sense?

Five stages of spinal evolution from horizontal to vertical.

After millions of years of evolution, uprightness came to be humans' innate structure. The spine and its musculature, still the central support, are now in a vertical line with spiral muscles supporting. The head sits not in front horizontally but leading on the top, vertically mounted. Arms and hands are free to manipulate tools and perform many other activities such as reaching out for love; they no longer have a weight-bearing function, except during crawling. The shoulder girdle is meant to be free; it's able to float above the rib cage, as it is suspended from above.

This innate freedom, however, is often lost because many people tend to use their arms in a collapsed way, with their shoulders dropped forward, thereby shortening the front of their body. The arms then become heavy and pull unnecessarily on the pectoral muscles that support the shoulder joint; this overworks the rotator cuff. In order for the shoulder girdle to work properly, the pectoral region must be released. You want to feel a widening across your shoulders.

I hope that this brief anatomy-in-movement lesson enables you to see that each step in evolution has created creatures that are unified in body and brain. The reason I spent so much time on this is because all the stages of growth and the accompanying characteristics that you read about here are integral parts of your human experience today. All creatures adjust to their environment with their physicality of muscles and bones, aided by the intelligent brain and nerve network.

One day, I was doing an exploration in class that involved starting on the floor as a single-cell creature and then growing into a fully upright human being. At the end of the exercise, one young man noticed that he finished the exploration long before the others in the class. He was standing for many minutes while the others were still exploring. As he described his experience, he began to cry, and noted that he rarely cries in public. He said that as he stood upright and saw all the others still exploring, he felt a pain in his heart. He also saw an image of himself growing up: his father had moved out, and his mother said to him when he was about six years old, "Now you are the man of the house." In this exploration, his implicit body memory showed him poignantly that he had been forced to grow up too quickly and lost much of his childhood.

In closing, let me ask: Did you wonder why I added "Sometimes" after this section heading? Well, if I sense my belly is tight, that tells my head there is trouble. Is this my head leading the body, or my gut leading the body?

Seeing a bear
I see a bear, and get afraid and run.
Or
I see a bear, run, and get scared.
What leads?

The following EX-ercises provide an opportunity to experience the feeling of balanced moving spirals and the potential for less compression, inviting the expanded Self.

A. EX-ercise: Early Stages of Discovering the World Is Safe

Early connection with child and caregiver.

1. Start lying facedown (on your belly) in a comfortable, safe place, arms by your side with elbows bent and palms facing downward close to and below your shoulders.

Lying facedown.

2. Push palms into the floor so the upper torso lifts off the floor. Look around and see that you are safe. Feel what that is like in your body. Can you get a nonverbal sense of safety?

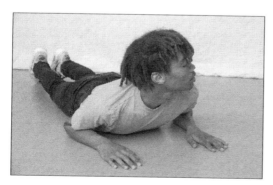

Spiral and look to the left.

Spiral and look to the right.

3. Come back down to the facedown position on your belly.

4. Repeat a few times.

> **DO** Whenever you want to feel the spiral muscles in your upper back.

B. EX-ercise: Spiral from Standing to the Floor

1. Start by standing in a comfortable position. Let your head look to the right, then to the left. As your head turns, the muscles in the front and back of your neck are activated, innervated by the accessory nerve, another cranial nerve that helps to regulate social engagement. A good way to start any exercise.

2. Add your shoulders to the rotation, then hips, and then rotate from the feet. Rest. As you spiral from one side to the other, feel where your spiral goes as far as it can go, and then spring back. Notice how activating the double spiral (the spirals to both sides) can support your upright stance.

3. If you are in reasonably good shape, try this next part. Start standing with your arms out to the sides, so your arms and legs form an X.

Spiral to the floor, step 1.

Spiral to the floor, step 2, back view.

Spiral to the floor, step 3.

Spiral to the floor, step 4.

Spiral to the floor, step 5.

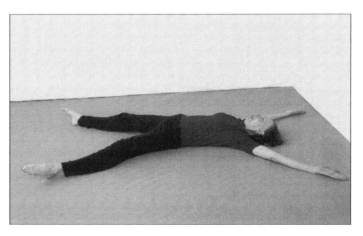

Spiral to the floor, step 6.

4. Keep spiraling in one direction until you get to the floor, and lie down on the floor.

5. Spiral your way up, and repeat in the other direction when you feel ready.

> **DO**   **Every once in a while, to enhance coordination. How easily you can get to the floor or get up from the floor is a measurement of health.**

C. EX-ercise: Spirals on the Floor

1. Start in an X shape lying on your back on the floor.

2. Circle to the right by bringing your left arm to your right arm on the floor.

3. Keep your left arm moving to the right as you sit up.

4. Keep the left arm making a circle so that you move to your left side and back down to the floor.

5. Land back in an X.

Spiral on the floor, step 1.

Spiral on the floor, step 2.

Spiral on the floor, step 3.

Spiral on the floor, step 4.

Spiral on the floor, step 5.

Spiral on the floor, step 6.

Spiral on the floor, step 7.

DO — When you want to feel the stretch and supportive spiraling movement at the same time.

CHAPTER

9

EMBODIED GRAVITY AND ANTIGRAVITY

We live in a gravitational field, including gravity and antigravity, and we need to adapt to that field to be upright. We don't consciously think about it, but unconsciously there is an aspect of us that monitors this field acutely so we don't fall over. *Gravity* aims down with a centripetal force toward the center of the Earth, while the spinning planet emanates a centrifugal force away from the planet called *antigravity*. These forces serve us as a web of support and suspension.

1. SUPPORT IS ESSENTIAL FOR HUMANS

Square one is the support you receive from the ground—your connection to the planet. There is also support from your relationships, through biological co-regulation. Your friends and family support your ideas or not. From

A web of support and suspension.

where do you get your support—a friend, a lover, or nobody? Or when you need support, who do you talk to, email, text, or call?

As we've seen so far, support is a core issue from the beginning of human life. In the womb, you are supported by liquid. Once you're born, you are influenced by how and when you are supported, both physically and emotionally: you are held and adored, or not. In Chapter 2, I noted that if caregivers do not hold children securely, with warmth and human contact, the children develop the belief that they have to hold themselves up. There is still support in the environment, but the child's awareness of it has not been fully developed. This often determines whether or not a person moving into maturity will be able to receive the inherent support from the ground and other people.

As humans, we like to complete things—both thoughts and actions. If someone is speaking, many listeners will find themselves finishing the speaker's sentence. Our brains fill in what we believe to be true; we invent a narrative. When a caregiver is not present to respond to the child's needs for support, the child completes the narrative: "I need to find ways to support myself in life."

The essential nature of support is not seen as a viable choice in this moment. As a result, all the built-in postural reflexes designed to respond to support do not get activated. The default system of voluntary muscular effort will impede the body's natural postural reflex, as I describe in Chapter 3, "The Two Basic Choices for Human Development." When you use voluntary mechanical support to hold yourself up, you are using surface muscles as opposed to the organically connected full-body, deeper layer of support that is closer to the bones (the red-fiber network). You might then have the experience of feeling chronically overworked, which can lead to adrenal fatigue or an inability to be fully present to life.

Additionally, because these surface muscles are needed when you go into activity, if they are busy holding you up, they are not free to move for activity and must do more work to accomplish the task. The additional effort produces excess tension, which leads to strain and discomfort. When muscles encounter strain for an extended period of time, pain is often a by-product. The pain then invites fear, which causes us to brace ourselves and contract, and the cycle continues.

In order to break the feedback loops, a full stop is necessary. In the moment, you first recognize your adaptive pattern of "lack of support," look into it. Find out how and when you are interfering—mentally, emotionally, and physically. We often move off of our support when we are "trying" to be something we are not, or "rushing" ahead of ourselves. Once you see what you are doing to "move away" from the support, you have the choice to allow or disallow the habitual patterns. In other words, you can cease to reinforce the inconsonant patterns that were developed in childhood and find the support that is now available to you.

One of my students had a bat mitzvah when she was fifty years old. She was so nervous in rehearsal that she kept pulling her upper body off her center and losing her support. We did a session on support. She told me after the ceremony that she continuously brought attention to her feet to enable herself to speak calmly.

In the human body, we have an inherent support system with specific mechanisms called *postural* or *righting reflexes* (in the eyes, ears, neck, muscles, and brain) that reassert balance moment by moment. When this system is engaged, the innermost support muscles (close to the bones) and the web of fascia (a thin sheath of fibrous tissue) take care of our basic uprightness. Surface muscles are then available for the activities for which they are intended—sports, dance, yard work, or typing on your computer—instead of just holding you up. Movement can be free and easy for an expanded sense of Self. There is grace and fluidity of motion with a sense of purpose and well-being as you go about your daily tasks and interactions with others. We see this in healthy children and wild animals.

Child with fluidity of motion
and a sense of purpose.

Tiger with fluidity of motion
and a sense of purpose.

To relate this to the polyvagal system that was introduced in Chapter 4, when you are not supported, it is hard to feel safe. And when you do not feel safe and supported, you cannot socially engage with others; you see "other" as some kind of danger. In this phenomenon, there tends to be a disconnect between your thinking brain and your primitive brain, and your thinking brain shuts down. Your primitive brain will do what it needs to do for you to survive, such as persistently looking for "the danger," or tensing muscles to get ready for fight or flight, which will take you farther away from available natural support.

2. "GROUNDING" VERSUS MY VERSION OF SUPPORT

When I am teaching support, my students often translate it into the popular idea of "grounding." But it is different. I make a clear distinction between what many people call grounding and my version of support. In grounding, most people sink down within their body to feel the ground; it's as if they are grinding themselves into the earth. The result is a feeling of heaviness, or weightiness. In my idea of support, you stay up within yourself while you become aware of the interface between your feet and the ground. You allow the ground to support you. That support can then rise up through your entire body.

Support, as I speak about it, allows upright suspension, which is light. It is somewhat kinesthetic in that you experience a feeling of lightness even though you have not actually lost weight. This is clearly different from going down into the ground metaphorically with your body, and staying down.

EX-PLORATION: THE SUPPORT NO ONE CAN TAKE AWAY

Earth is spinning, which produces centrifugal force. It is an upward force on the planet, moving from the planet Earth toward the sun. As you plug into Earth in the way I just described (in a light way, with awareness), you receive this support. And it's not just physical. It's support for your sorrows, thoughts, dreams, and imaginings, too. Although we can run, walk, or dance through life—connected to our support—support does not necessarily entail movement. Support is also standing in the stillness of potential. Allow the ground to support you there as well.

I find it fascinating that our bodies are so affected by our planet. Take, for example, this little nugget of information from a space science archive: "If the Earth were not spinning, you would be heavier, as you would feel the full force of gravity. Since there is more centrifugal force at the equator to cancel gravity, your overall weight at the equator versus at the poles is even less. If you weighed 100 pounds at the North Pole on a spring scale, at the equator you would weigh 99.65 pounds, or 5.5 ounces less."[39]

From a standing position, bring your attention to your feet (without looking at them). More specifically, tune into the bottoms of your feet. Obviously, the ground is under you, but it might not be so obvious that the ground is under you and supporting you. Let the support come up through you. Receive it all the way up. Note that the "up" is something that you receive, not something that you "paste on" to look more upright. Feel the support rise up through your ankles, knees, hips, whole back, torso, arms, neck, and head. Then let your head turn, and see what the world looks like with support from the ground. It is a combination of tracking yourself in relationship to the larger upward force at work. A truly expanded Self.

Before closing this section, I'd like to emphasize that I am not negating or trying to change any part of you that does not feel supported. Maybe you made this choice and are happy with it. My point is that it can change if you desire, and that sometimes a lack of support in life is not something people consciously choose. After jarring experiences, we can feel, physically, as if the ground underneath us is gone. How do we find it again? I'm wondering if there might be a new willingness in you to look at the support that is available from the forces on the planet. If you have felt, in life, like the rug was pulled out from under you, or that you stepped off the proverbial cliff at one point or another, connecting your feet to the earth and receiving support from the ground may help by offering you a fresh experience.

> **DO**   **Bring your attention to your earthly support as often as you can, as it invites relief, breath, and self-regulation, and a connection to the planet.**

Write about your experience of support in your *HUM Journal.*

3. SUSPENSION AND TENSEGRITY: A PERFECT BALANCE

Imagine a structure with elements of expansion and contraction acting simultaneously and in perfect balance. This is a *tensegrity* structure. A simple example is a bicycle wheel with its tensioned spokes balancing the hub. This is different from a wooden wheel on a cart, which has immovable parts.

The principle of tensegrity was discovered by an innovative contemporary sculptor named Kenneth Snelson and popularized by Buckminster Fuller, architect and designer of the geodesic dome. The word is a combination of two terms, *tension* and *integrity,* and describes a structural relationship principle that, when applied, produces stabilized structures through continuous tension or "tensional integrity," rather than through continuous compression.

Physically, a tensegrity structure is composed of firm struts that do not touch one another, but

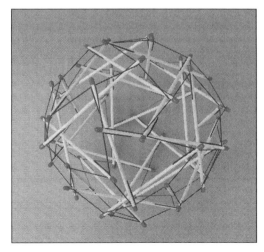

A tensegrity structure.

are suspended and made strong by the simultaneous action of a network of tensionally balanced stretched parts. Most buildings and skyscrapers—made from bricks, wood, or steel—are not tensegrity structures. They are compression structures, in alignment with gravity, rising block upon block, with a foundation for support. Tensegrity structures are different: they are self-supporting and distribute forces and strain evenly and omnidirectionally throughout their form, giving them an ability to yield.

In Fuller's geodesic dome, tensioned cables are always working to reduce the length of the struts, like very strong elastic bands, while the rigid struts are limiting how much the cables can do this. It is the interaction between these two activities (and simultaneous forces) that allows for the suspension. The tensegrity system balances itself in the most stable position of equilibrium with minimal energy, demonstrating the link between structure and energy. We can see this suspension in Snelson's sculptures and in human movement.

Suspension in human movement.

Suspension in Snelson's sculpture.

I use the tensegrity model in the following sections. The floating and balanced qualities of tensegrity structures are in some but not all ways metaphorically similar to our human design. Fuller sees it this way: "Indeed, the human frame with its many tensile muscles, ligaments and tendons pulling up on the rigid bones of the body, thereby stabilizing and supporting them against the force of gravity, is a prime example of tensegrity at work."[40]

4. SUSPENSION SYSTEM VERSUS COMPRESSION SYSTEM

Let's see what it looks like when we relate some elements of our human structure to a tensegrity model, instead of the old model that saw the body only as a mechanical lever system. Why is this mechanical model outdated?

Picture a dinosaur. How does that Brachiosaurus, with its long neck (sometimes up to sixty feet long), balance mechanically with the body? It doesn't. In the mechanical model, it would topple over. Or picture a horse: How does it jump over fences and land so easily on those skinny legs with its two thousand pounds of weight? Imagine yourself lifting large, heavy weights over your head. Your system would crush under that weight if standard mechanical techniques were our natural design.

There are two possible structural systems—suspension systems and compression systems. In many movement techniques, people talk about "alignment." This implies a view of the body as a building-block system—one block on top of another. If you stack everything up neatly, then you have your alignment. But this is a compression system.

If you actually look at a human skeleton, we don't stack up this way. You can't pile up the bones and make them balance: bones do not have horizontal surfaces upon which to balance or rest. That tells us that compression is not our design. Instead, we—just like dinosaurs, horses,

Group suspension with tensegrity in the air.

and other animals—are a suspension system; our form takes its shape through expansion (tensional integrity). Although the suspended expansion involves your whole self—body, mind, and spirit, including your energy and life-force—it is easy to see and understand in the physical realm.

The muscles and connective-tissue systems are expanded by the bones to give us our shape. So, our connective web fabric is pulling inward while the bones are resisting this pull and stretching the system outward, combining gravity and antigravity. In most tensegrity structures, the dowels cross each other, but in humans, the bones do not. We are a tensegrity-like structure, as we do not follow the model exactly. When operating optimally, the suspension system gives us the potential to experience our expanded, suspended Self: the whole of you expands, and our design is always looking for this expansion—mentally, physically, emotionally, and spiritually. When you receive the support that you need, on all levels, and feel safe in the world, you are less constricted (defended), and the whole of you can expand.

EX-ERCISE: FIND THE TOP OF YOUR SPINE,
SO THAT YOUR HEAD CAN FREE AWAY FROM YOUR SPINE

1. Place your fingertips just in front of the hole in your ear.

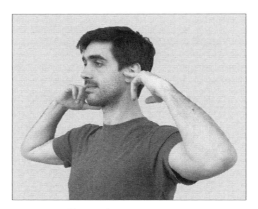

Fingertips at your ears.

2. Where your fingertips would meet in the middle of your head is the top of your spine. Sense the top of your spine, and feel how your head moves from there.

3. It is a slight "Yes" movement. Freedom at this primary head, neck, and back joint allows the potential for freedom throughout the system.

Finding the top of your spine with guidance.

4. You can also find the top of your spine by putting your tongue on the roof of your mouth and taking your tongue as far back as you can. If you could keep going, you would come to the top of your spine.

5. Now try placing your thumbs under your cheekbones, and fingers on the back of your skull.

Thumbs under cheekbones and fingers on back skull—front view.

Thumbs under cheekbones and fingers on back skull—side view.

Thumbs under cheekbones and fingers on back skull—back view.

6. Allow your head to release slightly upward, away from your spine. It is a very slight lift of front and back skull, allowing your whole back to lengthen and widen as you lift.

7. You may feel a large spontaneous breath, as there is now more space in your torso. Remember the expanded Self often has more space.

DO   Often.

EX-PLORATION: FIND THE TOP OF YOUR SPINE TO ENHANCE SOCIAL ENGAGEMENT

Place the palm of your hand on the back of your upper neck, feeling the ridge of your skull. This is where your brainstem is housed, along with the connections to your ventral vagal social engagement system. Movability and connection here allow self-regulation and also prevent a sympathetic defensive response.

First, just keep your hand there, becoming aware of any tension that might be releasing, followed by a sigh or swallow. (This can enliven your social engagement system.) Then slowly use your hand to nod your head in a slight "Yes" motion. Rest. Then make a "No" motion with your head, looking side to side, as in orienting. Rest. Keep your hand there until you feel some shift in your whole body. It may be a breath, a look around, or a tingling sensation. This may take a bit of practice. You can do this lying down or standing up. Try one hand, then the other.

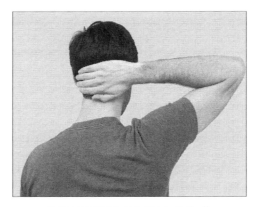

Palm on the base of your skull.

> **DO** When you want the back of your neck to release to support ventral vagal communication and freedom and ease throughout your whole body, mind, and self.

> **Write in your *HUM Journal* about your sense of suspension now.**

5. SUSPENSION IN MOVEMENT

When this primary suspension system works well, muscles do not strain but are active and toned, and joints are not compressed. The respiratory, circulation, and nervous systems can function with maximum ease and minimum effort.

Because we are living in a gravitational field, the skeleton maintains stretch on all our elastic-like muscles, while these muscles and connective tissue maintain tension or tone to support the bones. This complex architectural design for upright support distributes the entire workload of the muscles over the connective and muscle tissues, so that the burden does not fall on just a few surface muscles to overwork in their effort to hold you up.

In this model, muscles do not really hold you up, nor do they contract to move you; they are more like sense detectors. When the muscles detect shifts in movement or instability, they respond by expanding and suspending you in an elastic web of adjustable support. It is like you are wearing an elastic suit that constantly adjusts to your needs. You then spring into activity by releasing the elastic. Does this dramatically change your idea of the effort needed for activity?

Suspension in movement.

When you interfere with the natural integration, you begin to think of and relate to your body as parts. You feel separate, or divided. This division becomes the default body position and inevitably leads to muscular or visceral pain. We can also lose our natural instinctual and intuitive connection to our body because the communication network between the physical systems has been disrupted. Support and suspension can help to restore this connection.

You can see how "light" animals appear to be when they move; a one thousand-pound polar bear can jump or run with ease. Or watch a cat stalking prey, or a gazelle running with such beautiful effortlessness and grace. These are all examples of tensegrity-like design at work and the easy, supportive, and almost "suspended-in-thin-air" appearance of this movement-organizing principle.

You see the principle at work in indigenous cultures where women may still carry heavy loads of water or sticks on their heads. The women carry the weight while maintaining a vertical spine and the expansion of the design of the musculoskeletal system. The load is distributed over their entire form, rather than straining specific muscles to hold the load with just their arms.

Head balance with expansion.

Allowing muscles to lengthen is a key feature of human expansion. The bones keep the muscles stretched so the entire system can provide support and suspension at the same time. This encourages maximum flexibility and movability.

EX-PLORATION: TENSEGRITY

You can purchase a small, inexpensive tensegrity model called a "skwish toy," composed of wooden rods and connecting bands. Feel how light and connected it is.

> **DO** Hold a tensegrity structure when you want to be reminded of the possibility of your connectedness and wholeness even though we do not fit the model exactly, as we are moving creatures.

Tossing the tensegrity.

Holding the tensegrity.

Or, if your hip is painful, you can picture your hip joint as a tensegrity structure. This has the potential to make more space, thus relieving the constriction. You can explore the potential of your whole body as an expanded structure, naturally integrated and balanced.

Feel the space at your hip.

6. EMOTIONAL TENSEGRITY: IF I FEEL SAD, WHERE DO I FEEL IT IN MY BODY?

Donald Ingber, Senior Associate at Harvard Medical School and a tensegrity pioneer, states that the entire body is a collection of tensegrity systems nested within more tensegrity systems, down to the tiniest detail.[41] Every bit of you is always completely connected to every other bit of you. We've already looked at how thoughts are connected. Let's take a brief look at tensegrity and emotions.

If you feel sad, where do you feel it in your body? Does your chest feel heavy? Is the heaviness really just in your chest? Probably not. The work of Dr. Candace Pert is illuminating. This American neuroscientist discovered the opiate receptor—the cellular binding site for endorphins in the brain. Her popular science book, *Molecules of Emotion: The Science Behind Mind-Body Medicine*, states that we feel emotions everywhere in our body: "Every change in the physiological state is accompanied by an appropriate change in the mental-emotional state, conscious or unconscious, and conversely, every change in the mental-emotional state, conscious or unconscious, is accompanied by an appropriate change in the physiological state."[42]

As you feel the sadness, see if you are able to locate it in other parts of your body and not only your chest. This way, your entire body becomes more like a container—a vessel to hold and support your emotions—with your whole musculoskeletal structure. You might find that this action lessens that heavy pull in your chest because you now have broader support from your entire structure. I call this *emotional tensegrity support*. Now try feeling joy throughout your structure.

7. BIOTENSEGRITY: CONNECTION IN EVERY CELL

Let's explore this idea more deeply as another myth-breaker and a departure from classical thought. Not until fairly recently, i.e., the last several decades, did scientists observe that these very same tensegrity principles (of self-inclusive support) underlie the integrity of all biological structures. Our entire body, from genes to cells, to arms and legs, is organized and constructed through a balance of expanding and contracting forces.

Tensegrity pioneer Donald Ingber tells this story of his discovery of tensegrity and the body: "As my art professor spoke, he pushed this round tensegrity sculpture flat, and when he let go, it leapt up in the air. This was interesting because I had seen the same behavior just days before when I first learned how to culture cells, across the campus in a medical school laboratory. Cells flatten when they adhere to a culture dish; but when you detach them, they round up and jump off the dish just like the tensegrity toy."[43]

Another pioneer in this field, orthopedic surgeon Stephen Levin, coined the term *biotensegrity* to describe the pervasive presence of tensegrity principles in biology. Dr. Levin observed that bones at joints do not touch each other and do not stack up bone to bone but instead seem to float at the joint.[44]

In observing cells, scientists find that all biological organisms are made strong and resilient by their balance of tensioned and compressed parts. Biotensegrity principles maintain the integrity of every structure of our body, including organs, glands, nervous system, and the rest, integrating the body as one entire biotensegrity form.

Dr. Stephen Levin writes, "What I had been taught during my residency . . . [was] the accepted mechanics as first described by Borelli, a mathematician and 'renaissance man,' in 1680. Nothing has changed. This is all based on Newtonian mechanics . . . It is impossible to explain the mechanics of a dinosaur's neck using standard Newtonian mechanics."[45]

Snelson's dinosaur.

EX-ERCISE: A MECHANICAL LEVER SYSTEM VERSUS AN ELASTIC WEB SYSTEM

1. If you bend your elbow as an isolated lever system—let's say to bring something to your mouth to eat—you are living with a control booth in your head giving orders to your body to carry out this movement. This produces one effect.

Compare with:

2. If you have a sense of yourself as one entity—an integrated elastic web of muscles and connective tissue—as you have the intention to bring something to your mouth, you are aware that your entire body will change shape to do it. Your whole body is always informed and participating in the action. Yes, your elbow will bend and your hips will shift and your feet will adjust. Thought and action take place in the whole body-mind-spirit self. You are lighter, more fluid, and less cut off.

Note that:

Number 1 is you and your body as two separate entities, one part directing another part. This is an example of disconnection—the tendency to objectify the body—which I talked about in Chapter 1.

Number 2 is you sensing the whole of you, with no parts controlling other parts.

The principle of tensegrity is precisely the relationship among connective tissue, muscles, and bones. We are a continuous web of connective tissue and muscle. When one part moves, the whole is affected. The slight stretch everywhere gives us a feeling of buoyancy or lightness.

> ### *HUM Journal.*
> **Can you see how this tensegrity suspension model could invite an expression of your expanded Self and your expanded Self that connects to others?**

Group tensegrity.

FORM AND FUNCTION MYTH-BREAKERS

I'm striving to convey an understanding of how the body functions best. There is a very clear map of optimal organization, related to both form and function. This knowledge helps you use your form to maximal advantage. For example, if you think you bend from your lower back, you are misusing those spinal joints and not accessing the very beautiful freedom available in your hip joints for bending. By exploding myths and utilizing facts, you will get more ease out of your human body. Recall that one definition of a myth is a widely held but false belief or idea.

This information need not be translated into some kind of ideal. That would imply a judgment; that is, if you don't do it "this way," it's not good enough. I do not mean this at all. When I'm talking about movement anywhere in *Humanual*, I am simply referring to our innate design and the optimal function that is available for health and well-being—something we are rarely taught. The acorn has the potential to be a huge tree, and we as humans have the potential to be our expanded selves.

Every section in this chapter lends itself to a **HUM Journal** entry; thus, I won't continue to repeat the suggestion to journal. But I do recommend journaling if you feel the impulse to do it. Once you learn the *how* of movement and you still have difficulty, then you may want to look deeper into your history of adaptive patterns, emotional overwhelm, or trauma. Each of these sections suggests a change in use that invites an expanded version of yourself.

1. HEAD AND NECK

Do you ever wonder how your head sits on your spine? The base of your skull has two little condyles or knob-like rockers. These rockers fit into two small cups in the first vertebra, called the *atlas*; it's like the guy in Greek mythology holding up the world. Your head can rock only forward and backward around fifteen degrees at this joint. To turn your head side to side requires help from the second vertebra.

Students often ask me, "How should I hold my head?" The more accurate question is "How is my head holding me?" Most people overtense muscles to move their head or hold their head still; both options overstress the neck muscles. The *Humanual* option, which I describe next, allows the head to be available for any movement, because head and neck reflexes are capable of integrating and coordinating the total pattern of neuromuscular movement.

When you are not holding your neck muscles tight, your head is poised on the atlas so that its weight falls slightly forward (there is more weight in the front of the skull). This stimulates the stretch reflex: the muscles in the back of your head and down your spine contract a bit to pull up your spine to bring your head to center. Remember when muscles contract, both ends pull together. It's a very delicate balance, but extremely economical, as you are not tensing your neck to hold your head. When you understand this concept, you see it is a myth to say that you "hold your head up."

Overtensing the neck muscles is a common habit with many negative consequences, the least of which is a "stiff neck." So many folks I meet, as I am traveling or teaching, live in their head and have no sense of what their body is doing. The cutoff is the neck. As a result, the body is not able to move in a way that coordinates thoughts and emotions.

Let's take a moment to consider all that passes through your neck—what the neck "houses." In front is your trachea, the air tube connected to your lungs. Then you have your esophagus, the tube that food passes through to get to your stomach. The upper few vertebrae of your spine, which houses your nervous system, also pass through your neck. And *your voice* lives in your neck in the form of the larynx. As you can see, the implications of over-tightening your neck muscles are numerous and far-reaching, because compression to nerves and other tissues impedes function.

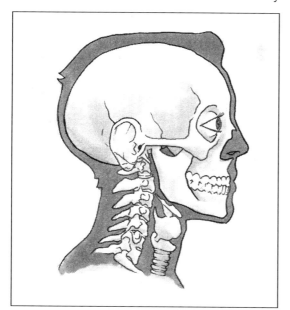

The top of the spine is between your ears.

A neck area that is free and unrestricted allows the ventral vagal complex to facilitate healthy self-regulation via the vagus nerve and our social engagement system. In social engagement, a person can remain calm, maintain a sense of humor, and cooperate with others. But if the neck is constricted, it is difficult for a person to feel comfortable in social situations.

Speaking of neck constriction, there is a new illness called "text neck." As you can surmise, the malady involves pain and damage sustained from looking down at cell phones, tablets, or other wireless devices too frequently and for too long. The degree of stress is related to how much you pull your head forward and down as you text or work, putting excess weight on the neck. This is shown in the chart below, which correlates the degree of forward movement to the extra weight of the head, which is generally 8–11 pounds by itself. This weight on the neck increases with a forward head position.

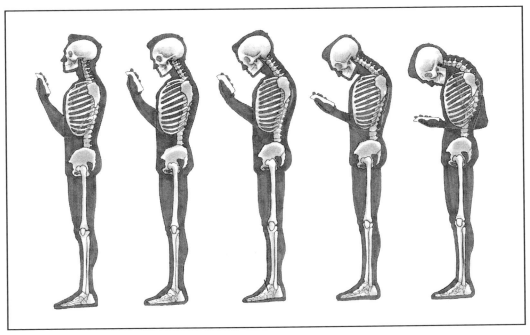

Text neck.

0 degrees = 10–12 pounds
15 degrees = 27 pounds
30 degrees = 40 pounds
45 degrees = 49 pounds
60 degrees = 60 pounds

Looking at your phone
with neck compression.

Looking at your phone
without neck compression.

You can imagine the potential problems that might arise with this use. As introduced in Chapter 8, the head–trunk relationship is the basic organizing principle in vertebrate movement. If you are lying down and want to get up, it is your head that moves first. This can be seen in the animal world: a horse's head will right itself first, then the body will organize to follow; and when you are riding a horse, you pull the reins and the horse's body follows.

Shell story

F.M. Alexander was visiting George E. Coghill, an award-winning physiologist, at his farm in Gainesville, Florida. Coghill was raising some chickens. F.M. noticed that one of the newborn chicks had an odd gait. He picked the chick up, examined it carefully, and discovered that a bit of yoke-covered shell, from birth, was imbedded in the down feathers at the back of the chick's neck. The shell was pulling the chick's head back and down. F.M. removed the shell and put the chick down. It resumed walking, but now with a normal gait.[46]

What a great story. If F.M. had not come along, that chick might have walked in that peculiar fashion for the rest of its life. When I share this story with workshop participants, I ask them to look for where their bit of shell is caught. How would life work better without your shell fragment? F.M. stated, "The hardest things to get rid of are the things that don't exist,"[47] meaning if you don't know it exists, how can you get rid of it?

2. JAW AND THROAT

The first hinge joint to evolve in the human body, the jaw is slung or suspended from the skull. One common complaint, especially among singers and people who use their voice frequently, is a lot of jaw tension.

Jaw tension is closely related to the way you hold your head. If your head is freely moving on top of your spine, then your jaw can hang loosely. But if you pull your head back and down by contracting the muscles in the back of the neck, your breathing is cut off, and the back of your neck curves and tightens, causing your jaw to clench.

With the head pulled back and the jaw tight, the throat's musculature is constricted, pulling the larynx from its naturally suspended position (which is like an old-fashioned microphone hung by guy wires). This interferes with breathing, speaking or singing (people gasp for air between phrases), and with overall musculature support, limiting our ability when upright to lengthen and not collapse.

Because of the throat constriction, in order to breathe or speak, you need to lift up to allow air in. The common habit is to lift the front of the throat up with the jaw and tongue. This lets you breathe, but the lifting work tightens the jaw and tongue, creating more tension.

Given these realities, we can see that all that jaw tightness could not possibly change much by massaging the area or wearing a nighttime mouth device. The tightness can change greatly, however, by altering the relationship of your head to the top of your spine.

Busted myth: You can change the active gripping in your jaw by massaging the sides of your face.

EX-ERCISE: JAW FREEDOM

The jaw is designed to hang freely in its resting state. Your mouth is open about half an inch, the width of one finger. It takes effort to close the lips together.

Jaw freedom with mouth closed.

Jaw freedom with mouth opened.

Start this exercise by allowing your jaw to just hang in its resting state, which you can find by opening your mouth until you sense a slight resistance. Then close your mouth. Be sure not to pull your head back as you open your mouth, or your jaw cannot be free. Repeat and notice.

Your jaw is part of the social engagement system, for mouth opening/closing, speaking and communicating, and kissing. And when defense is needed, the jaw in animals, and humans, growls to show teeth, snarl, or bite.

> **DO** Whenever you feel tightness or holding in your jaw or throat.

3. SHOULDERS

Many people hunch their shoulders up around their ears. They are told by others, "Pull your shoulders down!" And they obey and put them down, but two minutes later the shoulders are up again. Why? Because everything else that is happening in their body, mind, and psyche requires that the shoulders be in the up position.

From a positional standpoint, we can see one cause for this dysfunctional habit. When you stand with your hips jutting forward and your shoulders back in space behind them, there is nothing under the shoulders to support them, so it feels like they need to be held up. As you learn to bring your hips back over your feet, and then your shoulders and upper ribs forward over your hips, your shoulders will not need to lift up because they can sit on your back. Shoulders widen. This is just one reason why the shoulders might be up. We read about other forms of habitual constriction in the discussion in Chapter 7 about muscle spindles.

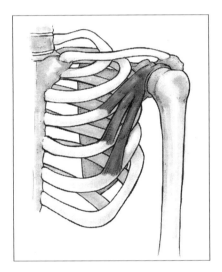

The shoulder joint.

EX-ERCISE: SHOULDERS OVERHEAD

1. Now let's see how your shoulders *are* able to move. Watch in a mirror, a side view, as you lift your arms over your head.

2. Do you notice that the whole upper torso moves? Why? Because your shoulders are not free in the joint, so the whole arm, upper back, and shoulder move together.

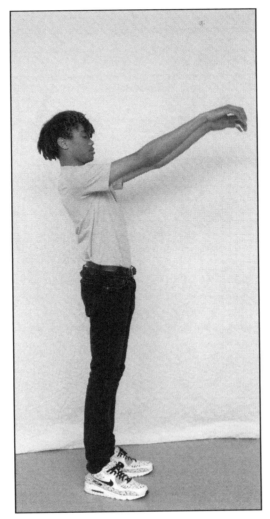

Shoulders not free with arms in front.

Shoulders not free with arms overhead.

3. But . . . the shoulders are the freest joints in your body. They are so free that they can dislocate. Imagine that. No other joint in the body can come apart and go back together like that.

4. Practice lifting your arms over your head with only your arm moving in the socket, keeping your upper back relatively still (but moving with your breath). No need to pull your shoulders back (the common directive). Instead, allow them to widen.

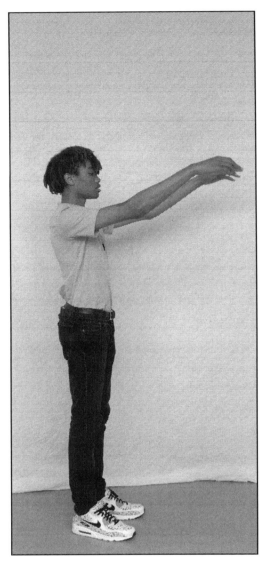

Shoulders free with arms in front.

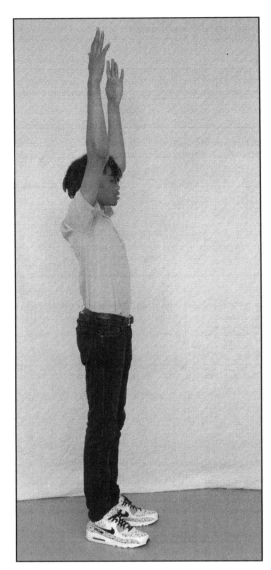

Shoulders free with arms over head.

> **DO** Whenever your shoulders feel restricted.

BIG myth: "Hold your shoulders down" or "Pull your shoulders back" or "Shoulders do not move as you breathe."

I find that your shoulders do come up a bit as you breathe. Shoulders are made to move. I am not saying they go up around your ears as in accessory breathing (which are situations of high metabolic demand). However, when you breathe, your lungs expand. And your ribs move on top of your lungs. And your shoulders sit on top of your ribs, so they move too. The conclusion is that your shoulders do move a bit as you breathe. And that is a good thing. Doesn't that feel refreshing?

4. RADIUS AND ULNA: THE BONES AND JOINTS OF THE LOWER ARM

The following information is invaluable for anyone who uses their arms for extended periods of time, such as musicians or hands-on practitioners. This includes anyone on a computer or phone, which is, of course, most people. Many end up with wrist and lower-arm problems.

The lower arm, from your wrist to your elbow, has two large bones. On the little finger outer side is the ulna. The bone sticks out at your wrist on one end and extends to your elbow. On the thumb side is the radius, and the bump on your wrist below your thumb is its lower end.

To discover important functional information, hold your forearm parallel to the floor with your palm up. Feel both bones parallel to each other. Lay your fingers along the ulna at your wrist. Rotate your lower arm so your palm faces the floor and notice that the ulna does not move very much in space. You can see that the ulna is the axis of the rotation—a stable center around which something can move. The ulna is like the binding of a book; it is the strongest part of the lower arm. The pages turn 180 degrees around the axis.

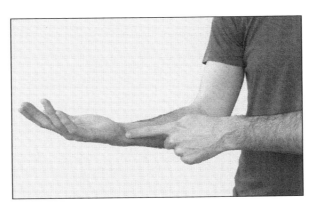

Finger on ulna (pinkie-side) at wrist.

Now, hold your upper (elbow) end of the radius and upper end of the ulna and rotate again. You see that both do not move. The ulna does not move at your wrist or your elbow, and the radius does not move at your elbow. So what moves for the lower arm to rotate?

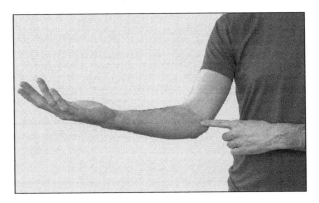

Finger on ulna (pinkie-side) at elbow.

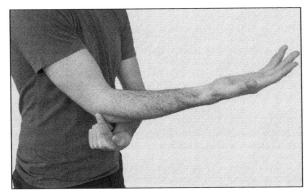

Finger on radius (thumb-side) at elbow.

This time, lay your finger along the radius side of your arm at your wrist and rotate your arm. You see that your finger moves 180 degrees.

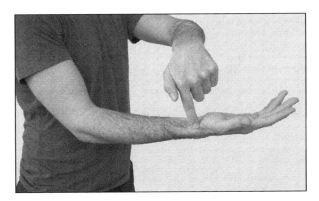

Finger on radius (thumb-side) at wrist.

The radius crosses the ulna in rotation. The ulna is stationary, and the radius moves in relation to it. The myth is that the axis is at the radius. Most people try to stabilize the thumb (radius) side of their hand and move the pinkie (ulna) side around. This tenses the lower arm and strains the elbow and wrist. Musicians, massage therapists, and people who use computers need to pay attention to how they use their hands, especially the angle at the wrist.

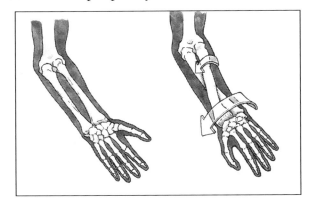

The radius-ulna crossing.

EX-PLORATION: RADIUS–ULNA RELATIONSHIP

To check your hand, lay your hand palm down on your lap to see the orientation of your hand.

Misuse = If you slip your thumb under your palm and it is in line with the radius at rest, then you see how this habit angles your hand in relation to your arm so that there is chronic contraction across the outer (pinkie-side) of your wrist.

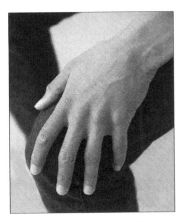

Misuse of the hand.

Improved use = Move your hand so that the little finger lines up with the ulna. Put your thumb under the palm again, and you see there is no chronic contraction on either side of the wrist. This can be called a rest position.

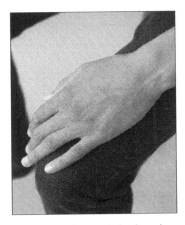

Improved use of the hand.

DO   **With any hand discomfort.**

EX-PLORATION: THIRD JOINT

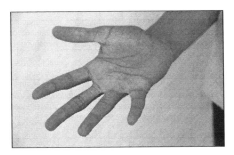

Pinkie-finger crease.

As you look at the pinkie-finger crease photo, you see a crease at the third digit of the fingers. Most assume this is where the finger bends. But if you explore on your own hand, you will see that your finger bends from the joint that is lower down.

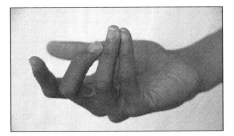

Pinkie-finger joint.

Now notice that the place where your thumb comes out of your palm is only the second thumb joint. This is the point from where most folks move their thumb. *But* it moves much more efficiently from the third joint, lower down the hand, near the wrist. Try it. Invaluable information for anyone who uses their hands a lot—to play the piano or type on a computer—don't you think?

Second thumb joint.

Third thumb joint.

DO   With any hand—arm discomfort.

EX-ERCISE: HANDSHAKE

1. With a partner, shake hands.

2. Practice the thumb and ulna placement described above.

3. Shake hands again and notice any changes in your arm, or whole body. How is your social contact different?

> **DO**   Whenever you shake hands.

5. ARMS: BRACHIATION

Let's see how this radius–ulna relationship affects movement. When discussing developmental movement, we can look at "development" in many ways. Perhaps the most obvious aspect

Child practicing brachiation.

is when babies learn to crawl and walk, thereby creating the movement patterns they will use in life. We can also look at developmental movement on an evolutionary scale. By studying other primates, we can learn more about our own use and body efficiency. One aspect of this evolutionary developmental movement is *brachiation*.

The term *brachiation* is derived from the Latin word for arm—*brachium*—and refers to swinging through the trees using only the arms. Children on monkey bars in a playground are technically practicing brachiation.

As you watch primates (apes, for example) on YouTube videos or *National Geographic* specials, you can notice that they reach for the next branch with the outside pinkie edge of their hand and arm. The first thing to grasp the branch is the little finger, lined up with the lower arm (as we saw in the photo "improved use of hand"). This reaching with the outside edge of the hand is one of the defining characteristics of brachiation, and it seems to be one of the major techniques that we humans have lost.

Most people reach for something by extending the index finger and thumb toward the object. But this is not the most efficient use of a human hand. Why would a primate reach with the little finger, rather than the index finger and thumb?

As we saw above, the strongest part of the hand is actually the pinkie side, not the thumb side. The muscles of the little finger connect through the hand to muscles in the outside of the forearm much more strongly than those of the thumb side, meaning that the pinkie side of the hand has a much more direct connection to the support muscles of the back and scapula to give you a more stable hold.

This is why martial artists who use weapons hold the weapon most tightly with the pinkie and most loosely with the index finger. They often refer to this hold as the "monkey grasp," recognizing the evolutionary benefits. The myth, of course, is that the thumb side is stronger.

This concept of brachiation can be extremely useful for humans, particularly when reaching for an item above head level. By reaching with the pinkie first, we can keep the shoulders released and the support muscles of the back engaged, allowing for better control of the object once seized. This is helpful when you are lifting your child, your groceries, or your phone.

Just as it's easier to carry a heavy load by getting underneath it rather than by hauling straight up from above, reaching with the pinkie allows the muscles of the scapula to do the work from underneath, rather than relying on the upper deltoids on the top of the shoulders. This not only makes it easier to lift any weighty object, it makes it easier to lift the weight of the arm itself.

6. ARMS ARE FOR REACHING: *HUMANUAL* TOUCH

Whether your arm is reaching for a pencil or a lifeline, there is an optimal use that sustains your expanded structure. When you go to pick up an object, what leads for you?

When you reach for something, for the sake of efficiency, you want to use your extremities—not your shoulder.

EX-PLORATION: REACHING FOR AN OBJECT

Reaching with fingertips leading.

Explore reaching for an object as you stand on your support, by leading with your extremities, your fingertips. To pick something up, fingertips move first. If that does not get you to your object, move your hand. If that is not enough, move your wrist, then forearm, elbow, upper arm, shoulder, then your back (as you bend your knees), and/or if needed, your entire body takes a step. You need your fingertips supported from your feet, the ground, and your whole body. Your arm is not a separate appendage.

| Reaching for an object. | Touching the object. | Reaching for an object with guidance. | Touching the object with guidance. |

Many people reach for an object by lifting their shoulder. If your shoulder leads and is closed in, you are moving forward with protection and that feels safe to you. But it is not the design in your arm and hand. Practice carving out space with your fingertips. As you keep your shoulder relaxed, there is an important connection from your head to your feet and out through your fingertips.

> **DO** Whenever you reach for something.

7. BACK AND TORSO

When I am teaching, I often use the expression, "Now you are in your back." When I say this, my students understand. They sense the strength of the back and torso muscles, and often feel confident with a strong sense of self, as in the phrases "strong backbone" and "a backbone of society." Can you feel the strength of your own back?

Your back/torso functionally includes your entire back from the top of your spine to your hip joints, including your spine, pelvis, and ribs. Your spine can be compressed or lengthened as you sit, stand, move, or do nothing. A shortened spine tends to compress everything in the torso; it also limits breath. A lengthened spine gives fluidity, spaciousness, and breathability to the torso. Feel the difference between your shortened spine and your lengthened spine.

The majority of people are shorter at the end of the day because they sink down on their spine. Between the vertebrae are discs composed of a series of circular bands filled with fluid. As you sink down, the discs flatten, and you appear to be shorter. After a night's sleep, they fill up again and in the morning you are taller.

Back collapsed.

"In your back,"
with guidance.

"In your back,"
lengthened.

8. MY ACHING BACK: DON'T "TUCK UNDER"

So many people complain of lower-back pain. The many reasons for this include the bracing that comes with a traumatic incident or injury, aging, conditioned habits, facing difficult choices, and so on.

A common misuse is a shortening in the lumbar region, the lower back. This is called "sway back," "over-arched," "slipped forward lumbar disc," or "tilted pelvis." Along with this shortening, the hips are usually jutting forward and off the center line. The body is falling forward, so something inside must come to the rescue and "grab you." The legs get involved. They tend to grab in back with the hamstrings and in front at the ankles or toes. This will

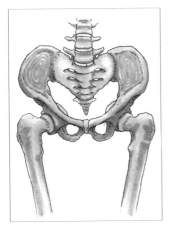

Front view of hip sockets.

keep you upright, but the tightness in your ankles, knees, and hips is not contributing to your overall health.

This may help you to understand why your hamstrings are so tight. You've been using them all day long to stay upright.

The common solution for the over-arched lower back, although not the most effective, is to "tuck under," which means to push your lower hips forward. This will solve the visual problem of your butt sticking out. But in reality, as you push your lower pelvis forward, it jams into your hips and tightens your hip sockets, which limits mobility. Most people cannot hold the tuck for long periods of time anyway.

Myth: It is good to tuck under to straighten your lower back.

Another common approach is to strengthen your stomach muscles, so that your stomach does not drop forward. Let us look at what that really does. The vertical, surface, abdominal muscles (your "six-pack") attach to the pubic bone on the bottom and to the lower ribs on top. These work more as you strengthen your stomach muscles by doing sit-ups or crunches. As a muscle works, it pulls both ends together. In this case, you are pulling your pelvis up and your ribs down. Yes, your stomach is a bit flatter, but you are also generally pulled down. Then you need to lift the front of your chest to expand. We usually do this by pulling down the ribs in back. This puts more pressure on the lower back. But that was the original problem we were trying to change!

EX-PLORATION: LOWER BACK

When you want less curvature in your lower back, instead of "tucking under," I suggest allowing your hip sockets to be free. Your hip sockets are where your leg bends just below the lower torso. While standing or lying on your back, lift your knees one at a time to sense that fold. Let your back, including your pelvis and whole spine, lengthen up from there, not squeezing, pushing,

My hip socket is here.

or pulling. As you lengthen your whole torso, your abdominal muscles will work a little bit to tone your belly and lengthen your lower back.

DO Whenever you want more length in your lower back.

9. BENDING: WATCH A TODDLER

When you bend over to take something out of the oven, or to pick up your nephew, or to hit a tennis ball, do you bend from your waist or your hip joints? In any event, if you bend without knowing how (i.e., in accord with your design of support, suspension, and breath, the *Humanual* Basics), you might be in for some trouble.

A major reason for lower-back discomfort is misuse or uneducated movement. Most people bend from the waist, thereby losing their support. When you bend over from your waist or lower back with your head pulled back and legs straight, you are repeatedly bending from the same fourth or fifth lumbar joint. Your lower back is not made for this. You never see a toddler bending from the waist.

Toddler bending.   Toddler bending and lifting.

All the spine's parts move in relationship to each other—when one part gets moved, the whole spine moves. It is not made to bend only in one place, again and again. This dynamic is very different from a hinge joint, like your elbow. You can bend and straighten your elbow a million times and not have a problem, but this is not true if you are bending from your waist or lower back, the lumbar area. As a matter of fact, your waist is not even an anatomical reality. It does not exist in anatomy books. If you only bend from your lumbar area, which is not made to function as a hinge joint, you will deteriorate the integrity of the joint.

For example, when you bend from your lower back to pick up an object (at arm's length) that weighs twenty pounds, you put at least four hundred pounds of pressure on your lower back. No wonder that after a while your back is hurting!

How does this happen? As you bend over with your legs straight, the weight of your torso is no longer supported from underneath. You become top-heavy as you increase velocity moving in the downward direction. Then you need to switch direction with the added weight of the object you are picking up. This multiplies the pressure put on your lower back. Repeating this pattern often results in back pain.

EX-ERCISE: DON'T BEND FROM THE WAIST

Bending, as in all movement with our natural design, is a full-body motion. The specifics outlined below aim to prevent habitual patterns. The movement for bending should take place in your hip sockets because they are a hinge joint—a beautiful ball-and-socket joint that can handle a large, free-flowing range of motion. This is suited for bending. To bend from the hips, you must bend your knees and ankles as well, so you can stay over your support.

When you bend in a "habitual" way (i.e., from the waist):

- Your legs stiffen.
- Your toes clench as you lose support.
- Your neck tightens.
- Your lower back gets misused as a hinge joint.

Bending in a habitual way.

To practice bending correctly:

1. Stand with feet hip-width apart. Stay over your support.

2. Allow your neck to be free from stiffening so that your head can release away from your spine, which then allows your back to lengthen and widen.

3. As your whole back (including your hips) aims upward, allow your knees to release slightly forward. Make sure your knees do not turn toward each other. They want to be over your feet. Your ankles, knees, and hips bend over your support.

4. As your head is freeing away from your spine, allow your torso to incline (but not drop) forward from your hips. Your arms hang freely and shoulders widen. Your back is lengthening and widening as you breathe.

Proper bending includes:

- Head free on top of your spine.
- Back lengthening and widening.
- Allowing your hips to move back and up in relation to your knees, going forward.
- Your body weight is supported over your whole foot.

Bending in a more efficient way.

Squatting with support.

There is no compression or strong pulling down of your torso in bending. It is a lengthening, an expansion of the muscles, and then a release of the joints. In reality, it is not really bending at all. It is one large structure-changing shape.

If you are comfortable bending farther, try a squat with weight on your heels, keeping your heels down, as you aim up and stay in your back. Hold something stable if you tend to fall over, or work with a partner and stabilize each other.

According to biotensegrity specialists Levin and Martin, "Movement is not bending of hinges, but expansion, repositioning and contraction of tensegrities. An instant repositioning of tensegrities allows for freely moving joints while the triangulation imparts stability of form and function."[48]

DO | Every time you bend.

10. PSOAS: LOWER-BACK PAIN IS NOT ONLY PHYSICAL

Lower backs get compressed and painful for many reasons: Your boss asks you to work one more night this week, and you feel overworked. Your date is now twenty minutes late, which brings on emotional exhaustion. You pick up a heavy object improperly. Lower-back pain is one of the most common complaints bringing people to doctors and healthcare providers. When life feels heavy and unmanageable, a typical response is to collapse out of your

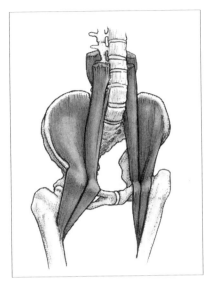

Front view of the psoas muscle.

wholeness. It is vital to understand the proper use of your lower back.

The psoas muscle influences your lower back, as it connects your lower spine to your legs. It detects subtle changes in weight and makes adjustments in movement. It is also part of the autonomic and emotional systems, with connections to the digestive and respiratory systems, as well as reproductive organs and pelvic movement. If there is a lot of misuse and pulling down in the torso, the psoas gets tight and shrinks; it loses its suppleness and cannot perform its designated functions. Have you ever felt a general constriction in your lower torso? Sitting at your computer? While playing sports? Or while standing waiting for the train?

The psoas is involved in the survival instincts of fight, flight, or freeze. When you are in danger, it is your psoas that prepares you to quickly move away and flee, or stand your ground and fight. When it comes to primitive fear responses, the psoas helps you make wise decisions in support of yourself. Moving properly as you bend or walk keeps the psoas healthy, well-functioning, and prepared for anything.

11. FEET: YOUR FOUNDATION

Your arm and leg gestures are very telling, but your feet also reveal a lot about who you are. How do your feet step into and walk in the world? Are you confident? Are you all over the place? Are your feet engaged fully with the ground? Is one foot always in front of the other, or turned out ninety degrees, as if you were a ballet dancer? Do you have disorganized feet, or feet that don't know where they are going? Do you shuffle, pound, or walk on eggshells? Notice your own feet now.

Your feet are the base of support for your whole body when you are standing and for your legs when you are sitting on a chair. Your feet stand your ground and simultaneously receive the support of the ground. They want to be "plugged into" the ground. When a connection is made, the energy from the earth spreads up your legs, into your torso and arms, through your neck and head, and out into the world. The expansion that you feel is an aspect of your expanded Self.

Each foot has twenty-six little bones with forty joints, and numerous muscles and tendons. With all these parts, your feet have a great capacity for gathering information. In an earlier time, before flat, even-surfaced floors, feet had to constantly communicate important warnings: "The ground under you is uneven; you need to adjust the rest of your body to balance." Or, "You are walking in dangerous terrain—quicksand—get out!" If you are holding a lot of tension in your feet, these messages do not get conveyed in a timely manner or at all to higher centers in the brain. Accidents can easily follow.

As you sit, it is most beneficial to have both feet on the floor. You can then let the floor support you. You always want as much support as you can get from below. And, ideally, this support is evenly balanced through both feet.

The habit of crossing your legs or lifting your feet up when sitting can be difficult to change. I once had a client with a severe back problem. I asked her if she kept her feet on the floor at work as she sat at her desk. She said she twisted her feet around the bottom of her chair. I asked her to try keeping her feet on the floor. Her pain disappeared when she engaged both feet with the ground. Not grounding, of course, but meeting the ground and receiving the upward force.

Sometimes the overwhelming or traumatic pattern that causes the feet to pull up, or the legs to retract into the torso, needs to be addressed first. The pattern could be from a moment you wanted to run away but could not, such as an interrupted flight response from a car accident, abuse, or a dangerous encounter. It could even be a result of a bad blind date. Your legs are saying, "Get me out of here!"

I had a student, Kathy, who had trouble keeping her feet on the floor. One day in class, we were doing an exercise while lying on the floor. It involved opening the arms. Kathy told me she was not able to do this. I asked why and she said she had no idea. The next week she came into class and related a memory. When she was young, she fell and hurt her knee. The pain was so great that she held her knee against her torso with both arms. When they took her to the hospital, Kathy would not let go of her knee; her arms held on tight. They had to give her morphine so her arms could release her knee. While the morphine did its job, the implicit memory in her body told her not to open her arms. Understanding the pattern helped Kathy shift her arms and put her feet on the floor.

EX-ERCISE: SHIFT WEIGHT

Head-to-toe movements engage the entire body. They also stimulate *baroreceptors*, the blood-pressure feedback loops. This will stimulate vagal activity to lower the arousal of your nervous system and allow you to feel calmer. I have noticed that many people tend to do a slight rocking motion as they stand.

Preparation: Stand in a comfortable space.

1. Notice as you are standing where you tend to put the weight on your feet. Are you often leaning forward on the balls of your toes, or more likely to be back on your heels? Explore what emotions come up with either one.

2. See if you can find uniform front-to-back and side-to-side contact of the bottoms of your feet as they touch the floor, so that the full weight of your body is distributed evenly over your feet and supported by the ground as you stand upright.

3. Your feet merge with the ground, as you are one with the earth.

4. Then shift your weight from one foot to the other: weight on the left foot and then weight on the right foot. Notice what happens. Repeat slowly many times.

5. Notice what happens in the rest of your body. Any settling?

6. How are your right and left sides different?

> **DO** When you want more stability in life.

MOVING INTO FREEDOM AS YOU SIT, STAND, AND WALK

In sitting and standing, there are two common options that most people adopt: they are collapsed down or stiffened up. Neither option is comfortable. That's why no one stays in these positions for long. This chapter offers detailed information on how to sit and stand with ease for longer periods of time. Isn't that a relief? Then you can take that greater freedom into walking.

Hunched over at a computer.

1. SITTING AND THE DOWNWARD PULL

How many times a day do you find yourself slouching down? Do you slump at your computer, in your car, on a barstool? How often do you find yourself "all of a sudden" in a slump? And as soon as you realize the slump, you hoist yourself up into "good posture"? Inevitably, I see many hands go up when I ask these questions to a group.

Sitting more upright at a computer.

Sitting in a chair, particularly for long periods of time, can cause a great deal of discomfort—especially if you are not using yourself well, including accessing your red-fiber system (see Chapter 7). But most people sit in a way that ignores our natural design of uprightness.

There is an aspect in us that always wants to be more upright. We try to sit up one way, or another way, but nothing seems to be a lasting solution. Enter *Humanual*.

You are designed to sit on the bottom of your pelvis—the *ischial tuberosity,* commonly called the "sitting or sit bones." Most people crunch down so that the pelvis gets tilted either backward or forward. As soon as the pelvis tilts, you're either tucked under on the back edge or over-arched on the front edge. Both result in a downward pull in your torso, which collapses and/or constricts your spine.

Slumping down, over-arching up, crossing legs, and wrapping feet around chair legs are all habits that are detrimental to the body's well-being. Slumping down occasionally is not so bad, as it can reflect a temporary emotional state. But how often do you sit slumped, and with how much zest or "attitude" are you pulling down? Parts of you may be getting chronically compressed and will eventually complain with pain. This downward slump can also reflect a posture of shame.

The following exercises will help you circumvent slouching and discover the most efficient way to sit—balancing the pelvis and spine. As you practice this, it is possible to experience spontaneous lengthening and upward movement. Remember, spontaneous lengthening cannot coexist with depression. If you tend toward depression, or other disorders such as back pain, difficulty with concentration, or poor digestion, it will be a productive exploration for you to try this way of sitting for a few minutes a day, working up to more.

A. EX-ploration: Sitting Bones

The sitting bones are little V-shaped rockers at the base of your torso. You want to sit on the point of the V. Experiment by sitting far back on the back edge of your pelvis, tucked under, and then way forward on the front edge, over-arched. Then rock back and forth until you find the middle. Let that middle spot drop into the chair as you aim upward through your whole back and head. In a way, the sitting bones are like feet at the bottom of your pelvis. They receive support from the chair and allow your actual feet to be in contact with the ground.

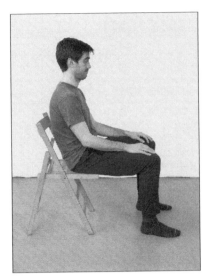
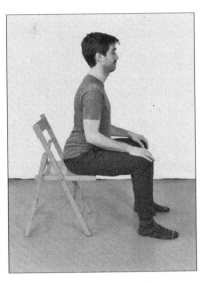
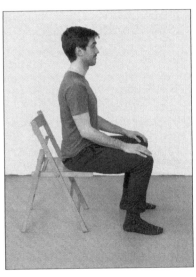

Sitting tucked under.　　　　　　Sitting over-arched.　　　　　Sitting bones dropped into the chair.

DO　　　　　**Anytime you sit.**

B. EX-ploration: From Slumping to Sitting Upright— in a Way You Might Be Able to Sustain

In order to sit up straight, most people pull themselves up by arching their back and pulling their head back. They remain there for about two minutes, then, finding it too much work, slump down again. The choices for sitting are: over-arched and pulled up, or collapsed and pulled down. Let's look at a different choice for sitting.

Recall that the head functionally leads all movement, and the body follows. Therefore, to emerge from your slumped-down sitting position, direct your head to aim toward the ceiling as you let your sitting bones drop into the chair, and do not over-arch your back.

Let your hip sockets be free, so that:

- Your whole pelvis and lower torso aim upward and widen.
- Your lower ribs and middle torso aim upward and widen.
- Your chest and upper back aim upward and widen.
- All follow the upward direction of your head, and your attention.

A breath may flow in.

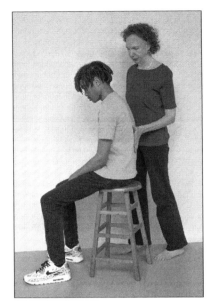

Sitting, step 1.

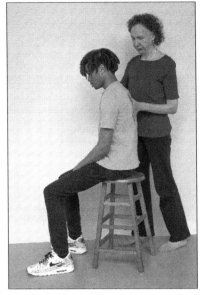

Sitting, step 2.

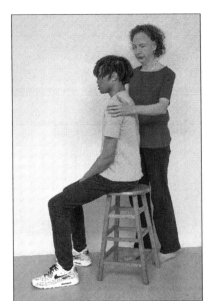

Sitting, step 3.

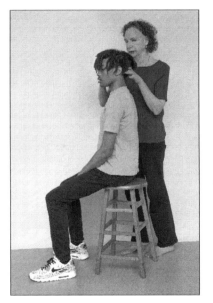

Sitting, step 4.

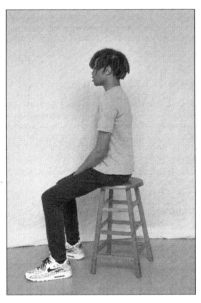

Sitting, step 5.

By sitting upright this way, you are saying "No" to the old habit of over-arching up, and "Yes" to the new habit of lengthening and widening. This sequence requires less work, and you can train yourself to sit for longer periods of time in a more upright way. You are now using more efficient muscles—the ones closer to your spine that are designed for support and for long-term sustained activity.

C. EX-ploration: Looking a Bit Deeper

As you are slumping, notice the desire to be more upright and follow the impulses from inside, instead of mechanically pulling yourself up. This might be easier after you develop a better sense of your inner workings through diligent observation. This might include noticing and then stopping your pulling down. *As you stop pulling down in your torso, you will rise up with less effort.*

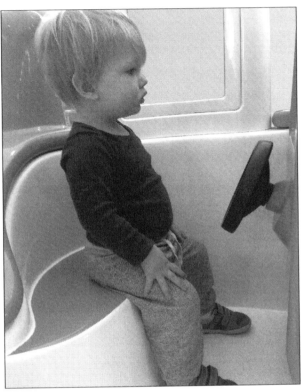

It is not about good posture. It is about good use.

DO   Anytime you sit.

The multiple facets of slump awareness

One of my students habitually went to a café at the end of her day to relax. She ordered a cup of tea and added many packets of sugar. She sat slumped down at the table as she drank her heavily sweetened tea. One day, she began paying attention to her suspension and support and sat more upright to drink. When she sat upright, she gagged at how awful the sweet tea tasted. Our senses are influenced by our use.

2. UPRIGHTNESS: IT'S NOT ABOUT GOOD POSTURE BUT ABOUT GOOD USE

From an early age, we are very interested in verticality. Our head wants to lift and aim upward—for food, connection, or to look around. At some point, we learn to sit up. Since the body so desperately wants to be upright, with many trials and tribulations we make it to standing. The quest for verticality seems to be innate and a sign of well-being. Why did humans evolve to a vertical position? According to Raymond Dart, the famous anthropologist, it was to see farther away.[49] What do you think?

The concept of uprightness has many metaphorical connotations: People who do the "right thing" and are conscientious are thought to have "upright behavior." There is also an implication that doing the "right thing" causes us to feel and be upright in our posture. The Bible mentions the word *upright* more than seventy times. The Book of Job says, "The upright man is the perfect man." Did he mean a person who has "good posture" and stands upright?

Dr. Jordan Peterson, professor of psychology at the University of Toronto, wrote a book called *Twelve Rules for Life: An Antidote to Chaos*. Guess what the number one rule is . . . Stand Up Straight! Although I do not agree with the phrase or the way he demonstrates it (too rigid and mechanical), I think the concept is correct. He notes that lobsters have innate hierarchical programming determining that the lobsters that flex their muscles more have more power and, therefore, dominate. According to Peterson, if you stand up straight you can be a top lobster. "Lobsters govern their postural flexion with serotonin. Serotonin governs status, emotional regulation, and posture in lobsters and in humans."[50] It's an interesting concept, whether or not it's why we desire to stand up straight.

In our society, we often equate uprightness with a kind of stiffness. This is unfortunate, and not the whole picture. According to our physiology, we can be upright and free, without rigidity. It's a built-in system, and it's based on the interaction and flow between gravity and antigravity, and our human reflexes. As a final point, true uprightness is something that we receive from deep inside; it's not something that we can paste on by tightening a few surface muscles. Observe yourself and others in life, and you will see what I mean.

The following EX-plorations aim to help illustrate balance and support in standing.

EX-PLORATION: STANDING UPRIGHT

Let's look at the common response to the command, "Stand up straight!" Most people lift their chest up and pull their shoulders back to have "good posture." They are usually stiff and held. This is not efficient. Instead, it's better to start where the body actually begins standing—on the ground, where our feet meet the earth. Here we start paying attention to use.

DO Lean forward a little and then back a little. Then less forward and less back until you have even contact on the fronts and backs of your feet. Now you have the potential for balanced support from the ground that can rise up through your entire body to allow you to stand upright. Notice that you do not have to hold yourself up stiffly.

DON'T DO In terms of the upper body, the common tendency is to pull the front up with the chest and chin, by pulling your shoulders down in the back. The muscles in your upper back are not designed for this and will either get stiff and overworked in their attempt to hold you up, or collapse back down to slump. Most people limit themselves to two choices: slumped down and "relaxed," or stiffened up and "rigid."

Neither is satisfying. *Humanual* offers a third solution.

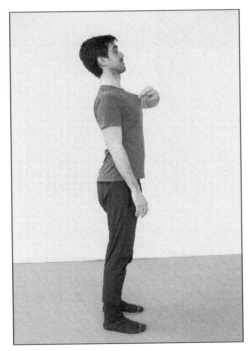

Stiffened up while standing.

DO

With your feet supported by the ground, place one hand on your chest and one hand on your middle or upper back. Lift both front and back equally, and let that lift ripple through your whole body. Feel your breath flow in as you stand. Your head is also releasing upward. When body weight is distributed properly, you do not slump down and your movements tend to be lighter and easier. This process is not the style of standing up straight such that "I will pull my shoulders back and heave my chest up." This process is "I am one whole expanded structure, with all muscles working a little bit." Can you sense all your muscles working a little bit? Now when you go to the gym or yoga class, you start with a more balanced body.

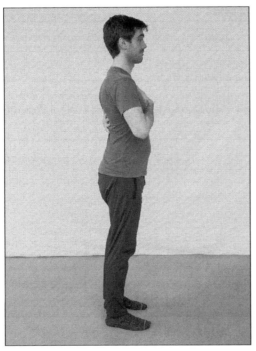

Using your hands to help you stand.

Standing with guidance.

DO   Whenever you are standing.

When I really look at the issue, I realize that the only reason for slumping down is because I am not paying attention to what I am doing with myself. If I were paying attention, I would feel my breath suppressed, shoulders contracted, and a general heavy pulling down. *If* I were unhappy, tired, shamed, or depressed, the slump would be accurate for the moment—the muscles and the psychology working as one.

> *"In the human vestibular system, the system that manages our sense of balance, the center point of neural activity, is based on the body being upright and erect. The vestibular neurons that fire most frequently do so during the least amount of body movement, indicating the importance of being upright as the center point for balance to operate around."*[51]
>
> — RODOLFO LLINAS

3. FULL STATURE AS YOU STAND: RECOGNIZING YOUR OWN UPRIGHTNESS AND UNDERSTANDING WHY YOU PULL YOURSELF DOWN OUT OF IT

A child in full stature.

Full stature is the term for inhabiting your uprightness as you move through life; it's a powerful concept. When you allow yourself to fully inhabit yourself so that every part is expanding to its connected maximum, you feel your full stature. Find your support and engage your suspension now as you stand.

Most people are collapsed and dropped down, or inflated and pulled up. As we've seen, these adaptive states are in place for good reason: they helped us deal with trauma, injury, accident, emotional turmoil, and more. The adaptive pattern of making ourselves small might allow us to survive, but what if life is now calling you to be full and visible? When and where in your life can you experience your full stature as you stand? Perhaps when you've completed a marathon that you trained hard for, or when a love interest sends a sweet text, or even when you make that perfect cup of coffee. Similarly, what pulls you out of full stature? Is it getting bypassed for a promotion, a bad grade, or the emotional turmoil of a family member?

It is most exhilarating to allow all of you—the real, authentic you—to fill with attention and awareness. You do not want to try to be bigger than you are by puffing yourself up artificially; you also do not want to pretend you are smaller than you are by shrinking in the world. What you want is to realize fully who you are and all that you are given. You want to begin to accept that "this is who I am when I am not doing my adaptive patterns" with your body, mind, soul, and spirit, and inhabit it fully.

When you are standing with full stature, you feel a kind of power, connectedness, and confidence; this invites your expanded Self. It's a kind of strength that is not easily shaken or dependent on outside circumstances. You can see animals in full-stature mode, especially when they are curious or alert, or ready for something to happen. You also see children this way when they are excited, stimulated, or interested.

An adult in full stature.

4. WALKING: HOW DO YOU WALK INTO A ROOM?

Once you have uprightness, you are ready to move into the world through walking. It seems like such a simple activity, but for many it is fraught with discomfort. When you walk into a room, are you comfortable? Do you establish power right away? Or do you look for the power person or people in the room and align to them? Maybe you prefer not to be seen and try to blend in with the background. Sometimes there is power in invisibility, as when a photographer is shooting candid images. Being unseen can be a plus.

Do you walk with self-assurance and confidence? Or do you feel awkward and walk with hesitation and self-consciousness? There are so many different versions of walking and, of course, each style has a different emotional tone. As you sit in the park or in a coffee shop, just notice the variety of styles of walking.

Walking is programmed in many species, but not in humans. A horse can walk soon after it is born, as this activity is already encoded in its fully developed brain. But since humans are born without a fully developed brain, walking must be learned. So, as toddlers, we explore. Eventually, we walk. Most of us continue with that particular style of walking for the rest of our lives and never look back. It works! But is it most efficient? Let's look. Think about your own walk.

Most people shift their weight onto one leg as they lift the other leg to begin the next step. Another habit is to shift both hips forward to begin walking; this has a similar motion to an arrested fall. Both habits usually create a drop onto the standing leg and/or a shortening in the lower back. This raises the question: If I keep my lower back lengthening and widening, how will I move forward? What leads the forward movement? The answer is in the exercise and photos below.

Knee leading forward.

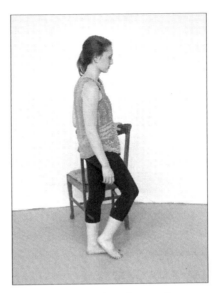

Knee leading forward with a chair for balance.

EX-ERCISE: WALKING

1. Allow your neck and the surrounding area to be less held. This allows your head to free upward, away from your back, which lets your back lengthen and widen.

2. With your spine lengthened, release your knee forward as you let your heel roll up, with your toes still on the ground. Shift side to side as little as possible.

3. Continue to lift your knee with your weight distributed upward and not dropped down to the side. As you bring your foot back down to touch the ground, aim your body up and do not stiffen yourself.

4. Try lifting one foot at a time, with your hands on your hips. Lengthen up along your spine to switch your weight. Do not drop side to side.

5. Or, try standing next to a chair and hold the back for balance as you lift one foot. Remember not to tighten your arms or hold your breath. Raise your knees alternately, as if you are walking in place. Lengthen your spine upward to maintain length and minimize hip sway.

6. Think about taking a step. You can feel your "get ready, set." Say "No" to it. Instead, aim your back up, and aim your head to the ceiling and fall up, as you release your knee forward to take your step.

7. Your knee leads you forward as you walk.

Remember: Shorter strides can help you maintain your lengthened back because you are stepping more under yourself. Shoulders release and spread sideways. Arms swing slightly. BREATHE.

The group walking
with knee leading forward.

Walking can be fun with
the knee leading forward.

When you feel the experience of walking as effort, it means you are thinking of yourself as a collection of parts that need to be moved independently. With this, the effort that you feel in your body is like the inefficient effort of "sitting up straight"; it is simply a concentrated force. But as we've seen, concentrated forces are not the most efficient model. Instead, you want forces dispersed throughout the entire form. That's what you are aiming for with every step you take.

DO   Always when walking.

HUM Journal.
**Next time you walk into a room full of people,
see if you have embodied any of these ideas.**

PART III

EXPANDED SELF

Undeniable Unity

CHAPTER

12

BREATH: CONNECTING INNER AND OUTER

Time to breathe! I cannot tell you how often a class participant says, "I hold my breath." There is not one simple solution to this issue, as the reasons for it are many and varied. For one person, it might be that they do not know the actual appropriate coordination; for another person it is their relationship to emotions, or shutdown.

Breath is one of your connections to the world around you. As you breathe in, or inhale, you take in possibilities from your surroundings. As you breathe out, or exhale, you are releasing what is no longer necessary. You don't need to do anything to make this happen. It is a built-in program. Your breathing is linked to every other part of you; and your breath will adjust itself accordingly, in each moment, to what you're doing, thinking, feeling, and sensing. When you walk, you breathe; if you walk faster, you breathe faster. How are you breathing now? How does that affect your inner experience of yourself?

Have you ever found yourself in a yoga class wondering, "Why is my breathing so shallow?" Or, have you been singing or performing onstage and suddenly realized you're running out of breath? Have you been exercising, driving, or even texting and noticed you're holding your breath?

You limit your breath for many good reasons. Maybe you are feeling overwhelmed, stressed, or just lost in thought. Sometimes your breathing changes in anticipation, or while holding in a difficult emotion. Essentially, breathing is a response to your activity and state of mind. Breathing can be both a voluntary and an involuntary activity.

1. OPTIMAL BREATH: MULTIDIMENSIONAL MOVEMENT

Ideal breathing coordination in humans is very specific. But if there was any overwhelm, trauma, or developmental or emotional dysregulation, this natural coordination has most likely been interfered with. Hence, most of us have some issue with breathing.

So, even though breathing happens automatically, and we really do not need to control it, most people benefit from some training to restore optimal function with minimum effort. You are looking for a spring-like, spontaneous breath that reflects the elastic quality of the body.

Breathing expert Carl Stough said, "Breathing is a process which will occur of itself, but proper breathing requires considerably more attention."[52] Let's take a look now at the complex process of breathing.

When our system detects too much carbon dioxide and not enough oxygen, the phrenic nerve, which sends motor information to the diaphragm and receives sensory information back from it, sends a message to the intercostals—the muscles between the ribs—to release and open. This creates negative pressure in the chest cavity, signaling the diaphragm, a hollow dome-shaped membrane-muscle-organ under the lungs, to lower and make room for the air as you breathe in. *Air enters the lungs naturally as a result of the increased negative space inside the chest, or thorax, not because you draw or suck it in.* During the exhale, the diaphragm rises, pushing the air out of the lungs. For the most complete breath, the diaphragm has to be free to move. But most people carry emotional issues that affect the diaphragm and, therefore, create muscular restrictions.

By the way, it is not a good idea to direct your breath metaphorically into your belly and to move stomach muscles, as is often taught in the yoga and music world; doing this bypasses the lungs and collapses the torso. Yes, for proper breathing, the belly responds to breath by expanding, but do not direct air into your belly area at the expense of not filling your lungs.

Your entire torso moves when you breathe—sideways, up and down, and front to back. It's what I call *3D breathing*, or multidimensional breathing. Also, keep in mind that the bulk of your lung tissue is in the back of your torso. Did you ever notice that when you go to the doctor for a checkup, they often put the stethoscope on your back first to check your breathing?

2. FLOW OF BREATH: A COORDINATED ACTIVITY

Ideally, your ribs expand, your diaphragm moves down, your lungs fill, and your belly expands to make room for the displaced organs.

I find a very efficient way to convey this is as follows. I put my hands on both shoulders of a client as I stand a bit to the side. At first, I just listen. Is there any movement in the shoulders? Perhaps I ask the client if they feel any movement, or if they believe shoulders should or should not move with breathing. Sometimes I have them explore the nonmovement. Is it comfortable? Restrictive?

Then I explain. "When you breathe, the lungs—which are elastic containers—move as they fill. The ribs sit on top of the lungs, so they move. Your shoulders sit on top of your ribs, so they move."

As I mentioned in the "Shoulders" section in Chapter 10, there is a common misunderstanding concerning the shoulders. Many instructors teach people to keep the shoulders still and down, or pulled back. But the shoulders are two of the freest joints in the body, designed to be free and to move.

When you breathe, let your shoulders move in response. I am not saying to force them up around your ears, but find the slight, easy flow in your shoulders as you breathe.

The explorations in this chapter investigate shoulder movement in relation to the mechanisms of breath, and the role of the diaphragm.

EX-PLORE: UPPER BODY MOVEMENT

Put your hands on your own shoulders. Is there any movement there as you breathe? Feel the stretchable containers of your lungs move as they fill. Watch the movement grow. As the *long, slow* exhalation increases, sense the movement in your torso and ribs. (There's now more vagal activity occurring, which down-regulates the sympathetic fight/flight system.)

Shoulders moving for breath.

The optimal breath brings fresh oxygen into your body; it fills your entire torso and spreads throughout your body to enhance your life-force. Then you can be present, alive, and able to engage in your next activity with fullness of body, mind, spirit . . . and breath!

Optimal breath can make you smile.

DO   Often.

3. THE IMPORTANCE OF EXHALE FOR SPONTANEOUS INHALE

As soon as you become aware of your breathing, you're in your body. When you inhale, oxygen goes via the lungs and bloodstream to your brain, which arouses the sympathetic nervous system and accelerates the heartbeat. When you exhale, you calm the parasympathetic nervous system, and the heartbeat slows down. Many major teachings emphasize the importance of the exhale, including wisdom traditions and chanting.

Shallow breathing, or "holding your breath," is not exactly "holding" your breath, but it is interfering with the flow of life-force in the body and the potential motion of the diaphragm. Any interference with the internal rhythm of breathing affects all our internal rhythms and cycles, which function best when there is coherence and flow among them, called *biological synchrony.* In fact, the respiratory muscles can weaken and lose their ability to move optimally if this rhythm is lost for an extended period. Shortness of breath can be a sign of some shut-down or immobility response, as we saw in Chapter 4.

When you notice a lack of breath, the common response is to inhale, taking a deep, forced and controlled breath. But let's look more at the design of the respiratory system and see what other, possibly more effective, choices are available.

Many say "take a breath" or "tank up" when singing. I find that this controlled inhale can actually place unhealthy pressure on the diaphragm, often tensing neck and chest muscles that do not need to be overly involved in breathing.

Because most people are busy taking an in-breath, they do not pay much attention to the exhale process. Without exhaling completely, excess carbon dioxide—a known stressor to the nervous system—may remain in the lungs. When this occurs, the system detects that there is too much carbon dioxide and not enough oxygen. Then it does the only thing it knows how to do—ask for more oxygen, which causes another inhale. Since the lungs are still partially filled with carbon dioxide, less oxygen can get in. Therefore, a cycle is set in motion that keeps you inhaling continuously for more oxygen. This habit can lead to shallow breathing, which is experienced as interference to the breathing cycle, or a feeling that you don't have enough breath.

However, when you exhale completely, your body naturally takes a "reflex" inhale. By releasing your ribs and expelling all air in the lungs, you engage the spring-like action of your ribs to expand and create a partial vacuum, and the air comes in as a neurological reflex. It is your optimal breath and will feel satisfying.

With optimal breathing, you don't suck air in to "take" a breath, or "push" air out to expel a breath. You simply allow air to flow in and out, so the lungs easily exhale carbon dioxide and effortlessly fill with oxygen. As your whole system slightly expands and contracts, your nervous system has the potential to settle and recover from stress.

Next time you catch yourself interfering with the motion of the breathing cycle in any way (such as holding your breath) in your tennis match or while you are watching TV or sitting at your computer, don't force an inhale. Remember the potential movement of your ribs and dia-phragm. Allow that.

A. EX-plore: The Silent "la la la"

As you exhale, let your tongue move as if you were saying *la la la,* but do not allow any sound, not even a whisper. Your tongue will move up and down, from the roof to the floor of your mouth. The silent *la la la* has the potential to extend your exhale. For best results, keep your jaw still.

> **DO**   Whenever you need to calm or settle your system.

B. EX-plore: Rib Movement

Try putting your hands on the sides of your ribs and gently pushing your ribs down and in a tiny bit as you exhale, and then let them spring open for your inhale. Be sure not to collapse your torso and shoulders as you exhale; instead, lengthen your spine and widen your shoulders. As your spine lengthens upward, your ribs drape or drop downward.

You can feel the springing ribs expand on yourself or someone else.

> **DO** Once in a while to get to know this spontaneous breath that allows the spine to lengthen.

> ### HUM Journal.
> **Sing a song with your new breath. In the shower is fine.**
> **What do you notice?**

4. BREATHING TO REDUCE STRESS

Ancient yogic traditions knew about the power of breath to affect both physical health and spiritual practices. Similarly, many modern approaches to the widespread problem of stress utilize breathing for its far-reaching effects on all aspects of being human.

A. EX-ploration: Breath and Safety

Sit with a partner to explore breath, emotion, and safety. Person A will breathe in for 7 counts and breathe out for 3. Do this for 3 minutes. Look at person B and your surroundings. See what your mind is telling you: Does that person look safe or unsafe? Do you feel critical or complimentary toward them? Let person B try it.

Then switch the numbers. Person A breathes in for 3 counts and breathes out for 7 counts. Look at person B and see what your mind is telling you: Does that person look safe or unsafe? Do you feel critical or complimentary toward them? Let person B try it.

When we exhale longer, the ventral matrix of the vagus nerve is engaged and inhibits the sympathetic nervous system. This means we are not on the defensive, and we see the other as less dangerous and can have an easier time connecting.

DO When you see others as a potential threat.
Learn to become less habitually defensive and to discover the power of the exhale to relax your body's vigilance (if this is an issue for you).

B. EX-plore Your Breath

You can do this sitting, standing, or lying down. If you do this exercise lying down with your knees bent and your feet flat, it allows you to feel the weight of your lungs in contact with the floor.

Be aware of support from the chair or the floor. Your eyes can be open or closed. Become aware of your breath. Allow the breath to come in and go out. Just watch it. Do not try to change it. What does breath feel like? What is your awareness of the breath? Does it easily go some places, but not others? Notice breath and body tension. Watch air moving inside; it may hit some tension. When the air hits tension, it can go around it or go through it. The tension may change. Feel the rhythm of the breath. Be mindful of breath. No sense of any inhaling or exhaling, no sound of breath being sucked in or pushed out. No tension in the belly to squeeze air out for a "deep" breath. Whatever is happening with the breath is fine, and you can allow it to change. The organism organizes itself.

We naturally seek to restore this self-regulation. Human breathing evolved to be a beautifully poised activity—an automatic dynamic balance between pressure differences in your chest cavity and the entire atmosphere of planet Earth, depending on your activity. Enjoy the elasticity of your ribs and lungs and associated respiratory organs.

Let your breath find its own rhythm. It affects and is affected by other body rhythms. Some breaths may be long and deep, and others shorter. Like the ocean waves, flowing in and out, all breaths are not the same—one of those miracles I talked about in Chapter 1. The combination of breathing and awareness ignites the alchemy of something new.

> **DO** Anytime to connect deeply with yourself and to be in the present moment, awake and alive.

C. EX-plore Your Breath with a Smile

A very slight smile (like that of a bodhisattva) engages the muscles in your face in a way that invites a breath. Notice how that changes your whole body: your feeling tone, your expression, your embodied sense of self. Can a simple smile and breath invite your expanded Self? Of course, we can also mention how your smile affects those around you.

> **DO** Whenever you need a slight lift.

> *HUM Journal.*
> Write about your breath today.

5. THE DIAPHRAGM CHAIN

Most people are familiar with the respiratory diaphragm and its role in breathing. There are other diaphragm-like structures in the body that can influence the respiratory diaphragm. I list four of them below, but there are others. They all communicate and work together. Freeing one can help free the rest.

From top to bottom in the body:

- The *tentorium* is a fold of the dura mater in the brain forming a partition between the cerebellum (lower brain) and the cerebrum (upper brain). It is like a sling or hammock between the older brainstem and the newer brain cortex. This area tends to get very tight and stuck for many reasons, including pulling your head back and down and living primarily in your head with constriction. Freeing the tentorium by releasing your head and neck can free the rest of the diaphragms for a freer flow of air.

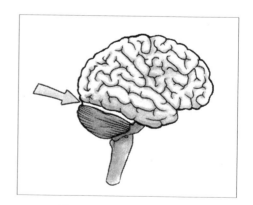

The tentorium diaphragm.

- The *thoracic inlet* refers to the opening at the top of the thoracic (chest) cavity. It is also clinically referred to as the *thoracic outlet*. Although not an actual diaphragm, the thoracic inlet functions as the seal at the top of the thoracic cavity. Its movement, or restriction of movement, greatly affects the respiration. Its opening also releases the muscles of the social engagement system (eyes, ears, voice, and breath) to allow more contact and communication.

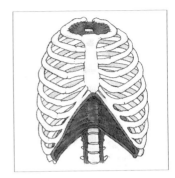

The thoracic inlet.

- The *respiratory diaphragm* (explained above) is next in line.

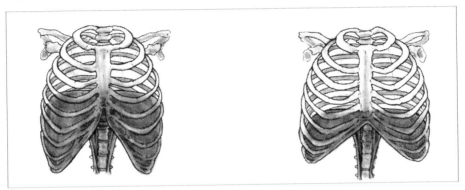

The respiratory diaphragm (exhale on the left, inhale on the right).

- Below the respiratory diaphragm is the pelvic diaphragm or pelvic floor, a muscular partition separating the pelvic cavity (above) from the perineal region (below). This dome-shaped structure often gets tight and stuck for many reasons; it is especially related to tribal (family) issues, sexual issues, or abuse.

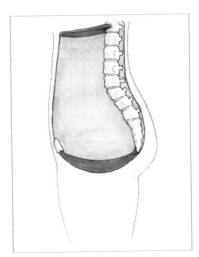

The pelvic-floor diaphragm.

- When you stand with your feet together, your *arches* form a dome shape. There is also a connection from front to back in each foot that creates a dome shape. These are considered diaphragms in function. They connect to the other diaphragms energetically and have the ability to convey a spring-like feeling throughout the entire body.

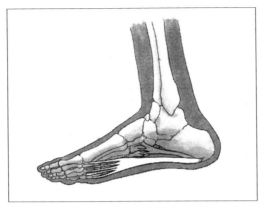

The foot diaphragm.

A. EX-ploration: Foot Diaphragm

Notice your toes on the ground. Are the front parts tilted upward off the ground and not really engaging? This indicates a tendency to fall backward, which is often related to fear, or retreat, or lack of comfort at the very least. Gently pull the five toes forward and down as you lift the metatarsals (ball of foot) upward.

   This activates a spine-like feeling along your whole foot, which is the engagement of the foot diaphragm. This connects to all the other diaphragms and allows the whole body to come slightly forward instead of leaning back.

> **DO**   **When you want contact with the ground to support you in moving forward.**

B. EX-ploration: Whole-Body Diaphragms

Lie or sit down in a comfortable position. Look at the pictures of the diaphragms. Imagine what they might look like inside you: the tentorium, thoracic inlet, respiratory diaphragm, pelvic floor, and arches of feet. Note your breathing. Note any restrictions or movement. Note the relationship among the many diaphragms. When all these diaphragms are pulsing together, you can feel the connection and expansion of your continuous, unified, evenly distributed tensegrity-like structure. When you do this exercise as a meditation, your body disappears and you are just breath, pulsing; there is no "me" and no self. You are not breathing, but rather, *breath is happening.*

> **DO** | **When you feel disconnected or disoriented.**

6. BREATH AND EMOTION

As you focus on breathing, you may contact any number of emotional states. Darwin's classic list of emotions includes fear, joy, sadness, anger, pride, disgust, and surprise. Emotions are vibrations that show up in the form of sensations—contracting or expanding, lifting or sinking, churning or pulsating. Some are comfortable, others less so. Darwin talks about emotion and action. Naturally, you feel emotion and want to perform an action, either outward or inward. Sometimes you are not able to take the action required to follow the emotion. Other times, you don't want to feel the emotion and push it away, because it is painful. Or, in the case of trauma, emotions actually shut down.

If you are experiencing an uncomfortable emotion and don't want to feel it, one of the quickest ways to *not* feel it is to hold or restrict your breath. Let's say you are in a restaurant and your partner says something very hurtful to you. You want to cry, but you are in public and don't want to risk the embarrassment. Your best bet is to clamp down on your breath, bracing around the area. *Voilá!* You are intentionally not breathing and, thus, not feeling.

You are bracing against experiencing the uncomfortable feelings of an emotion. The emotion wants to express itself, but you continue to brace and hold it down. Do this occasionally and no harm done, but if this continues and builds into an adaptive pattern, it can lead to obvious problems.

It is important to train yourself in timely, healthy, emotional responses that are appropriate for the moment. If someone insults you by implying that you are not competent, you can respond by sharing your feelings (anger, hurt, etc.) in the moment. An unhealthy response would be to let all your past hurts (insults, affronts, etc.) and limiting beliefs ("I'm not worthy") rise up, causing you to lash out at the person. Flying off the handle affects your nervous system and body and, as a pattern, can lead to chronic illness and pain. But remember that you always can use your breath to self-regulate.

CHAPTER

13

EMBODIED EMOTIONS

Shouting at the driver who cut you off, or dancing with your loved one under the stars on a moonlit night—both give you a visceral, embodied experience of your emotions. Emotions affect your breath and inner organ function, for better or worse. Lingering negative emotions can lead to pain.

Emotions often repeat themselves. You may tend to cry often for "no reason." If you try to just stop crying, it probably will not work. You need to understand that emotions are preceded by bodily sensations, such as a tightened shoulder or heavy chest. If you tend to the sensation and allow that to change, you have a better chance of not recycling the emotion over and over. This is true with both positive and negative habitual emotions. In the case of positive emotions, you want to encourage the physical sensations that precede and support desirable emotions.

1. EMOTIONAL CONSTRICTION EVOLVES INTO PHYSICAL PAIN

Let's see how emotions relate to pain, and possibly illness. We all have a low tolerance for certain sensations/emotions, like anxiety or fear. Instead of trying to get rid of it, try to explore the actual experience of anxiety—for many people it is a pounding sensation in their chest cavity.

It brings a certain level of discomfort, right? Maybe this sensation means you cannot speak or breathe well. With such a low tolerance for anxiety, you have probably come up with a way to suppress this energy: You tighten your breathing system around it to avoid feeling it. Then, it feels less intense, and you feel more in control.

As a result, the energy or emotion is trapped in the body as tightness or constriction. When you stop feeling one emotion, you stop feeling many, so your emotional range becomes limited. And you take in less oxygen, which presents its own challenges. The body tends to collapse, sometimes a stiff, braced collapse. Unabated, the emotional constriction potentially evolves into more discomfort and pain, and sometimes shame.

You can easily see the collapse associated with the shame posture: the back is curved, chest hollowed, gaze down. Shame is universal, and similar across mammalian species. The antidote to this collapse is full stature with healthy determination or aggression. We can see both in a YouTube video of Patti Smith performing in front of royalty at the Nobel Prize awards in Stockholm. She is singing Bob Dylan's "A Hard Rain's Gonna Fall." Partway through the song, she forgets the words. She drops her head as her chest collapses. As you watch this, you can feel her pain—the burn and the embarrassment that she is experiencing. But she was able to recover, become more upright, and sing the song with pride.

I also saw the shame posture in a contractor who was doing work on my house. He made a mistake, and each time he offered a new idea about how to fix it, his chin dropped lower toward his chest. Then, he would look up at me as if I were his mother and he a young boy looking for her approval. He was so ashamed of his mistakes. The shame posture comes from relational encounters in which you end up feeling bad about yourself. You will be either more agitated and stiff, or more collapsed with resignation. Either way, it is such a physical, somatic expression that chronic holding of the posture from the shame very often evolves into "mysterious" pain.

Research shows that the receptors in the brain are the same for physical pain and emotional pain. Much pain is the result of bracing against an unpleasant feeling or sensation. The bracing causes a disconnect between the brain and the muscle spindles, which should be telling you that you are tightening your muscles. When your head is disconnected from the body's feedback loops, the brain is no longer able to regulate to help heal. Pain is one of the consequences of that dissociation; the body is essentially "crying out" for help. Like F.M. Alexander said, the sensory feedback loop is the problem, regardless of where the pain might be.

If, as a child, you were playing in the playground and a friend pushed you down, you might run to your mother, crying for protection. But if your mother did not protect you from the other child and instead told you to "get out there and be strong," you would tighten down your muscles and breathing so as not to feel those hurt feelings and also to defend yourself from further betrayal. Eventually, all that bracing and pulling down could cause pain. Is that physical pain or emotional pain? They are often difficult to separate.

Pain is dependent on several factors. You hear of people with whiplash from car accidents who continue to have pain years later. Yet some athletes are hit with more force and have no pain the next day. The difference, in this case, is that the athlete *expects* to be hit; the person in the car does not. The startle or surprise element influences the reaction of the muscles. As you know, if you expect to be hit, you prepare for it and protect yourself.

Another role of pain is to protect an injured part of the body. If you break your leg, moving it could make the injury worse. Thus, the body produces pain so you don't move too much; then the affected part can knit itself back together.

The EX-plorations in this chapter are for sensing, "being with," and tracking pain and emotions.

EX-PLORATION: PAIN

What is underneath the pain? Usually there is tension and muscle holding. In the holding is constriction. Constriction can be followed by expansion. Muscles constrict to get ready to move. Allow the small micro-movements within the constrictions. This will lead you to the next step, which includes more flow. Also notice: Are you pulling your pain in toward yourself, or letting it move out away from you?

DO Anytime you feel pain.

EX-ERCISE: BE WITH

1. When a pain or sensation arises that you are not comfortable with, instead of denying or ignoring it (as you may want to do), feel it as pure sensation. Leave out your dramatization of the story.

2. The sensation will often shift slightly within a few seconds. You may feel trembling, the urge to cry, or another emotion. Don't fight it. Typically, this will pass rather quickly.

3. Keep your attention on the area that has pain and feel it. Most of the time, when you feel pain you do everything you can to avoid the sensation. This perpetuates the pain.

4. Inquire into this: Does the pain have a color, sound, or image associated with it? Does it change as you pay attention (better, worse, maybe morphing into something else)? Does it relate to the areas around it? Does it move or change texture? Is it a part of you that you forced into exile? How old do you feel?

5. Find a pleasurable sensation (breath or warmth) and move or "pendulate" between the pleasure and the pain.

It is important to remember that any emotion or feeling or pain that is in your awareness is only a part of you—even though in the moment it feels like it has taken over.

Searching for the cause of pain

Isabella came in crying about the pain in her left shoulder that just kept getting worse. The pain kept her up at night and prevented her from living the active life she was accustomed to. Isabella lived in New York City. She told me that the first time the pain showed up was just after 9/11. Then, a few months later while delivering her baby, the pain got much worse.

I began working with her left shoulder after establishing some support and suspension. Getting some freedom in her shoulder joint helped a bit, but not enough. I then worked on her right shoulder, which actually seemed tighter. I asked her about any falls, car accidents, or trauma that might be related. She said there was none. I then asked her if she noticed any images or emotions around the pain; again, she said none.

I decided to have her lie down so we could work on the table.

As I put my hands on her right leg, I felt incredible tightness. I tried to move it and could not. It was almost immobile. I asked Isabella if it hurt. She said no. I stayed with it a while, asking if anything strange had happened to her leg. Again, she said no. Given that I know from my professional career that tightness in the body is often one of two things—misuse or some kind of trauma—I persisted, gently asking again, "Are there any images that come to mind as you sense the tightness in your right leg?" Still, she answered no.

Then, as if a light bulb went on, from her implicit memory Isabella recounted, "Oh yeah, I had rheumatic fever when I was three years old and could not move my right leg." Bingo, this was the answer.

As it turns out, young Isabella was in the hospital without her parents; she was very afraid. The only image she recalled was of her three-year-old self in the hospital crib looking out the window and yearning for her parents. As she remembered that moment, something in her body, mind, and spirit shifted. I was then able to move her right leg. With that, her pelvis released, which explained why she had so much trouble in childbirth. Her right leg was gripping so tightly that her pelvis could not open.

I believe the pain showed up after 9/11 because the events of that day brought up her thwarted flight response. She was not able to escape from the city on that day, just as she was unable to escape from the hospital so many years before.

When Isabella got off the table and stood up, she was no longer tightening her right leg. She looked much more balanced and relaxed. Prior to our work together, she had been pulling in and tensing her right leg when she stood and, therefore, not putting any weight on it. Because of this, she leaned over to the left side of her body and *into* her left shoulder. As her right leg dropped to the ground, she stopped leaning to the left, and her left shoulder became free of tension and pain. The pain really had nothing to do with her left shoulder.

Now, as she walked around the room, Isabella said she felt like her legs had the suppleness of a cat; they were bending and contacting the ground with much more ease. As she left, she said with a beaming smile, "I feel the skip in my step."

Pain is not always what we think it is.

2. GAMMA MOTOR SYSTEM: THE UNSEEN PATTERN BENEATH THE LEVEL OF CONSCIOUS AWARENESS

Different rhythms in the nervous system are classified by frequency. In this book, I introduce the *alpha* (8–12 Hz) and *gamma* (30–80 Hz) systems and how they relate to conscious movement, inherent support, and the non-doing aspect of movement.

You read about the alpha motor system in Chapter 2. It originates in the cortex and is associated with conscious sensations; it is also responsive to your commands. When we think, "I want to walk," the alpha system engages active skeletal muscles, tapping into energy so you can walk.

The gamma system is a separate, less-known motor system. It originates in the reptilian or primitive brain and produces no conscious sensation. Instead, it works "behind the scenes" to control the length of muscle fibers. Even though we aren't consciously aware of the actions of the gamma system, they are essential for the overall coherence of our movement system and for sensory and supporting activities, such as reinforcing our desire to stand up for long periods—a tonic activity.

The two systems, alpha and gamma, are linked in the spinal column. Any movement or impulse initiated by one will trigger the other. As you decide to move your arm, the alpha network mobilizes muscles to move your arm. But the underlying network that organizes everything else in the body to support or allow or balance the arm motion is the gamma system.

Bracing patterns, or patterns of contraction, are created when there is emotional suppression and/or physical pain; they are protective in nature. The gamma system can produce an underlying bracing pattern (a high sympathetic tuning), most typically experienced with chronic pain, emotional or physical. However, the associated anxiety and depression create feedback loops that keep the pain in place, often a somatic, body-related syndrome. Most back and neck pain is related to the bracing patterns created by the gamma motor system. The fibers of the bracing pattern communicate to the brain, warning of threat; so we brace, and then feel fear, and then brace further against the fear.

Sometimes with all that bracing going on behind the scenes, you bend over to pick up a towel that fell to the floor, and all of a sudden, there is a terrible pain in your back. The cause is not really a back problem, but a whole-body gamma bracing problem.

In an experiment reported in the *New England Journal of Medicine*,[53] doctors examined patients who complained of back pain. Then the patients had X-rays and MRIs taken of their back. Radiologists were given the scans. The doctors could not match up those who complained the most with those who had the worst configuration at the joints. In other words, some people had visible degeneration but little pain, and the reverse was also true. There was no correlation between the amount of pain and the damage shown by the scans. So what is causing the pain? Look into the gamma nervous system. It is the bracing pattern—change that.

> **HUM Journal.**
> **Think about your own bracing pattern(s).**

EX-PLORATION: HUMANUAL BRACING PATTERN, PART 1

As you stand, notice one aspect of your holding pattern (for example, that your right shoulder is forward).

Are you actively holding or pulling it forward?

No.

But some part of you thinks it needs to be forward.

If you were actively pulling it forward, it would be your conscious alpha muscular system doing it. But since you are not consciously or actively doing it, the gamma neurons will keep the muscle spindles taut, thereby allowing the continued firing of motor neurons, leading to muscle contraction.

There is probably good reason from your recent or distant past.

You think you are not pulling it forward, but who or what else is? It may not be the conscious (alpha) you, but the gamma (subconscious) you wanting to protect or fight.

I think recognizing that the action is done by *you* is the key. There is no "it" doing it. Understanding that some systems operate on a different level of conscious awareness is also key.

The gamma system is not a conscious system.

Now bring conscious awareness to the pattern of holding (your right shoulder forward).

Just be aware of the pattern. Do not try to change, fix, or manipulate it into something else.

As you stay with it, notice it can shift ever so slightly, just from observation and this explanation.

Also, as you stay with it, you might notice it is part of a larger pattern: your whole arm wants to come up to defend, your head tilts away, your leg recoils into your torso, and you see a more encompassing defense pattern.

But in this moment, do you need to defend?

You may choose to explore completing the defensive pattern by moving toward or away.

But somehow that is not enough in this moment.

The message you are getting is that you need to have this pattern ready in case you need it. And you think you are going to need it.

You have the program ready, so you don't have to think about it.

Your right arm is standing by and ready to defend you from that side.

When you become consciously aware that in this moment you do not need to defend yourself, the pattern subsides a bit.

In that moment, you come to a full stop. You are not doing anything—not protecting, not running, not fighting, not freezing. Not even not-doing.

Ah. There is a breath.

Make a full stop, and you will realize the unity of the system.

No habits, no one thing is more important than another; the system is alive with all the possibilities available to you (tensegrity unity). Your right arm goes back on the shelf with all your other possibilities. It is no longer the main attraction.

You now have the absence of the pattern.

You feel a bit hollow and empty.

All the inside pieces need time to readjust.

However, you can feel yourself (gamma system) less braced. Your right shoulder is less ready to protect and takes its rightful place as a part of your full tensegrity expansion, which says, "Don't mess with me."

And *that* will protect you if you need protection.

You are without your habitual defenses, but you have the unity of the universe supporting and defending you.

DO Whenever you become aware of an unconscious holding.

EX-PLORATION: HUMANUAL BRACING PATTERN, PART 2

If your pattern (right arm) is still holding, you become conscious of an unconscious holding.

Lie down and allow yourself to actually be on the floor or mat. Receive the support of the ground.

Notice how your body releases.

Then, notice where you are still holding.

Choose one place.

Notice that you are not consciously holding there, but "it" is still holding even though you are not actively doing it.

Stay with that.

Then:

Consciously hold or tighten the area that you are unconsciously holding.

Be aware that you are holding it unconsciously and consciously.

See what else emerges—perhaps a larger pattern of holding or expressing, or an emotion.

When conscious and unconscious meet, there is a clash for a second, a spark of electricity. And then you are under the pattern for a moment. Try to catch the moment and stay with it. See what else emerges—often a breath, a swallow, a wake-up feeling, or a wave of emotion.

DO | Anytime you feel pain or discomfort that is there for "no reason."

3. UNDERSTANDING AND RELEASING ANGER

The emotion of anger is related to the sympathetic nervous system and the fight response. The sequence is often frustration, anger, then rage. As the process builds, we accumulate "steam." If the anger is not expressed as healthy anger, it builds to rage; then it feels powerful enough to overtake you. It is usually more appropriate to deal with the anger in the present moment than ignore it, which allows it to keep its hold on you.

There are so many levels of anger. Let's distinguish between justified anger and just being grumpy and annoyed all the time and letting everyone know. Being angry about abuse is different from lashing out at someone who is a poor driver. Anger is an emotion that most of us have been taught to suppress. But it is a natural response to someone invading your physical, emotional, or psychic boundary.

Anger occurs as a boundary defense. You defend with anger—*but* it is healthy anger. This all happens in present time; you are responding only to the event that is happening right now. If, on the other hand, your boundary is invaded and you recruit all your past hurts and injustices and respond with that backlog of defenses, that is not appropriate to the moment. This anger is said to be unhealthy anger or unwarranted, because it is reaching far beyond this one incident. It is not meeting the present situation as it is.

A basketball player in one of my workshops told me he got very angry every time he played a certain team. A guy on the other team ridiculed him because he was shorter. This made him angry and so tense that he could not make the shots. I kept telling him to let himself be mad at the other player, and to experience the sensations and let them move through. He finally said, "I am so angry. If I feel what I feel, I'm afraid I'll punch him out." I said, "Good—feel the sensations of wanting to punch him but, of course, don't. Feel what the anger wants to do. Just tell him that he does not get to ridicule you." With our work (sorting out some of his unmet needs as a child), he finally built up the courage and told the other guy to back off. And he began to feel freer and make the shots. Sometimes we need the "felt experience" of anger to motivate us.

Feel what is there and allow it to move through your body. You can experience it and choose to express it or not. But do not stifle the emotion because that is your adaptive pattern from childhood, from not getting your needs met. Recognize the energy of it, and allow that to transform.

To correctly feel the signs of your anger coming up, notice the heat and the constrictions—where are they in your body? Ask yourself: Is this anger appropriate for this situation (healthy anger), or is it triggering an old wound, apart from this situation, that needs to heal? If the anger is warranted, speak up and defend yourself!

EX-ERCISE: THE JAW AND ANGER

A tight jaw can restrict vocal expression and contribute to a feeling of being stuck or held back. This is why the jaw is sometimes called a "linchpin for anger." Many self-help techniques offer an exercise to release the jaw.

An out-of-position jaw can compress the vagus nerve. When the jaw and throat are tight or withdrawn, the personality may not have access to healthy expressions of vocalized anger/aggression. Have you ever felt yourself tightening your jaw to not speak or to hold back anger? When you have access to your expanded Self, you are able to speak the truth of the moment.

1. Think of something amusing, so that you smile a little and engage your facial muscles.

2. From there, allow your jaw to just hang in its resting state, so that you open your mouth until it meets a slight resistance (about the width of one finger).

3. Let out a whispered *ahhh* sound.

4. Then close your mouth, and breathe in through your nose.

5. Repeat and notice what happens in your body. Be sure to not let your head drop forward or back and collapse as you exhale.

6. Now, as you open your mouth wider, let the whispered *ahh* get more aggressive. Make animal sounds like growling, or *ahhhhrr!* Feel the bite in your jaw. Explore whispered and vocalized sounds.

7. Let the sounds come out your eyes. Feel your whole body expressing the anger outward.

8. Think of saying, "Don't mess with me," "Notice me," or "Get away from me!" or whatever comes to mind for you.

9. Allow your hands to come up to shoulder height and push forward slowly to clear your space by pushing something or somebody away. Rest and feel your inner responses.

Hands up to chest.   Hands begin to push away.   Hands push away and arms straighten.

Be sure to stop between any of these steps if the energy builds too much and needs to settle. If it gets uncomfortable, you may want to do this exercise with a therapist.

DO   Anytime you feel anger.

This exercise can also be used to express pleasant emotions. After step 5, the *ahh* sound can lead to excitement, delight, laughter, or joy. Let the expression and words follow these emotions.

Hands up for joy.

4. THE EVER-PRESENT FEAR PATTERN

Another common emotion is fear. Generally, one feels fear in relation to danger, real or perceived. You want your fear pattern to be in good working condition when you need it, and to be turned off when you don't need it. If you feel fear, you want to run from the danger. But often, for one reason or another, you cannot run. In this case, the urge to run becomes a somatic pattern and continues to fire as it remains stuck in your body, often your legs.

The body's fear pattern is usually the same, whether you realize the parking meter has expired and you run to not get a ticket, or you run to escape a fire. The body pattern of constriction is consistent, varying only in intensity. Yet each person has a somewhat individualized response. Fear is often some version of the startle pattern—head pulled back and jutted forward, shoulders up, knees locked, and a startled face.

The outside environment is constantly sending messages of fear or safety to your senses, and the quality of your hearing affects your fear response. As human primates, our middle ear bone is detached, and our hearing focuses on the higher-pitched frequencies such as the mother's voice. Dr. Stephen Porges calls it *motherese*.[54] Biologically, your mother's voice is supposed to be comforting and soothing. If you are frightened as an infant, your mother's voice can settle you. Think of the tone of voice we often use when we talk to babies.

Danger, on the other hand, is frequently a low-pitched sound, like the ominous noises of a horror movie that evoke fear. If you have auditory sensitivity, the middle ears tend to be tuned to detect more low-pitched sounds—then every sound is "What was that?" In this case, a person becomes highly focused on lower frequencies in order to detect danger and misses out on the higher-pitched motherly voice. We see this problem in children who live in unsafe neighborhoods, where they are forced to scan and listen for danger all the time. When they arrive at school, they are still in danger mode and unable to feel safe enough to hear the teacher's moderately pitched voice. They miss out on learning and creativity. In truth, children under these conditions are rarely relaxed enough for optimal learning and function. The fear and insecurity then increase, and the cycle continues.

5. EMOTIONAL EXPANSION

Joy, happiness, gratitude, relief, triumph, and contentment all have very specific bodily sensations in the direction of expansion, fluidity, and ease.

Getting the news that your friend has recovered from a serious illness or accident, watching your child learn to walk, receiving praise for a job well done, or seeing a spectacular sunset can bring immense joy and happiness. Personally, I feel the most unimaginable joy and love when I am visiting my grandchildren, Axel and Vaughn. It is a unique kind of love that goes so deep and feels so special.

When you feel appreciated, seen, welcomed, or wanted, which everybody desires, you recognize it as a positive experience. Feelings of goodness, caring, kindness, and love are little treasures that you want to hold on to. It is necessary for us to consciously make a place for positive thoughts in the mind and body. Practicing having pleasant thoughts of love and compassion for yourself and others has been proven to have a positive effect on your life. This work of Mindful Self-Compassion is taught by many qualified teachers.

> **HUM Journal.**
> Practice consciously maintaining your positive thoughts.
> What do you notice? Does this practice make more room
> for your expanded Self?

Focusing on the positive thoughts brings us to joy. I have a colleague who is filled with joy, responding with joy every moment. I was curious about this, so I once asked him how he genuinely experiences so much joy. He shared that life was challenging as a child, but he had wonderful family and friends to help support him. From these experiences, he came to the conclusion that joy would be his chosen emotion whenever possible.

The modern world trains us early on to strive to be successful and to advance in life, but it's equally important to play and have fun. Play and laughter are crucial for human interaction as well as a joyful life. They are not meant to be an "add-on"—something that we do after all the work is done.

Researcher Jaak Panksepp published an unusual paper in the journal *Behavioural Brain Research*.[55] His findings showed that rats laugh, affirming that they have a type of social behavior with playful activity. Panksepp describes his discovery of the phenomenon: "Having just concluded perhaps the first formal (i.e., well-controlled) ethological analysis of rough-and-tumble play in the human species in the late 1990s, where laughter was an abundant response, I had the 'insight' (perhaps delusion) that our 50-kHz chirping response in playing rats might have some ancestral relationship to human laughter."

> **HUM Journal.**
> **What is your relationship to play and laughter?**
> **Recall the last time you had a really good laugh with friends.**
> **Do you ever feel the rhythmic sway in your body as you walk**
> **down the street with a song in your heart and joy in your step?**

PRESENCE: YOUR MULTIDIMENSIONAL ALIVENESS

We tend to want to hold on to the present moment if it is pleasant and to be done with it if it is unpleasant. Whether or not you want things in life to change, they will; you cannot make life stand still. Perhaps you fervently wanted the romantic relationship to stay the same. It did not. Or maybe your dream job is no longer "it" and you find yourself wanting to move on. It is not possible to hold on to the present moment, but it is possible to hold on to being present. This is sometimes experienced as non-doing or doing nothing, which is often the hardest thing to do.

1. THREE-DIMENSIONAL PRESENCE

Modern culture is obsessed with "progress" and moving ahead. Presence seems to be a way of life that most of us in Western civilization have lost. Even in the circles that do talk about being present, the idea has become very

Your presence includes your past.

two-dimensional—kind of flat—and taken for granted, a bit stale. In actuality, the present reality is always dynamically changing, so you want to be able to adapt multidimensionally. The present includes your past hurts and triumphs.

You are constantly affected by what you think, sense, and observe; and you respond to that in the moment with action, expression, or relative stillness. Your biological systems are either in sync with the present moment or not—meaning that your breath, muscular effort, and nervous system activity are appropriate for the moment or not. When you are consciously present and responding with even the slightest movement, there is a kind of embodied, non-judgmental, participatory cognition that encompasses the deepest levels of your body, mind, spirit, and even your soul, which intuits some kind of deeper, more inclusive aspect of human life. In presence, you suspend judgment for the moment. As Tommy Thompson, well-known Alexander Technique teacher, says, "You suspend definition." Try it.

> ### HUM Journal.
> **Can you suspend judgment and definition in this three-dimensional present moment? Is it enough to just observe and be interested?**

Because presence lives in many dimensions, as a powerful and substantial energy of the moment, it is not just one thing but encompasses many possible or potential impressions and thoughts that are felt and experienced.

Perceiving his feet in the moment

One time, as I was working with a client, I said, "Let your feet connect to the ground again." He asked, "How did you know my feet came up?" I told him I saw the energy rise in his whole body, as if he were getting ready to lift his feet; yet they were firmly planted on the ground. What happened? Most likely, his mind wandered. In that moment, he lost awareness of his body and the support of the ground; he was no longer present in the moment in which we were working but instead was visiting the past or future through a thought. He declared somewhat defensively, "You knew what I was doing before I knew what I was doing!" Most others respond with genuine curiosity about the guidance, as they see that my direction is helping them develop the skill to perceive these nuances for themselves.

Many thoughts, feelings, and emotions can pull us away from inhabiting our expanded Self. We can develop the skill to perceive these nuances in present time. When we believe that we are free to choose to make changes and adjustments (or not), the potential for deep change is endless.

EX-ercises in this chapter focus on paying attention to moment-to-moment reality, including your relationship to the environment.

EX-ERCISE: SENSING PRESENCE

Stand in a comfortable space, and become aware of your *Humanual* Basics.

1. Sense the space in front of you as far as you can see.

2. Sense the space to your sides.

3. Sense the space to your back.

4. Sense the space above you.

5. Sense the space below you.

6. Sense all the directions together while remembering support.

As you sense the surrounding space, you can experience greater three-dimensional presence. One acting student said after doing this exercise and then a monologue, "I was 100 percent present and doing absolutely nothing."

DO   Often.

If you are really paying attention and being present, then your responses are likely to be appropriate for the moment, all systems working together with coherence. If you grip your toothbrush tightly and use a tremendous amount of tension to brush your teeth, are you truly present to the reality of the moment? Or have you lost accurate feeling of your own muscles, joints, and breath?

Presence includes meeting the reality of the moment. The toothbrush is light; it takes very little effort to brush. Recognizing this, you have less contraction. You are more "filled out"— and actually three-dimensional. More of you is present. It is possible that one day you might gain the perspective that you are angry in this moment, and gripping the toothbrush is your way of expressing that anger. If that is the case, go ahead and grip, but note why.

There is a wonderful story of an Alexander Technique teacher whose apartment was robbed. The police collected fingerprints and then asked the woman what she did for a living. She answered, "I teach the Alexander Technique. Why do you ask?" The reply: "We took many fingerprints in your apartment, and none of them were smudged." This means that every time she touched an object, she used exactly the right amount of pressure to lift it and no more. That is being present and meeting the moment.

EX-ERCISE: PRESENCE IN THE MOMENT—NO SMUDGES!

1. Think of picking up your phone.

2. Feel your arm tense to get ready. Are you tensing your shoulder? Elbow? Hand?

Holding your phone with smudges.

3. Now pay attention to how much effort you actually need to lift your phone.

4. Lift your phone with just enough contact and pressure. No smudges.

Holding your phone with no smudges.

5. Try this with many objects in your day.

> **HUM Journal.**
> **Write about your smudges today.**

2. LACK OF PRESENCE: STUCK THOUGHTS = STUCK JOINTS

Do you ever find yourself lost in thought? Next time try to notice what happens in your body in that moment. Often when you recognize the distant thoughts and come back to the present moment, you can feel that your body was held in position and not moving. The stiffening (or bracing) of the joints is *unconscious*, occurring through fixated thinking. You lose access to information in the body, which prevents informed movement and inhibits decisions made in the next moment. It is as if being stuck on a thought blocks awareness—not just of the flow of consciousness, but the flow of feeling or sensation as well. So, if you continue to be stuck in thinking, obsessing about thoughts, you miss what is happening in the flow of consciousness—*the present moment.*

Dissociative patterns, which involve problems with memory, identity, emotion, perception, behavior, and sense of self, cause us to space out and lose presence. Are there other implications of losing presence in addition to unconscious stiffening of the body? Here's an example: You are having a conversation with Judy about how much fun you had last night at the movies. At one point, Judy says something that reminds you of an errand you need to do later that day. Your mind has essentially left the conversation. Does this sound familiar?

Later, you recall that conversation. One part of you was gone for a few moments. Judy thought you were there, but you were not fully present with her, and you missed something. You were pulled away and busy with your future obligations. If you tune in to yourself, you will see that you are uncomfortable about the moments that your mind was somewhere else. Your legs may tighten and your breath may be held as you think about juggling this dual presence.

Then, you might even begin to feel like you owe her those few moments. Do they have consequences in the larger picture? If you find a way to reflect on those moments and not let them pass unnoticed or ignored, might that help you to not repeat the pattern?

To take this a step further, is not paying full attention to Judy a symptom of a larger dissociative pattern? In other words, do you have a need or habit of not being present so that you don't feel the discomforts and pain of unresolved trauma? In the moment, there is often nothing painful to run from. But if you have a habit of running or leaving, then your pattern will not allow you to remain consistently present.

Daily life is always handing us our lessons. Simply be open to look at what is coming up in the moment.

> ### *HUM Journal.*
> **How often are you fully present when you are talking with someone?**
> **How often do you notice that your mind is elsewhere when you**
> **are speaking to others or performing tasks? Why might you do this?**

3. 50-50 AWARENESS: INSIDE/OUTSIDE FIELDS OF ATTENTION

Presence brings awareness, both inner and outer. The presence I find most useful, and teach to my clients and students, is what I call *50-50 awareness:* 50 percent of your awareness pays attention to what is happening inside you while 50 percent pays attention to what is happening outside in your environment. Through this practice, you create an expanded field of attention. You see the relationship between the two. For example, if you witness something unpleasant, you may feel sick in your gut. But if you see something pleasant, you may feel pleasure in your heart. Or, if you have physical pain while doing certain activities, like bending to pick something up, it may be helpful to pay attention to what is happening in your musculoskeletal system while you are bending. As you read this, it is possible and may be helpful to try 50-50 awareness. Notice your use, and change it if needed.

Expanding to sing

I was working with a group of singers in a master class in a large auditorium. A man got up to sing; he placed himself just the right distance from the piano and his feet the perfect distance apart. It was almost exaggerated how he prepared himself in the way he thought would be helpful. But as he sang, his voice was limited and small; it never traveled more than two feet in front of him. It never reached the audience.

I watched this six-foot-tall, well-built, powerful gentleman sing. He had a fine voice, but I felt as if he were putting himself in a small, perfectly organized, two-dimensional box and just singing in that box.

I worked with him in a *Humanual* way, pointing out that he wanted to sense himself present in the whole room with his 50-50 awareness. As he began to sense how he was shrinking himself and diminishing his body, especially his torso, he was able to make another choice and be present to new possibilities. I showed him how to connect to the ground in a different way—a way that would allow a more expanded version of himself, including the hall. Now, as he began to sing again, his voice was clear and booming, carrying to the balconies. After just one or two notes, the audience of class members, sensing the difference, began to cheer madly for him. He found his present, three-dimensional moment that included himself and his environment.

F.M. ALEXANDER wrote of a person he once observed,
*"The apprehensive fear that he may be wrong and his intense desire to do it right . . .
are the secrets to his failure."*[56]

4. NEUROCEPTION: SOMETHING IS OFF

Related to presence is *neuroception*, the detection of risk or danger in your environment. It refers to your *felt-sense* of safety, meaning it's something you feel inside. This inner sense is not cognitive, not of your rational mind. *Neuroception* is a word coined by Dr. Stephen Porges.

Neuroception detects danger from below the conscious level. Your mind may tell you that a person is safe, but your gut tells you something is off. You must have some degree of presence to detect this. Neuroception is neurological detection without awareness; it is subcortical information that is then brought to a level of perception and conscious thought.

One of my clients, Daniel, an avid tennis player, had an accident and badly hurt his arm. He went to see a physical therapist. She touched his arm, which caused it to hurt more, so he became nervous about letting anybody touch his arm.

When he was in my studio, I asked if I could approach him, and I promised not to touch his arm. Daniel said it was fine to walk toward him, and that he would feel safe if I did so without touching his arm. As I walked toward him, however, he began to feel uneasy. Notice that even though he said that he wouldn't get anxious when I approached, he did. Cognition said, "No danger," but neuroception said, "Yes, there is danger approaching." He was surprised by the reaction.

Being aware of what's happening below the surface of conscious awareness and cognition gives us another glimpse into how our expanded Self serves us.

5. MIRROR NEURONS: A PRESENT-MOMENT PHENOMENON

Long known to science, ordinary motor command neurons, located in the front of the brain, fire when a person performs a specific action. For example, if I decide to pick up a pencil, the firing of these neurons allows me to do it. If I then throw the pencil across the room, other neurons will fire.

In the 1980s, researcher Giacomo Rizzolatti found that a subset of these neurons—maybe about 20 percent of them—will fire in the present moment when I'm looking at *somebody else performing the same action*. This was first observed in monkeys and then in other species, including humans.

Like all neurons, these "mirror neurons" distribute electricity in the body. Because the brain activates as if the observer were actually doing the action, this subset of neurons is said to allow the body to mirror the behavior of others. As such, mirror neurons are an aspect of presence.

For example, if I watched you go to a table and pick up an apple, my motor neurons would fire as if I had picked it up. The same goes for any activity. If you are teaching me a new dance step, as I watch you my mirror neurons are firing, which allows me to better execute the step. It's easy to see the mirror neurons in a baby: when a baby and loving caregiver are present to one another, the baby will often imitate facial expressions and/or actions. Neuroscientist Vilayanur Ramachandran said, "It's as though this neuron is adopting the other person's point of view. It's almost as though it's performing a virtual reality simulation of the other person's action."[57]

Mirror neurons explain present-moment aspects of the mind such as empathy, imitation, synchrony, and the development of language. When people are in sync with each other, they tend to stand or sit in similar ways, and their voices take on similar rhythms. The imitation of more complex skills is what we call *culture*, and it is the basis of civilization.

Baby mirroring loving caregiver.

6. NON-DOING OF THE HABIT OFTEN BRINGS YOU TO PRESENCE

The non-doing of any habit allows you a moment of choice. It brings you to presence. When you are able to stop acting on your past adaptive behaviors with awareness, you have the potential to be in the present moment. Between stimulus and response is the moment of freedom and choice. For example, you are stimulated to write a text message. Then your shoulders tighten (habitual pattern). Instead, recognize the stimulus (decision to send a text), see the moment of choice, and make your decision—to tighten or not to tighten your shoulders. Once you become aware of the present moment, you have the freedom to change.

In the present moment, you can also recognize the need for letting go of some of those adaptive patterns. Richard Rohr, a Franciscan friar known for his stimulating talks about man's relationship with God, says, "The spiritual practices of all great world religions teach us letting go: how to step aside and be flexible. . . . Let go and let God."[58]

After fifteen minutes of paying attention to not doing her habits as she sits and stands, one of my clients, a professional ice skater, said, "I've never tried so hard to do nothing."

SPIRITUAL LIFE: THE WAY OUT OF THE BODY IS THROUGH THE BODY

Can a practical technique end up opening doors to a spiritual life? For some people, the answer is an emphatic "Yes."

In 1984, I was teaching a master class in the Alexander Technique to vocal students at the New England Conservatory. It was a class of young pop singers, one more outrageously dressed than the next. Many had purple, sticky hair that stood straight up, making it difficult for me to even find their neck and head.

One of the participants, a young woman, requested private work at the end of the class. I said yes, adding that although she had a beautiful voice, the tightness in her back was preventing her from experiencing her full voice. I knew additional lessons could help this. She said, "Yes, but what I really need the lessons for is my spiritual life." I gulped and nodded. I was astonished. I had given what I thought of as a standard, straightforward "vocal master class," never mentioning meditation or God. Where did she get the idea that the Alexander Technique would help her with her spiritual life? What I knew, however, is that there is something about being *in* our body—in an organized, coordinated way—that allows us to be free to leave and enter larger realms. This is a type of spirituality; as some say, "the body is a temple."

1. WHY (AND HOW) YOU MIGHT WANT TO EXPLORE A SPIRITUAL PERSPECTIVE FOR YOUR OWN SANITY

Modern life is chock-full of identifications, adaptive patterns, and delusions. A spiritual life offers a refuge from the temptations that promise fulfillment but often do not deliver, and it gives access to a more enduring source of contentment and joy.

The reasons for following a spiritual path are many: It helps us to cope with stress; to improve life; and to attain physical, emotional, and mental health. A spiritual life can wake us up to, and directly and deeply connect us with, the ever-present source of life, which is much greater than our limited personality and ego. Ultimately, the spiritual life can transform our inner world until individuality merges with the unchanging source of the universe.

On this path, one encounters big questions: Who am I? Why am I here? What does it mean to be fully human, embodied, and alive? Does having a spiritual life affect me as a human? Does it affect my body? These central questions have been pondered for generations past and will likely be pondered for as long as humanity exists.

There are three fundamentally different ways to explore a spiritual life. The first follows an outer path of organized, belief-centered practices called *religion*. The second follows an inner path of direct, internal experiences, often termed *mysticism*. The third follows neither religion nor mysticism and is not organized by or related to any tradition. It is based in the fundamental respect for nature, including human life, and the inner wisdom of the mind and heart. Which path makes sense to you? What happens inside your body as you read these choices? Do you feel any attraction or calling or even mild interest?

> ### HUM Journal.
> ### Who am I? Why am I here?

Belief-centered religions, such as Christianity, Judaism, Islam, and Hinduism, are found in both Eastern and Western cultures. A primary concept shared by all religions is that you and God are separate; therefore, the religious establishment is the intermediary. Religion has the answers for you. This comforts many people.

Each outer religious tradition has its parallel inner mystical tradition: Christianity has Gnosticism; Judaism has Kabbalah; Islam has Sufism; Hinduism has Yoga. These traditions share the mystical concept that God does not exist outside of you. In other words, you can connect directly, and without an intermediary, to this unnamable larger consciousness. Practitioners of Buddhism and Zen could also be in this category, as they do not believe in a divine being reigning over the universe.

The mystics were independent spirits, self-motivated individuals who sought to function from the drive of their own inner awareness rather than external conditions and circumstances. They knew that mystical practice is not detached from daily experience, nor is it conditioned by it. No events get "swept under the rug," as nothing stays unresolved in mystical practice.

"Theologians may quarrel, but the mystics of the world speak the same language."
— noted German philosopher and mystic MEISTER ECKHART[59]

Over time, these two paths have created sanity and a level of peace and purpose for some people in some way. Both religion and mysticism offer practices of meditation and/or contemplation, chanting and/or singing, charity and/or selfless service.

The third category comprises people who have no organized spiritual life but have principles by which they live. The Golden Rule of "Do unto others as you would have others do unto you" is a prime example of a guiding spiritual-moral-ethical principle. While people in this category may refer to themselves as atheist or agnostic, they consider themselves upright, wholesome citizens. They may define spiritual work as singing, or gardening, or caring for animals, or healing trauma. It can be any and all of those and much more when higher consciousness and full presence are brought to the activity.

But do any of these paths pay enough attention to the body? I have been in spiritual circles where the body was thought to be insignificant: "You are not your body." At the same time, many of these people complained of lower-back pain during meditation and asked for my help! The body is the vehicle for your human experiences and, as we've learned, it has a specific design for maximum function. When you honor and work with this design, you can be free to let your spirit soar.

All spiritual, religious, and mystical practices grew out of ritual and involve the body in one way or another. The body is our vehicle for feeling and expressing our connection to the sacred. How could it be otherwise? The circular dance of Sufis known as "whirling dervishes" creates a trance state that facilitates unity and oneness. Tantric teachings offer ecstasy with divinity through sexual practices. Buddhists sit very still to meditate. Pilgrims walk to Mecca or other religious holy sites. Orthodox Jewish people rock back and forth as they pray. Many people sing or chant as a spiritual activity. Some religions even practice a form of self-mutilation or infliction of bodily harm to prove one's devotion. Whether you fast or celebrate with special foods; or dance, bow, or sit quietly, the body is always part of your spiritual experience.

A failure to recognize the integral place of the physical body in spirituality is related to something else I want to mention here, called *spiritual bypassing*. This refers to the avoidance of one's own difficulties, challenges, or issues in the name of spirituality. For instance, one may fail to release or process anger because he or she thinks that being angry is not okay for a spiritual person. Or, someone cannot cope with working to support himself and decides to live in a monastery instead of having to earn money for rent. In essence, the spiritual practice is bypassing, or taking the place of, dealing directly with underlying issues. The bypass can also be related to trauma: instead of facing the reality of the trauma, a person can escape to other realms. Spiritual bypassing is a form of delusion and is unlikely to produce the intended results of authentic spiritual inquiry.

Before we move on, it is important to note that trauma and spirituality sometimes share common physical states such as seeing bright lights, experiencing the slowing down of time, or feeling awe. In fact, the awakened *kundalini* (primal energy) in yoga has been likened to the awakened survival energy in trauma. Both produce very strong psychophysical responses. We hear stories of kundalini-awakened saints carrying out miraculous feats, and of human adults lifting a car to save an imperiled child. While rare, this incredible energy needs to be recognized and properly integrated into daily life.

2. PARABLES AND HOW THEY MIGHT INFLUENCE YOUR OUTLOOK

Spiritual teachings are often told as stories or "parables" that contain a message for us to contemplate. Because they are engaging, narratives tend to make a more memorable impression on us than facts, lessons, and lectures. Here are a few examples:

A monk spent many long hours on the mountain alone, meditating and contemplating life. Occasionally, he would come down to the town and walk around the streets. One day, a young boy asked the monk, "How can you manage being in town after being on the mountain for so long?" The monk replied, "When I come to town, the mountain is under my robe."

So true. How do *you* manage "being in town"? Do the flashing lights, the noises, and the cars whizzing by put you in a mild startle response? Do you feel fearful and anxious, expecting danger? Do you keep the mountain under your robe, or do you let the town change your inner sensations and take you out of your calm, embodied, inner sense of self?

A blind man is in a room alone with the door closed. He wants to get out, so he puts his hands on the walls and walks around the room, searching for the door. But every time he gets close to the door handle, he feels an itch, and as he takes his hands off the wall to scratch, he walks right past the door, thereby missing his chance to escape.

Every time I read this story, I get goosebumps. How often in my life do I see my own patterns running the show and preventing me from escaping that room and uniting with my expanded Self? This experience is so physical. My adaptive patterns pull me in, not letting me get to the handle to open the door and free myself.

Long ago in a faraway kingdom, a crime was committed that was punishable by death. Two men were accused. Both stood before the king, both saying they were innocent. But one was the king's friend, and he had actually committed the crime. The king needed to make a decision about whom to kill, without looking like he was favoring his friend. So he took two pieces of paper and wrote "die" on both, meanwhile telling the men and the guests that one piece of paper said "live" and the other said "die." He allowed the innocent man to choose first. The innocent man was clever, and he knew the king was up to no good. He took one piece of paper and put it in his mouth and swallowed it. "This is the one I choose," he said. The crowd assumed it said "live," because the other paper said "die." The guilty man had to face his punishment.

I heard this story when I was about ten years old and remember thinking how clever that man was. Faced with a traumatic survival situation, he used his own cleverness to save his life. I can only imagine the sensations in his body as he paced the floor, trying to figure out a solution, not only to save his own life but to see justice prevail.

Last but not least, the following Sufi teaching has long impressed and guided me on my journey:

Past the seeker, as he prayed, came the crippled, and the beggar, and the beaten. And seeing them, he cried, "Great God, how is it that a loving creator can see such things and yet do nothing about them?" And God said, "I did do something. I made you."

3. SPIRITUAL PRACTICES FOR LEADING YOU TO YOUR EXPANDED SELF

Now the journey really expands. You are not only thinking about your body and mind in relation to your environment, you are venturing into the spirit, the non-matter, the non-material. How do you even know it exists? The explorations below are for developing deeper awareness of other realms of consciousness by turning inward and seeing with fresh eyes. Seen meets unseen while potential emerges.

EX-PLORATIONS: SPIRITUAL PRACTICES

Most spiritual practices involve some kind of inquiry or questioning about topics that we do not usually take the time to ponder. Some involve quiet time alone, and others invite consideration of spirituality embedded in everyday activity. I recommend some practices that allow you to stay involved in life and others that take you out of daily life for a different perspective. All involve some recognition of, or change in, your bodily experience.

> ***HUM Journal.***
> **All these practices can be supplemented by**
> **journaling about one's thoughts and results.**

A. Practice—Turn Inside

The four *turn-inside* practices lead you to be in your body as a method of going beyond your body. Noticing and carefully observing the inner sensations allows embodied change and transformation, and hones your skills of perception and differentiation.

1. **Turn inside to see.** Most spiritual paths include some form of inner exploration or reflection, observing inside your self. In the Bible, Christ says, "The kingdom of Heaven is within." In the Bhagavad Gita, Lord Krishna says, "He who finds his happiness within, his delight within, and his light within, this yogi attains the bliss of Brahman." What if going inside means checking to sense what your body is doing? Do you have support? Can you feel your own expansion? Is your breath flowing multidirectionally? What if the expanded Self *is* the kingdom of heaven? The inner journey allows you to take a moment to receive guidance, to examine your life, or to just *be* in the energized present. Pay attention to both mind and body when you look inside.

2. **Turn inside to see emotional activity.** When you turn inside, an entire world of subtle feelings and sensations begins to arise in your awareness. You notice the emotional landscape in your experiences and responses. Your vagal tone and gut feelings certainly have input here. You want to notice whether these responses are connected or disconnected to your reality. Are you sad or happy all the time, even though a situation does not call for sadness or happiness? What's the dominant emotional flavor of your life, as you look from inside?

3. **Turn inside to see mental activity.** Look at the activity of your mind and its thought process. What you think greatly affects you. For example, think of a lemon. It's difficult not to salivate. That's a tactile, physical example, but you may not be aware that energetically our thoughts strongly influence outcomes in the world. Is the tenor of your thoughts mainly positive or negative? Do you recognize an inner space that is timeless, empty mind—where your body feels spacious and light as a feather? Can you rest in this presence? Every once in a while, look inside and take a screenshot of mental activity to see which arena you are occupying. Be honest with yourself, and not judgmental.

4. **Turn inside to see physical activity.** As you look inward, notice your physicality, your vitality. Notice how stressed or relaxed you are. Is there constant rocking or foot tapping, or do you find stillness? In your life, do you get fatigued easily and feel like you're slumping? Is your life sustainable utilizing just your life-force or energy; or do you need to supplement with caffeine, drugs, or a vacation? If you need a holiday to regenerate, why isn't rest and recovery included in your daily life? What recharges you? And the classic spiritual question: What gets you out of bed in the morning? And may I add, *How* do you get out of bed in the morning?

B. Practice—Virtues and Shadow

Practice the virtues: prudence, justice, temperance, courage, faith, hope, and charity. What are the postures and patterns that go with these character traits? Also, recognize your shadow side and the seven deadly sins: pride, greed, lust, envy, gluttony, wrath, and sloth. What are their associated postures and patterns? Everybody has both. Many folks try to show their virtues while trying to hide and ignore their shadow side. This behavior becomes problematic. Just as our physical nature has a down (the ground) and an up (the lengthening), life has the virtue and the shadow. Thus, spirituality must include an earthly, grounded component that teaches you how to integrate your shadow side and not suppress it. Embracing your virtues and your shadow together seems to be a key to wholeness.

"Enlightenment is not imagining figures of light but making the darkness conscious."
— CARL JUNG[60]

C. Practice—Look at Your Outside Perceptions

How do you evaluate the feelings of people around you? Do you have compassion and empathy for their life's journey? How do you pick up these cues?

You engage in the world in many ways, including through your senses—both physical and spiritual senses. You derive information from your physical experiences of seeing, touching, feeling, hearing, and tasting the contents of your surroundings. And this seems to be what is real. Your spiritual or intuitive sense, on the other hand, takes in information on another level when it perceives the world around you. What cannot be heard or seen, touched or tasted, also appears as real.

Subtle, delicate receptors "read" the world around you: they pick up the words you do not speak but feel and the thoughts you transmit to and receive from others through your vibrations. We often call this the subtext. Which data do you actually rely upon the most—your outward senses, or what you pick up intuitively by other receptors?

D. Practice—Curiosity, Creativity, and Novelty: Seeing with Fresh Eyes

"Every human is a question in life. We have a chance to change it. We all start as a question. Release fixation and I become a walking answer. This is creativity."

—THOMAS HUBER, contemporary spiritual teacher[61]

Life energy and information come in and go out of living creatures. Is this energy fixed, habitual, and stale in your life, or is it creative and free-flowing? Are you entangled in symptoms, syndromes, and the tension of past experiences, or are you creatively opening to your expanding Self?

As you have learned, how we perceive things can be changed by shifting our inner neurophysiology—our breath, our use, and our healing of trauma. How you move and breathe affects how you see the world. Can you change the lenses through which you see? Instead of being fearful, can you explore looking with fresh eyes, withholding definition?

Can you bring curiosity to your daily life? Habit is strong. We tend to fall asleep on all levels and become a collection of recurring patterns. With this, novelty and creativity are left out. Look at your relationship patterns, your surroundings, and your social network. What is it like to see these things for the first time? Actually look closely. Who is this person? (Not what I assume is there.) Practice this every day: see something new in a person you know, or in your familiar environment, or in yourself. Otherwise, tomorrow is just a replication of yesterday, especially if much of that past remains unresolved.

E. Practice—Being Conscious

Instead of setting aside an hour a day to be mindful, what if you combined mindfulness and "bodyfulness," so that you are more consistently aware of your whole system, your mind and your body—your support, suspension, and breath, the *Humanual* Basics? Don't just practice for an hour; engage many times during your day. Invest in being conscious. Embody consciousness.

Being conscious shows you that the most essential moment is the present—the essence of life while it is happening, and *not* what I think it should be. Notice and let that miraculous unity be part of your life. It is not always pleasant, but neither is it always unpleasant.

F. Practice—Making Up Stories (the Right Kind)

I see my mind making up stories. I understand that these are stories based on my past experiences. As I make up stories (about how badly things can turn out), both my body and mind are involved with their specific sensations and vibrations. When I imagine that something unpleasant might happen, my body cringes, and fear sets in. The stories I make up may have very little to do with the reality of what is happening outside of me, but in my head the movie rolls on.

When I really think about it, I realize I can make up any story that I want; I am in charge. I can make up stories that are pleasant and cause me to feel good, that feed my hopes and dreams. That's far better than negative stories. When I stop making up stories about my interpretation of what is out there, I am more connected to what is actually out there.

Also, remember that the brain has a negative bias (an evolutionary imperative to detect danger and unpleasantness). The other day I turned toward a wall, and for a split second I thought I saw a bug crawling there. I watched my mind get scared and make up a story, as my body mobilized to get rid of the insect so that it could not hurt me. I very quickly figured out that it was a string hanging with a wooden knob on the end. But I clearly saw the moment of negative bias in my reptilian brain as I watched my neocortex—the thinking brain—working hard to quickly figure out this threat.

Neuroscience is now proving that holding a pleasant thought for a few minutes actually changes the brain such that it feels happier. Catch your mind if it's doing the opposite, and say to yourself, "You're making up unpleasant stories." Notice the accompanying physical pattern—a tight throat, tense stomach, or held breath. Just stay present to it, with awareness, and allow it to change. It's just energy, and energy will always change. You may also want to get to know the part of you that makes up unpleasant stories. Is this habit, compulsion, or some need of yours? Can you let it change?

Find something pleasant to make up a story about, and feel those happy neurons firing! If you cannot find pleasant, find less unpleasant. Wouldn't it be better to imagine your suspended self, with your breath flowing easily through you, and your resilient nervous system, adapting to pleasant events? At the deepest levels of our being, it's a choice.

4. SELF 1-2-3: LAYERS OF BEING HUMAN

Neurophysiologist Sir Charles Sherrington wrote in 1961: "Each waking day is dominated for good or ill, in comedy, farce or tragedy by a dramatic persona, the self. And so it will be until the curtain drops. The self is a unity. The continuity of its presence in time, sometimes hardly broken by sleep, its inalienable interiority in sensual space, its consistency of viewpoint, the privacy of its experience, combine to give it status as a unique existence. Although multiple aspects characterize it, it has self-cohesion. It regards itself as one, others treat it as one. It is addressed as one, by a name to which it answers. The law and the state schedule it as one. It and they identify it with the body, which is considered by it and them to belong to it integrally. In short, unchallenged and unargued convictions assume it to be one. The logic of grammar endorses this by a pronoun in the singular. All its diversity is merged in oneness."[62]

Which self/Self did he mean?

Self-1

Self-1 is the oneness that no one can take away. It is often called Self (with a capital S). It is the unity, the essence, the coherence, the built-in organization that hurls evolution forward at a minutely adjusting and advancing pace. This is the Self you don't need to work to have or become, because you are born as it. Some people call Self-1 their Higher Self or True Self; it is the Self that is one with all that is.

Most people have fleeting moments of the oneness, our unified Self, a few times in life. But it is never far below the surface, waiting to be recognized and honored—the one, the all, "the nothing" and "the everything" simultaneously. Every spiritual practice and religion describes it and gives suggestions on how to feel it and live it, so we can be lifted above the day-to-day doldrums of human life and its associated egocentric existence. It is both the seen and unseen, the goal and the attempt.

"The knower and the known are one."

— MEISTER ECKHART[63]

Self-2

Life as Self-1 could be called a peak experience, but for most of us, this is not our everyday experience of self. Enter Self-2: More often than not, underneath your persona (personality) is a "you" that wanted to be held and supported but didn't get enough of that. Babies cry when they want something, and their caregivers ideally respond to their crying. As we all know, the response is not always adequate. This Self-2 felt hurt, twisted, knocked out of place, interrupted, injured, abandoned, and did not get sufficient love, care, nourishment, and support. Self-2 is the unhealed aspect of us. Some call it our shadow self, the part that did not get what you needed (but simultaneously believes somehow that it was your fault), so it hides in resignation and shame.

Self-3

To survive in everyday interactions and relationships, Self-2 needed to establish functional behavior patterns. These adaptations became your day-to-day presentation, which is Self-3: The "you" that knows how to function, to interact, to get along, and to make decisions and carry them out. It's the "you" that is the familiar character—the personality, the ego, the likes and dislikes, the identifications. Self-3 adapted to get love or to survive; you wanted nurturing but couldn't get it, so you found other behaviors and created another version of yourself to get what you needed. Self-3 is the healed-enough-to-function version of you.

Total Self

Self-1, Self-2, and Self-3 are aspects of our self/Self. Self-1 is essence and true source, and the other two selves are shaped by circumstance—by adapting to existence. The spiritual life is the practice of recognizing this truth and harmonizing our various selves and parts—mental, emotional, physical, and spiritual—to create an existence that is a true reflection of our natural being and divine nature.

Humanual work is not about getting rid of things but rather integrating all parts and restoring useful behaviors that got hijacked. Begin to give some thought to the patterns and habits that have affected you in your life.

Working with Self-1, Self-2, and Self-3: An Example

Self-2 struggles. I ignore her. I don't even believe that I exist much at that level because Self-3 is so strong that she is able to overpower Self-2 to get things done. One day, I was in a meeting with some very clever people, and I began to watch myself trying to keep up. I saw myself struggling to maintain my participation; I wanted to be accepted as equally clever, intelligent, and innovative. Yet, I felt my insides churning, and my muscles, particularly in my neck, were so tight that they felt sharp. My legs also had pain, but it was different from my neck pain; I felt dull contractions and a constant ache.

Later that night when I got home, I wondered about the difficulty I experienced. I searched inside and to my surprise found Self-2. I knew her vaguely from the thoughts (and resultant feelings) that I occasionally experienced when I judged myself as "not okay." As I reflected on this message, I felt the twisted muscles, the closed heart, the struggling failed attempts to get what I needed as a child, the cries, and the language and sounds that I made up out of desperation for a connection. This is me also—the part that felt ignored, silenced, and knocked off track.

Then Self-2 showed me: "This is what I *wanted* to do." I let Self-2 move slowly and make sounds as I recognized the stuck energy inside. To get to know Self-2 and work with it, I tried slow-motion, dream-like movements that did not use my voluntary (alpha) muscular system. Instead, I focused on observing the micro-movements within the whole of my tensegrity-like structure. My body knew exactly how to move to release the life-force that was stuck. I felt shudders, quivers, and flutters throbbing inside.

I then noticed repressed emotions coming up, but I did not turn away. Instead, I chose to stay there. As I watched the feelings and sensations moving in my body, I began to accept this aspect of myself as vulnerable—this "damaged goods" me. My Self-2 had been hiding inside, afraid to emerge, covered up by Self-3 all along.

In that moment, I realized that Self-2 would lead me to Self-1. After I recognized and moved with Self-2 (as described above), I could create a new reality: I let my feet meet the ground and unconditionally engage as I allowed myself to truly receive the support from the ground. In that moment, I felt totally supported like never before. I had no need to hold on or to overly contract. Every cell was in tensegrity, floating up against its own edge. The expansion created a lightness that I had never known. My body was still, my mind clear; I had entered the silent, spiritual realm of Self-1.

Explore what Selves 1-2-3 are for you in body, mind, and spirit.

EX-PLORATION: GOING INTO YOUR BODY TO GO BEYOND YOUR BODY

Find a comfortable place to sit or lie down.

1. Start by watching your breath moving out and in. See the rhythm, the flow, the restrictions, and the movement.

2. Be aware of your body—pay attention to your feet, and then dwell in your feet, continuing to: lower legs, thighs, pelvis, spine, torso, shoulders, upper arms, lower arms, hands, neck, and head.

3. Be aware of and then dwell in your visceral organs, whatever you know of them—your heart, lungs, liver, spleen, kidneys, stomach, intestines, reproductive organs, etc.

4. Be aware of and then dwell in your sense organs—eyes, ears, mouth, nose, and touch.

5. Be aware of and then dwell in your systems, whatever you know of them—circulatory, digestive, nervous, musculoskeletal, immune, fascial, and respiratory.

6. Be aware of and then dwell in your mind—focus on one thought or image, then let that go and watch all the thoughts that appear.

7. Let your bodily awareness expand out to the space around you. Dwell there. Include the people you know and don't know. Include the Earth.

8. Keep traveling in that outward, expanding direction, and go as far as you can imagine, to the planets and stars as you continue to dwell in your expanding body.

9. Find the silent emptiness beyond the beyond. Rest there. Dwell there.

10. When you are ready, retrace your steps and make your way back. Take time to arrive back into your body.

"No particular thought can be the mind's natural state, only silence. Not the idea of silence, but silence itself. When the mind is in its natural state, it reverts to silence, spontaneously, after every experience, or, rather, every experience happens against the background of silence."

— NISARGADATTA MAHARAJ[64]

CHAPTER

16

MEDITATION: A QUINTESSENTIAL PRACTICE

The inner depths of your soul that reach to the stars can be accessed through meditation. You can discover the process of quieting and focusing your mind, for health and well-being, and for raising consciousness. Even five minutes a day can make a positive difference.

"The unchangeable can only be realized in silence.
Once realized, it will deeply affect the changeable, itself remaining unaffected."

— NISARGADATTA MAHARAJ[65]

1. MY MEDITATION STORY: THE LIGHT OF BEING MEETS THE GROUND OF DAILY LIFE

Having begun meditation more than fifty years ago, I feel qualified to say a few words about it. People sometimes ask me why I started meditating at such a young age; it was not something my parents suggested or even knew about. I had an inner sense of this other world, but nobody I knew talked about it. With meditation I experienced it, and I loved the practice from the first moment of attention.

I have practiced many forms of meditation over the years, finding each one to be most beneficial at the time. In meditation, the daily challenges of life can be diminished within the larger cosmic realms of consciousness.

As a young teenager, in 1966, I heard Maharishi Mahesh Yogi speak at Harvard Divinity School. I was initiated into transcendental meditation the next day and began my relationship with the inner world. I had longed for this inner world without knowing what I was longing for. I practiced for twenty minutes in the morning and twenty minutes in the evening. My brothers laughed at me, and my friends thought I was odd, but it made perfect sense to me.

As I studied macrobiotics, I practiced Zen and Shinto meditation at home and abroad, in Japan and Korea. Meditating in the temples of Japan, in the early-morning dew-filled atmosphere, surrounded by Buddha statues hundreds of years old, was a transcendent experience I shall never forget.

I became interested in *The Course in Miracles* and the beautiful lessons I read every morning. As part of the study, a group of us traveled to Assisi to honor the spirit of St. Francis in the beautiful towns of Italy.

For a while, I practiced the Centering Prayer, The Cloud of Unknowing, flowing out of the Christian mystical tradition and the contemplative experience of the Divine presence.

When I met the Indian spiritual guide Gurumayi at the Siddha Yoga Meditation Ashram, I was moved to follow this path for fifteen years, in India and the US, with a mantra and the blessings of a living guru. No words are strong enough to convey the sublime, divine experiences.

With a growing interest in psychology and the works by Gurdjieff, I joined a Diamond Heart group and practiced the teachings for thirteen years. Inquiry brought me to understand myself and my patterns of thought, as I pondered the meaning of truth and presence.

Now, most often I return to simply watching my breath go in and out. No control, no counting. I just make a point of being with what is while breath comes in and breath goes out. If I notice a thought or a body sensation, I stay with it a moment; it shifts, then back to my breath. Breath comes in, breath goes out.

Although the outer forms varied, for me the inner process was similar. It is so important to take the time to sit—to stop my busy activities of life, and to stop the rambling in my mind and running in my body. The practice continues to envelop the depth of my soul and shower me with delicate perceptions that grace my path.

2. MEDITATION FOR MODERN LIFE

In daily life, the majority of people focus their energy outside themselves, concerned with events happening around them. This focus is necessary for navigating life successfully, but it is only half the story. How can you welcome your expanded Self with only the outer half of the story?

There is an entire world inside you that has just as much to offer, and this inner world is also necessary for navigating life. You are probably already aware of many signals and informative cues from inside. This inner world also offers a place of healing or refuge. *Meditation* is based on the Latin word *mederi*—to look after or to heal.

Meditation is a process through which you can come to experience and expand your relationship with your inner self. Focusing your attention inside, instead of on the activities outside, can be a welcome state, even if only for a moment.

Meditation is a direct perceptual knowledge or experience of a subtler level of reality than we ordinarily sense. In meditation, you bring your attention inside to what is occurring within you (vibrations, sensations, emptiness, or passing thoughts) and/or to your inner self, or what could be called your True Nature. In some traditions, the inner self is identical with "God," Self, Source, and/or Divinity.

Meditation enables you with your everyday consciousness to experience a direct personal connection with this ever-present universal "God" consciousness from which all phenomena arise. At its height, your small ego is submerged in the larger energies of life. You realize the divine oneness of which you are a part.

For some seekers, to discover or be in touch with this Self (which I called Self-1 in Chapter 15) is the goal of human life. You meditate to reveal your inner being. As it unfolds, you become more complete and centered because you now have an inner life to balance your outer life. Having this balance can diminish anxiety. (Sometimes anxiety will increase, usually briefly, before it diminishes.) *One cause of anxiety is our separation from our inner self—our complete self, our true self.* Without your complete self on board, it is hard to feel secure in life.

When there is a disconnection in body, heart, and soul, as often happens in trauma and conditioned behavior, spiritual dissonance results. Specialized meditation or mindfulness training can help to repair that disconnect. Classic meditation is not for everyone. Contrary to popular opinion, calming down is not a comfortable state for everybody, especially if you were in a calm state before an unpleasant incident. For a traumatized person, simply beginning to find safety in becoming aware of the inner self and sensations can be a huge step (more in the EX-plorations below). Meditate not to attain something but to realize that what you're looking for is already in you.

3. DISRUPTING THE PATTERN WITH A NEW OBJECT OF ATTENTION

We are all engaged in a continuous internal dialogue in which the meaning and emotional associations of one thought trigger the next, usually without our being consciously aware of the process. We create "grooves" in the mind, neural pathways that make thoughts flow in the same direction. Hindu psychology calls this process *samskara*, referring to the subtle impressions (or grooves) of our past actions and mental circuits. The literal meaning of the word *samskara* explains the phenomenon well: the prefix *sam* means "well planned, well thought out," and *kara* means "the action undertaken."

Your personal samskaras are created from the memories of your past and can prompt you to react in the same limited ways over and over again, as we saw with adaptive patterns. Most people build up an identity on the basis of samskaras without even realizing they are doing this.

In meditation, it is possible to disrupt the unconscious repetition of thoughts and emotions by focusing on a new object of attention. This can be anything that you repeat or focus on silently in yourself—a sound (mantra), an image (your deity), and even emptiness (nothing). With less meaning or emotional charge to trigger associations, the mind can detach from its usual preoccupations and experience the spaciousness and peace within.

Meditation is a powerful way to loosen the grip of adaptive patterns, physical and emotional. Thus, it paves the way for you to connect to your True Self, which unlike the limited fearful self is infinite, pure consciousness.

I want to recognize that this is not always easy or comfortable. We become very attached to and familiar with our limited and fearful selves, no matter how much pain they cause. You want to be sure to tend to these selves and not push them aside. The sacred space inside, with spirit shining, may need to be tolerated in small increments as the habits or fears are processed and diminished. Or, it may be more accurate to say that little by little the fears are no longer necessary. Because now you realize and know in your body, mind, and spirit that the moment of fear or constriction was a long time ago, and the situation is different now.

4. WANDERING ATTENTION VERSUS RESTING IN THE SILENCE OF THE MIND

Meditation takes you from activity into silence, giving your whole self a very deep level of rest (remember the rest and digest of the dorsal vagal system). When you rest, you can heal, letting go of accumulated stress, fatigue, toxins, and rigidity. Old physical and mental patterns of thinking and feeling can begin to fall away of their own accord. When this happens, the mind is actually learning to heal itself, "mederi."

Studies in neuroscience show what wisdom traditions have known for centuries, namely that the physical and emotional health benefits of meditation include stress reduction. This manifests as decreased stress-related cortisol, better sleep, lower blood pressure, control of blood sugar in type-2 diabetes, decreased depression and anxiety, improved cardiovascular function, strengthened immunity, and general well-being.[66]

This merely scratches the surface of the significant health benefits of meditation. It is an opportunity for you to say to the world, "This time is for me." When meditating you can just *be*. Perhaps the greatest gift of meditation is the sense of calm and inner peace it brings to your daily life. When you meditate, you go beyond the mind's noisy chatter into an entirely different place—the silence of a mind that is not jumping into the past or the future. Meditation can bring you to the peace of the present moment.

"The faculty of voluntarily bringing back a wandering attention, over and over again, is the very root of judgment, character, and will. . . . An education which should improve this faculty would be the education par excellence."

— WILLIAM JAMES, American philosopher and psychologist[67]

Witness Your Thoughts and Actions

You use your mind all day long to focus and work out multiple details for yourself, from "What should I wear?" to "Should I have one more cookie?" to "Should I continue life support for my aging parent?" The mind is good at this, but again, it is only half the picture.

As you meditate, you want your mind to quiet down. Many people think the mind is a major distraction or obstacle when trying to meditate. The mind is spinning off to many places while you are trying to bring awareness and focus to one place. As you may know from experience, it is very difficult, if not impossible, to *stop* your mind from spinning endless streams of mental chatter. The goal of meditation is not to battle the mind but to direct it, or watch it and just be interested in where it goes, since every thought in your mind is expressed as a muscular reality in your body.

How do we do this? One solution is to simply witness the thoughts as they arise and subside. You can watch the mind streaming along instead of becoming entranced by it. A thought comes up. See it. Let it pass. Thoughts are not concrete material, just different forms of energy or consciousness. "Mind" is a form of consciousness with a tendency to congeal into thoughts and images, "grooves," or samskaras. If you see it as consciousness instead of concrete images, there is less of a problem. The world is made up of continuously moving particles, and everything is a configuration of them. It is all consciousness.

Mantra Aligns the Mind with the Deeper Self

Most meditations bring attention to something particular in order to focus your mind, which typically tends to be all over the place with random thinking (often called *monkey mind*). For meditation, you want to guide your mental energy and give your mind something to focus on—perhaps a word or *mantra* (a sacred sound), something internal like a body part (heart), something external like a candle or nature (a tree), the breath, and even the mind itself (to watch the thoughts). Or, you can simply *be with* whatever is happening. Mantra means "that which redeems and protects the one who contemplates it."

If the object of attention is a mantra, you can repeat it silently to yourself or chant out loud. A mantra is pure sound, like *OM* (called the primordial sound). It allows your mind to detach from its usual preoccupations and be immersed in the spaciousness and peace within. A word or mantra can be very influential. Words have certain vibratory patterns of sound that resonate inside us. The sound can bridge the gap between surface thinking and the consciousness underlying reality—the inner Self. These vibrational patterns are formed into syllables, such as OM, that have been used for thousands of years to transform cells.

Musical instruments were developed to duplicate the sounds and vibrations that experienced yogis heard during their meditations in their inner sacred spaces. Devotional music is still widely used today, along with mantra, in yoga and meditation circles to generate increased resonance with the inner self.

5. POSTURAL COMFORT WHILE MEDITATING

How you sit to meditate greatly affects your meditation. I have taught in meditation centers all over the world and can tell you that it's not unusual for folks who sit for prolonged periods to be in pain somewhere in their body. This pain often distracts them, which interferes with focus on the object of attention. Instead, the pain becomes the object of the meditation.

It is well known that certain body postures and gestures are associated with automatic brain responses. If you stand bent over, you feel one way; if you stand erect, you feel another set of feelings. Your ordinary life is made up of personal gestures. They keep your personality and identifications intact by way of repetitive patterns of thought, movement, and perception.

Over time, sages and yogis have observed that an erect or upright spine is most effective for deep meditation. This may be related to the energetic connection between heaven and earth (gravity and antigravity), or the support and suspension we have been practicing.

Many styles of sitting can work. If you are comfortable sitting cross-legged on a cushion on the floor, that is fine. If you are more comfortable sitting in a chair with your feet on the floor, that is also fine. Wherever you can sit steadily will work best. Even lying down is fine if that position allows you to meditate. If you are restless and keep fidgeting and moving your body, the mind will also become restless. If your body is steady, then your mind can become steady. Again, it's not always easy. If you prefer to move, a walking meditation can also be very potent.

6. MEDITATION AND MINDFULNESS PRACTICES: THE BEST MEDITATION IS THE ONE YOU WILL DO

Find one technique you would like to explore, and stay with it for a while. Numerous books, talks, audio applications, and YouTube videos are available to help you learn. And there are some wise masters and teachers who can guide you, especially if you desire personal direction and support.

These explorations are for learning to go inward to focus your mind, or to witness the fluctuations of your mind.

A. EX-ploration: Simple Meditation

Choose something to bring your awareness or attention to, like a word or a phrase. You could try "OM" or "I invite the divine." Start by giving attention fully to it, letting go of everything else. Allow yourself to become absorbed in it, even for just a few minutes. Without stress or strain, gently open to an increasingly stable presence. This exploration is best done with the eyes closed.

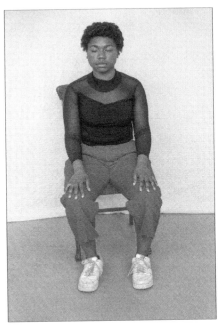

Meditation.

Group meditation.

DO   Once or twice a day.

B. EX-ploration: Meditate on Your Breath or Heart, at Home in Your Body

For meditation, you want your mind and breath to be linked and become one. The word *respiration* comes from the Latin *respire*, "to breathe"—composed of *re*, "return to" *spiritus*, "spirit." If your breath is quiet, your mind will be quiet.

Find the natural rhythm of your breath, or let it find you.

Begin from an effortless position sitting, standing, or walking. Observe your breath. Don't try to change it. As your mind becomes absorbed in your breath, accumulated layers of tension and stress can shift. If your mind wanders, bring it back to your breath. Don't try to force thoughts away. And when thoughts come and "talk" to you, don't talk back. You are only interested in your breath coming in and going out.

It may be helpful to notice movement and sensations as you breathe: your chest, stomach, and inside your nose and throat. The front, back, and sides of your torso can move. Remember the multidimensional breathing.

Meditating on your heartbeat may also provide a useful focus, as well as augment feelings of love. In any position, sense your heart beating. It may take some time to start perceiving it. Feel the vibration, like water drops into a pond, reverberating in your chest, especially in your back. Feel your heart beat in your back.

> **DO**   One minute every day is a good start. Twenty minutes is great. One minute on day one, two minutes on day two, etc., can build quite nicely.

C. EX-ploration: Non-doing Meditation

You begin with a willingness to be quiet and listen to the stillness. Allow your mind to be empty. If necessary, use the phrase "Give me nothing" or "Empty mind," over and over. There is nothing to do, nowhere to go, no one to be.

> **DO**   When life feels overwhelming.

D. EX-ploration: Meditation and Trauma

For those who carry the effects of trauma, chronic pain, or strong conditioned adaptive behaviors, meditation may initially seem extremely challenging or uncomfortable. En route to the refuge of the inner self, you may bump into uncomfortable buried experiences, traumatic memories, and emotional wounds. If you are able to integrate these experiences, your meditation will be enhanced. If not, you may grow confused or dissociated. Not everyone is advised to, or able to, meditate. If you have experienced trauma, it might be difficult to focus inside your body, mainly because at one time the body was a painful place to be. To be comfortable with self-discovery and accessing your deeper authentic self, it is best to learn to meditate in small increments. If you begin to become activated, open your eyes and look around at the present circumstances. Chances are the activation happened in a very different time and place.

If you tend to get flooded with painful emotional or physical feelings when you relax into yourself, then try to find the bodily sensations that occur *just before* the flooding, and be with those as your meditation. You know when you are going to sneeze; there is a buildup of sensation just before. The same is true for flooding.

If you feel a contraction, find it in your body, watch it contract; see the movement, and then allow or encourage it to slowly expand. Expansion follows contraction. Continue to contract and expand until you find a comfortable resting place. If you feel pain, find a place inside that has no pain and pendulate with that.

If putting your attention inside your body is still too painful or anxiety provoking, another option is to make some distance by projecting the pain (physical or emotional) outside your body. You can imagine placing it across the street, or even in the next town or another country. How far away do you need to put the pain? Engage your imagination and visualization. Use the elements—melt it in fire or drown it in water. See if that gives you some distance from the pain while still allowing you to settle a little deeper into yourself without becoming activated.

If you tend to dissociate, consciously watch yourself leave your body. What do you see when you look back at yourself? Where do you go? Stay there as long as is needed. When you return, notice that you are able to come back into your body.

DO — When necessary.

E. EX-ploration: Dual Consciousness

There is a concept called *dual consciousness*. Sometimes when you start meditating, an unpleasant flashback will occur. At that moment, recognize the flashback but also acknowledge "that was then" and "this is now." To help you come into the now, look around the room. Name three objects in your visual field. It can be helpful to shift your body with rhythm or small micro-movements to feel your support. Hold the unpleasant memory of the past and the pleasant memory of now, together. You are not going into the old trauma; instead, you are bringing the old trauma into the present in order to help dissipate its influence. This dual consciousness of holding then and now, including body sensations, is key in trauma recovery and in accessing your authentic self or True Nature.

Here is a simple exploration for this: Think of one mildly uncomfortable memory and one unpleasant sensation in your body that comes with it. Then recognize the support from underneath—either the floor or the chair. In that moment when you recognize the support, notice if there is a pleasant sensation somewhere in your body, a flow or space, like water through sand or a breath of fresh air. See if you can hold the mildly unpleasant sensation with the newly found pleasant sensation. Go back and forth between the two and see where you land.

> **DO** When you feel a mildly unpleasant sensation inside.

F. EX-ploration: Contemplation

Perhaps the word *meditation* sounds too esoteric or alternative for you. If so, I can offer a contemplative practice. Most of you have a continual flow of thoughts, ideas, images, and/or feelings to which you cling—so much so that these ideas actually have *you*. Do you have any idea who the "I" is behind them? For example, who is the "I" behind your self-image? The goal of contemplation is to find out who is the "I" prior to any thoughts of right and wrong, good and bad. You might also ask, "Who is the 'I' before *I* defined the 'I'?"

The practice: Imagine you are sitting on the bank of a river and boats are sailing by. Each boat gets a name based on your thoughts and judgments. One boat may be called "anxiety about work," while another is "fighting with my partner," or "I want to win." You get the idea.

See the boat and let it move on. The tendency is to jump on board and identify with it, which allows it to pick up steam. You are not trying to make your mind blank or quiet; you are just letting things come and go, and not jumping aboard any one boat. You say, "Not this," "I'm not only that." Let it go. Do not hold on to anything either pleasant or unpleasant.

Name them, but right after naming them, say, "I am not just that." For example: "Anxiety about work . . . I am not just that."

You do not want to destroy the boats because these thoughts are part of you, and you do not want to reject any part of yourself. You just don't want it ruling you. As Dr. Richard Schwartz, founder of Internal Family Systems (IFS) Parts Work, says, "All parts welcome."[68] If "dissatisfied" parts continue to show up, you may want to get to know them and sort out their story with some form of therapeutic help. IFS or Somatic Experiencing® have proven to be helpful.

> **DO** When you are overrun with thoughts.

These are just a few ideas for you to begin or continue to deepen your meditation practice.

CHAPTER

17

FEELING AT HOME IN YOUR EXPANDED SELF: WHOLENESS

The body, the mind, the emotions, the spirit, and more all contribute to the wholeness that exists as you, and as the larger universe. Whether you see it or not, the wholeness encompasses every aspect of human life.

"The right way to wholeness is made up of fateful detours and wrong turnings."[69]
— CARL GUSTAV JUNG

1. HOLOGRAPHIC WHOLENESS

Now that you have a better understanding of the many intricacies of your being, what should you do to heal yourself? My answer to this question: whatever makes sense to you and leads you to a deeper sense of yourself and your own humanity. Go with whatever you feel attracted to. Where is the door open? Your task is to notice what happens to you when you perform different jobs, or eat different foods, or behave differently. Ask yourself, "Is this contributing to my health and well-being, and a fuller version of myself, or not?" If you really tune in, you will know.

In my fifty years of exploring and studying the body, the self, and the psyche, I have heard many opinions about what part of the self is most important. They say, "If you fix _____, everything else will be fine."

Foot reflexologists say "the foot." Acupuncturists say "the meridians." Some say "the breath." And yet others say the mental, the physical, the emotional, or the spiritual is most important. Which system is primary, this one or that one? My opinion is that *they are all primary*. I believe, as some scientists do, that humans are holographic. The key understanding of a *hologram* is that every part is represented in the whole, and the whole is represented in every part. This implies that the whole of our being is represented in every cell of our body. Let's take a closer look by examining a hologram of an apple.

A hologram is produced when a single laser light is split into two separate beams. The first beam is bounced off the apple. The second beam collides with the reflection of the first, creating an interference pattern of colliding waves, which is recorded on film.

To the naked eye, the image looks like concentric circles. But when a laser is shined on the hologram, a three-dimensional image of the apple appears. You can view it from all angles and see it as the apple. However, when you try to touch it, there is nothing there. It is a virtual image.

The interesting thing about a hologram is that you can cut it in half, and the whole image will show up on both halves. As a matter of fact, you can cut it multiple times and every tiny piece will display the image of the whole apple.

I hope this reminds you of the movement of tensegrity structures. If you recall, pushing one part of the structure causes the entire structure to move. Or, it could remind you of the gamma nervous system, which makes an adjustment in the *entire* body to support a change taking place in *one* part of the body.

I was teaching a group of musicians and one very clever, observant young woman said, after watching me work with a half-dozen singers, "It's fascinating to watch you work. You show each new person their suspension and support, and their singing improves greatly. There is more resonance, an easier flow of air, and a clearer sound. The interesting thing to me is that they all had different problems: one had a tight jaw, one had shoulder pain, and one felt shy. But even with these different problems, the suspension and the support helped every one of them. You didn't really need to fix separate problems," she observed. "You just took care of the whole."

The explorations in this chapter are for embracing the larger picture of human existence. With balance and the experience of wholeness, you can reach for what you want in life.

EX-PLORATION: FEELING YOUR WHOLENESS, PART 1

Experiment with sensing yourself (I) as a whole. Your attention will search for it and then find it, and then lose it and find it again. Connect to yourself as one unified whole, with no parts, no doing, and no effort. Does your sense of wholeness (I) include sensation, breathing, viscera, muscles, bones, etc.? Sense moment by moment, and be present in consciousness, as your unified whole. Not so easy. But if you picture yourself floating in the ocean or a swimming pool, it is easier; you don't feel parts, you experience yourself as whole: I am floating.

DO	When you want to feel whole.

2. CONNECTIVE TISSUE AND WHOLENESS

Connective tissue is what it says it is—tissue that connects. One aspect of connective tissue is *fascia*, an uninterrupted elastic-like layer that surrounds, attaches, stabilizes, separates, and penetrates all body structures, from head to toe. Fascia is a three-dimensional web that holds everything together and keeps you from coming apart; you might remember the stretch reflex discussed in Chapter 7. The fascial system creates a continuous tensile and compressive balance that unifies and seamlessly distributes the force of any movement throughout the entire body via the sensory gamma nervous system. When something moves, everything moves, including our support, suspension, and breath, *Humanual* Basics.

The fascial system perceives instantaneously, communicating roughly three times faster than the nervous system. Fascia's underlying fluidity and connectivity form an internal communication system that is constantly informing the body where it is in space as an aspect of *proprioception*. This term comes from the Latin *proprio*, meaning "one's own." It is the sense of what is happening *inside* our body, including information such as balance and the location of various body parts in relation to one another. Proprioception also indicates what is happening at our joints, and whether the body is moving with the required effort.

Proprioception is part of interoception, the process of perceiving what is happening within the body. Messages from the body travel to the brain—to the insula and cingulate in the medial prefrontal cortex—and are processed by the brain. Through this messaging activity, we gain body awareness, which is one of the main ways we "feel" or "sense" who we are in our form. A major part of this sensing involves fascia, as an intelligent, whole body-mind system, constantly sensing itself and offering feedback to itself. The recognition of your inner world is available at any moment, informing the unity of your inner and outer movement.

As we discussed in terms of tensegrity, bones do not actually touch one another and thus do not pass loads directly to each other, as they are suspended within the matrix of muscles and fascial weave. Fascia contains and incorporates muscles, bones, and joints into one whole system, managing all movement globally, with resilience, strength, and holistic integration. The fascial system is always trying to distribute load and strain evenly throughout the body.

Stephen M. Levin and Danièle-Claude Martin describe it well in *Biotensegrity—The Mechanics of Fascia*: "The mechanics of tensegrity structures . . . Forces are distributed throughout the system rather than locally concentrated as they are in lever systems. The system functions as a single unit. All this makes for a more energy-efficient system."[70]

One can learn to improve "use" by engaging the entire skeletal system and the fascial core to release strain on the afflicted part. Strain in one part of the body affects everything else. If you are unbalanced or stuck (energetically and/or physically), your fascial tissues don't distribute strain as effectively, and some areas and/or joints and muscles take excessive strain. The tighter you hold yourself, the more you brace and compress; the result is often some kind of discomfort. In order to alleviate pain in one part, the whole system must be restored to its tensional balance, which means addressing or resolving emotions, dissonance, trauma, and other overwhelming events as they show up. Thus, one can learn to handle strain in a system-wide manner, and to identify or establish new patterns of movement that create suspension and release into a more expanded version of oneself. The EX-ercise in Chapter 9 (section 4) called "Find the Top of Your Spine, So That Your Head Can Free Away from Your Spine" can help with this.

3. MOVING WITH COHERENCE

When you discover the fabric of the connective tissue, it serves as an underlying template of wholeness that supports a variety of movement in your dynamic exploration of life. Combined with the buoyancy of breath, you feel both a solid connection to the ground and a lightness of being. It's the type of lightness that allows a cheetah to run at lightning speed, as if it weighs practically nothing.

One of my clients ran on the treadmill at the gym often but would always feel tired and sore afterward. When she began to run with awareness of her natural expansive structure, she was able to run longer distances with less fatigue. She felt the lightness and buoyancy. The unity of all parts working together allows this coherence.

The potential for freedom, ease, and play is hidden underneath all discomfort. Restrictions in body and mind are limiting, but they can change. Our system naturally longs for freedom of expression, a kind of play, which we can foster through subtle and rhythmic movement. The coherent micro-movements that we explored in Chapter 3 are a wonderful entrée to the world of play. Opening to swaying, rocking, rolling, and bouncing invites aliveness.

As you explore any kind of movement, recognize that you will most often go directly into alpha muscular movement (voluntary, active effort) using habitual patterns, because this is what we are predominantly taught. These patterns are often jarring and could interrupt your experience of the more subtle forces of sensory awareness that are available.

As you move with awareness of fascia, micro-movements, and fluidity, you begin to feel the subtle coherent undulating forces throughout the body. One part moves, and all of you moves. Every movement has the potential to be seen (and felt) holistically, like a *multidimensional blueprint*. It is as if you are watching the ocean and its layers. On top, we see the waves with their ebb and flow, or turbulence, and deeper underneath are the steadier currents and tides.

In the next section, we explore what happens when you expand your view and include the environment as an extension of your fascial web. This encompasses all the forces around you, including gravity.

4. GRAVITY, WHOLENESS, THE EARTH, AND YOU

The majority of people think of gravity as a force that moves downward toward the Earth, pushing anything with mass into the ground. They rarely remember, however, that anti-gravity also exists, which means that any up has a down, and any down has an up.

It is less known and understood that physicist Isaac Newton, in his later years, conceived of gravity as a mutual attraction between the mass of objects. In other words, because of gravity, objects act in relationship to one another, not independent from one another. Thus, gravity is intrinsic to the interaction between two or more objects. There is some gravitational force between you and the sofa, or the planet and the sofa. In fact, there is gravity between *every* object in the entire universe and *every* other object. Hence, I am attracted to everything and everything is attracted to me = universal mutual attraction. I have heard this called the "love principle." Could we not similarly see gravity as one vast fascial web of connective tissue, linking everything together?

In truth, without gravity we would be floating in space like astronauts. Gravity gives us the mutual attraction of an equal pulling of two objects toward each other.

There is the mutual attraction of a person and a planet. But because the planet is so much bigger, the person stands on the planet. When you pull equally on two objects, if one is a feather and one a lead ball, then the feather is going to move more toward the lead ball. Thus you, the feather, stand on the planet, the lead ball.

When you stand on the Earth with the recognition that the ground does support you, actually pushes up into you, you feel secure and stable. The whole of you is being held in the fascial web of one grand tensegrity-like structure. And when you feel this security of stable support, you feel safe and held. Then the interoceptive messages tell the brain that *all is okay*.

The body relaxes, as there is no need to prepare for danger, and you can engage socially with another.

When I teach a master class—whether to performers, medical professionals, or therapists—I often include a walking exercise. I first ask participants to walk as they normally do; then I ask them to walk with the support of the Earth. The most frequent comment I receive is "I feel lighter." When you stop weighting yourself down and start using the upward support of the Earth's force, you feel lighter. Try it in this next exercise.

EX-ERCISE: HUMANUAL CHAIR BALANCE™

1. While standing, take a four-legged chair and tip it onto two legs.

2. Explore while it is on two legs where the chair is heaviest and where it is lightest, by tipping it forward and back. Where does it balance?

| Exploring the chair forward. | Exploring the chair back. | Balancing the chair. |

3. Do the same experiment with yourself. Lean forward and back, and see where you are heavy and where you are light.

4. Find your lightest place. Find your balance.

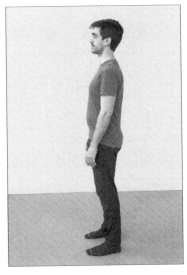

Exploring your weight forward.　　Exploring your weight back.　　Balancing yourself.

5. Walk around with that.

DO　　**When you feel out of balance.**

The Rainmaker

This was one of Carl Jung's favorite stories to tell. He allegedly told it in every possible seminar.[71]

> Once upon a time there was a Chinese village suffering a great drought. The village people thus sent for the rainmaker, who lived in the farthest corner of China. When he arrived and the elders of the village gathered around him, the rainmaker merely asked for a place to stay in solitude. He was provided with a small hut, where he sat and meditated for three days while the entire village population impatiently waited. On the third day, the rain started to come, and the rainmaker left his hut. Excited and grateful, the village elders gathered around him curiously. "What have you done?" they asked.
>
> "Nothing," he replied.
>
> "But you have brought the rain after so many months of drought."
>
> "I don't know about that," answered the rainmaker. "In the village I come from, people live according to the ways of the Tao. We maintain the dynamic balance of Tao, so people are sad and people are happy, babies are born and

people die, the sun shines and the rain comes. When I arrived at this village I felt that I was totally off-balance; I couldn't think straight or calm down. It has taken me three whole days to retrieve my inner balance."

EX-PLORATION: FEELING YOUR WHOLENESS, PART 2

There is a difference between your subjective experience of your weight and your objective experience, as we just saw with the chair exercise. Subjectively, you can feel quite light, but your objective experience is different when you step on a scale and look at the numbers.

How do you feel your own weight? It is a delicate balance between the centrifugal force (antigravity) coming up from the Earth, and the centripetal force (gravity) coming downward toward the Earth. This means you would feel weightless if you were simply allowing the universal forces to act. This is sometimes hard to feel unless you have had a direct (hands-on) experience of this with a qualified Alexander Technique teacher, or some other skilled practitioner who could help you experience yourself this way.

On the contrary, if you are holding yourself up, then you are not letting your full weight drop into the ground. In this case, the Earth can only match a portion of your weight, so you are not getting the full upward thrust. Or maybe you are dropping your weight down too much (slumping, etc.) and not using the body's natural suspension and support; then you have so much downward effort that you cannot receive the upward forces from the Earth. In both situations, you will experience yourself as "heavy."

You want to be able to perceive your whole expanded self on the ground, wherever you meet it. At that place, you receive the support or mutual attraction upward from the planet. When you equalize the forces, you have the potential to not feel heavy. Then, if your body feels weightless, you (body, mind, emotions, and spirit) will feel lighter and less "pulled down" by your own circumstances, on every level.

I repeat once more: If you pull up too much or drop down too much for whatever reason, you miss the delicate balance of the merging of the mental, physical, emotional, spiritual, and cosmic presence. Instead, you will get pulled to a part and lose the sense of the whole.

DO Your whole life.

5. WHOLE-BODY THINKING: THE EXPECTANCY WAVE

This wholeness, or oneness, that I talk about is not the common way of understanding the psychophysical connection. Most people incorrectly believe that the mind controls all activities—that the experiential living "you" in your brain will move your body "you," a separate object that responds to your commands. This idea not only creates division within you, it is inaccurate. If you look closely, there is more going on than that; the response occurs long before you move.

As far back as 1965, an arresting neurological fact came to light. Changes in electrical potential take place in the nerve cells in the frontal lobes of human brains *before*, as well as during and after, voluntary muscular movements. Two German neurologists, Deecke and Kornhuber, found that while an individual is thinking about carrying out an action, the action is being preceded by a slow, negatively charged wave occurring in the front region of the brain. Drs. Falconer and Walter affirmed that negative waves of this sort precede and accompany every conscious, spontaneous, voluntary decision and action, from deciding to walk or talk to starting and stopping your car. They termed it the *expectancy wave*. A good deal of later research confirms this observation.

Every thought manifests as a change in the body; that is, it has a muscular response. To observe the power of thought, think the word *down* over and over and see what happens. Then try the word *up*. Or *lemon* for fun.

In the words of Rodolfo Llinas, author of *I of the Vortex: From Neurons to Self*, "That which we call thinking is the evolutionary internalization of movement."[72]

Llinas continues, "Our brain has a periodic control signal reflected in our muscles as the 8-12 Hz physiological tremor. This premotor control is designed to save time and synchronize motor apparatus. In the last 15 years or so, it has become clear that the 8-12 Hz rhythmicity of physiological tremor is observed not only during voluntary movement, but also, and perhaps to a greater extent, during maintained posture and in supported limbs at rest."[73]

Voluntary movement is just a continuation of the always-present physiological tremor. In the expanded version of Self, there are no parts; you are one continuous system. There is no controlling point that directs all the rest.

In the old, outdated model, the brain was not influenced by the body. The body was simply a mechanical thing that the brain executed specific behaviors on. This is now mildly ridiculous, given what neuroscience has revealed.

6. WHOLENESS IN THE MOMENT

When something is off, most people ask, "What should I do to fix the problem?" They want to *do* something. But you really want to be curious and ask, "What am I actually doing in this moment?" Thus, the real question is always, "What am I doing that is causing or contributing to the problem?" Do this with no blame.

Meet the moment that feels "off" and stay there; don't rush in and try to change it. Give yourself permission to live this moment as it is, you and your surroundings. Simply accept it, and choose to allow the wholeness of reality to be what it is. Then, try to follow the wisdom and guidance of this poem by Rumi:

The Guest House

This being human is a guest house.
Every morning a new arrival.
A joy, a depression, a meanness,
some momentary awareness comes
as an unexpected visitor.
Welcome and entertain them all!
Even if they are a crowd of sorrows,
who violently sweep your house
empty of its furniture,
still, treat each guest honorably.
He may be clearing you out
for some new delight.
The dark thought, the shame, the malice.
Meet them at the door laughing and invite them in.
Be grateful for whatever comes,
because each has been sent
as a guide from beyond.

— JELLALUDIN RUMI, translation by Coleman Barks[74]

7. WHOLENESS AND HEALING

The word *wholeness* is the root of the word *healing,* which literally means "to make whole again." You will think of yourself as whole unless you are misinformed enough to think that you are not whole. Then, when you stop that, you become whole. Wholeness can be gauged from the perspective of how we use ourselves, both physically and emotionally.

In the physical realm, when your arm hurts (not from an injury), you think you are fine, other than a little discomfort there. You are neglecting to consider that your arm is part of your whole body (self), and your whole body (self) is working *in a pattern* that includes a hurt arm.

Let's imagine that the arm with the pain is only 5 percent of you. If you were able to get rid of the pain, the rest of you, 95 percent, would continue to operate in the same pattern as if the pain were still there. In many cases, the pain would return or show up somewhere else. If you just treat your arm and not your whole body (self), you won't shift the pattern, which is the underlying cause of the problem. A metaphor for this notion might be having lost your keys in a messy room. You could just look for the keys in the messy room, or you could clean the entire room and you would probably find your keys—and be less likely to lose them there again.

In the emotional realm, restoring wholeness begins by seeing why you lost your wholeness. What part, or parts, of you did you lose? For each of you, it will be different aspects of your essential self; you lose parts that are not properly recognized or nurtured. For example, if you were not shown compassion, you would not know it existed.

As a child, you need your center, and you need your essential self reflected back to you in a full-bodied way. You take direction from that inner knowing of your inherent wholeness. But maybe you had to separate from your essential self to survive. When you move away from your authentic, essential self, you will have conflict in your life and in your role in humanity. How could it be different?

Another example of wholeness: "I didn't want to change myself; it was what I was born with—my heritage, my roots—and I wanted to live with that." —Barbra Streisand, commenting on why she did not change her nose.[75]

> ### *HUM Journal.*
> ### What is your experience of wholeness?

As you move toward inhabiting your whole authentic self, you begin to heal the parts. If, as a child, you were not permitted to voice your opinion, then your voice might be meek and restrained. But now, as an adult, you are free to speak, and nobody is preventing you from speaking. Then, as you begin to feel more comfortable speaking your opinions, you can feel more whole and expanded, and less held back. But it's not always an easy journey. Support, suspension, breath, and recognition of the emotional circumstances can help. I have seen these practices help so many people. One middle-aged client, a tall, full-bodied woman, had a meek voice. As we worked together, it was clear that she was trying to be a good, polite, soft-spoken female. But in truth, she had a big, belting voice that began to emerge.

EX-ERCISE: REACH FOR WHAT YOU WANT IN LIFE

In Chapter 10, you learned *Humanual* touch—how to reach with your fingertips. Now it is time to reach for what will give you the wholeness you want in life.

1. Think of something that you would like to reach for—perhaps something that would allow you to feel more complete, like a strong voice, or a sense of confidence, or greater compassion. What would make you more able to feel your expanded Self?

2. Using your imagination, place it in the room with you.

3. Remember, our bodies are designed to do things in the most efficient way possible. If you want to reach for something, your extremities will reach first; your fingers will lead the way.

4. Allow your fingertips to head toward the object of your desire.

5. That will probably not be enough. So, invite your fingers, then your hand and forearm, and then your upper arm to reach for your goal.

6. If that is not enough, let your shoulder move, or take a step until your fingertips can lead you to your goal.

7. Touch it.

8. Bring it to you. Take in that strong voice, or that sense of confidence, or your long-lost compassion.

9. Hold it with both hands and bring it toward your chest, as you allow it into your heart.

10. Reclaim your wholeness.

DO — To feel satisfied.

Wholeness shows up in every aspect of daily life. It is reflected in our diet, as it is always best to eat as much whole food (unprocessed, in its natural state) as possible. Wholeness shows up in our life energy, including movement *and* stillness. Life sometimes involves moving ahead and plowing on to the next project. Other times, resting, regrouping, and recharging are best. Wholeness shows up in our awareness patterns. Are you aware of the larger universal information? I was, but . . .

The expanded Self—or a mere coincidence of thought?

While writing this book, I took a break and went to the grocery store. I had finished picking out my bunch of kale and was continuing on to find some ginger. As I passed the avocados, my body was strangely drawn to them; something in me said, "Buy some avocados today." But my head and its reasoning jumped in and countered, "You have two avocados at home that will last you the week; you don't need to buy any more now." So I didn't. But my eyes kept looking over at the avocados, continuing this strange attraction. Later that evening, as I was preparing my dinner, I began slicing one of my two avocados. Somehow it had rotted, even though it was not that old. I took the second avocado out and began slicing. It, too, was no good. How did that part of me know that I needed to buy avocados? Some kind of connected wholeness must exist. I wondered to myself: *Is this one way we lose touch with our expanded Self—by not following the intuitions that come through to us?*

18

THE UNIFIED FIELD OF UNIVERSAL LOVE

Congratulations if you have made it this far in this epic journey! Fasten your seat belts a little tighter. The unity that holds our world together is unfathomable and beyond our wildest dreams.

1. THE INVISIBLE AUTHORITY

In Chapter 1, page 1, F.M. Alexander begins his first book, *Man's Supreme Inheritance*, by acknowledging the invisible Authority.

> I should like in passing to point out that the theory and practice of my system are influenced by no particular religion nor school of philosophy, but in one sense may be said to embrace them all. For whatever name we give to the great origin of the universe, in the words of a friend of mine, "We can all of us agree . . . that we mean the same thing, namely, that high power within the soul of man which enables him to will or act or to speak not loosely or wildly, but in subjection to an all-wise and invisible Authority." The name that we give to that Authority will in no way affect the principles which I am about to state.[76]

Religious and spiritual teachings from all over the world recognize this invisible Authority, or oneness. This oneness is the place we never leave. It is the internal organization we see most readily in healthy children and wild animals—the place they cannot leave. No matter what is going on, there is a unity, an underlying connection that links us to ourselves and to everything. The thread of evolution. It's the eternal flame that never goes out, the endless flow of time and space.

2. UNIFIED FLUID BODY

"It is my belief that we carry in our cells, in our tissues, in the very throb of our existence an underlying flow that urges, inspires, flares our nostrils and beats our heart. This encompassing atmosphere of love has its own destiny—perhaps using humans as its messengers, this love has arrived on Earth."[77]

— EMILIE CONRAD

We are conceived in liquid, and our entire structure was formed in liquid. Liquid continues to be the primary physical constituent of which we are made. From your earliest beginnings, your awareness within your fluid human body holds the potential to change the inner landscape of sensation, feelings, and form. If you can be aware of the fluid aspects of your body, you can connect to a primordial aspect of yourself. The fascial system is one such aspect:

> Recent research shows there is a micro-fascial system (a tensegrity structure) within every cell. Inside the cytoskeleton of the cell lay microtubules of fascia that have a hollow core, through which fluid flows. Energy, information and consciousness flow within that fluid. Consciousness flows through every cell of our bodies. The fluid within and around every cell performs the important function of being the transport medium of oxygen, nutrients, chemicals, hormones, toxins, energy and information throughout our entire being, almost instantaneously.[78]

Fluidity provides unity. Cellular intelligence is more than an amalgam of its parts and functions, floating and fluid. Every cell is awake, alive, and self-aware—whether at the microcosm of the cell, the macrocosm of the human being, or the grand macrocosm of the universe. Cells do what other organisms do: They float, they move, they relate, they metabolize, and they make choices. They are full of fluid. They communicate to their own inner environment and to the family of cells to which they belong. Thus, they are individually organized while also working together to create body systems that range in size from the tiniest amoeba to complex, evolved organisms such as humans.

In the human structure, because of the inherent flexibility of muscle and connective tissue, the fluids are able to distribute forces of movement and weight multidirectionally. This fluidity provides many options for movement.

Allow the EX-plorations in this chapter to include venturing into the unknown to experience the unified field of your expanded Self.

EX-PLORATION: FLUIDITY

There is so much fluid inside the human body, your organs and bones are literally floating inside you. Lie down on a comfortable surface and sense your own fluidity. Feel the fluid movement; it may take a few minutes to sense it. Notice what happens to your breath, your perceptions, and your sense of self as you get in touch with this reality. Perhaps think of your favorite body of water, the ocean and its waves, or a placid lake.

Also allow fluidity of your thoughts. Let one thought flow into the next with less lingering. Remember stuck joints = stuck thoughts.

DO   Whenever you feel rigid or constricted.

HUM Journal.
What does *fluid unity* mean to you? Words, a photo, a song?

3. CONSCIOUS ATTENTION—THE SPARK

Many of our daily actions happen in an unconscious manner—how we walk, speak, sit, stand, eat, or communicate, as a few examples. Even what we think is often unconscious. By and large that is convenient. You don't have to think about the route every time you drive to work, or concentrate on the piece of music you have played many times. But when you are unconscious with these actions, you don't get to make decisions about how you will carry them out. And with the piece of music, if you get interrupted midway through, it is harder to know where you are. Bringing conscious attention to activity enlivens it. The Bhagavad Gita mentions "the doctrine of unified action," recommending that you decide what you are going to do, then do it fully and consciously.

When you sit or stand for any reason, the body sustains a type of background muscle activity in order to maintain upright balance. You are not normally aware of this because it is unconscious and automatic, but if you pay attention to the muscular activity in your legs, torso, or arms when you stand, you can feel this work that goes mainly unnoticed. *Bringing conscious attention to this activity gives it the spark.*

As you stand upright, the lengthening that takes place in the head and torso produces the conditions under which this muscular support network can work optimally. When we stand truly upright, with full stature, we experience the feeling of "I am in myself," which is at once stabilizing and elevating. More than one client has exclaimed to me (with a beaming face and an alive body) after working this way, "I feel like I could do anything!" Humans feel safe and supported when they are consciously *in themselves.* Then they can engage socially with their fellow mammals for connection, companionship, love, and sex. *In these attentive, nonoverwhelming moments, the conscious awareness can override the adaptive implicit patterns.*

But, make no mistake about it, when you respond to an overwhelming, uncomfortable stimulus, like loss or injury (real or imagined), the natural poise of the head is disturbed and constriction or collapse will follow. When your heart is broken, you will probably collapse your chest. As physical tension and pain increase, so do mental and emotional pain; and it becomes more difficult to handle life situations. Even simple tasks such as reaching or bending can become a burden when the body's support systems are compromised or lost. The spark is gone.

The vast majority of people are aware of localized muscular discomfort but do not detect the general pattern of tension or the overall bracing as a response to a challenging situation or environment. We often assume that the act of tensing is random and uncontrollable, but in fact, muscular tension follows a predictable and observable course in the wake of pain, misuse, or an adaptive response. When you understand the main elements that trigger and organize it, origins of the tension can be identified, completed, integrated, and repatterned.

You are an active, moving creature, able to respond in the moment to whatever life presents. You don't need to always be moving, but you need to be able to move in response to the environment. You are not meant to be completely relaxed or overly tight. Your embodied self serves a concrete conscious function in support of movement and activity in unison with your intentions. This is your spark.

When you observe from this greater, conscious, unified context, you can identify how this human system-wide supported unity works together to create harmony and a feeling of acceptance or love.

REEDUCATION—THE UNIFIED FIELD INCLUDED IN EDUCATION

A very effective tool for change is to identify what you are doing while you are doing it. Since this learning has not been prioritized in our school systems, it needs to be addressed by your own desire. In school, as you were learning to write, what mattered most was to form the letters perfectly. But what about that poor little crunched-up hand, that rounded back, and the frayed nervous system created in response to you feeling petrified by possibly doing it wrong? Survival depended on those perfect letters, not a well-organized body or a calm nervous system.

People tend to think that physical problems can be addressed by exercise. But in truth, although fitness efforts and body work can sometimes help, *no amount of stretching, strengthening, exercising, or massage can replace your conscious awareness of what you are doing in the moment.* If you go to the gym and work out for one hour and then spend the rest of your day unconscious of your use, then what have you gained? Your knees are still locked and you have little fluidity in movement, and you are still breathing in a very shallow way, limiting your life-force.

The reeducation process can be easier than you might imagine. You are born with conscious awareness. It can be used to make decisions about how you move, and how you react or respond. As you learn to work with the deep-seated emotions, feelings, and physical structures, you have more choice, and less stress. You have a path to regain your human capabilities to socially engage, to triumph, and to have your defensive responses ready at your disposal, to be used *only* when you need them.

That does not mean relaxing. Many people want to eliminate their stress by relaxing. Many tend to relax by collapsing or directing "relaxation" actions to a specific area—like "relax your shoulders," ignoring (again) the totality of which it is a part. What we call relaxation—slumping in front of the TV—usually produces collapse, which impedes the larger expanded structure.

We are all affected by the pressure and stress saturating the socio-economic environment of our world today. Learning to self-regulate and co-regulate can help minimize the damage to our self, our families, and our communities. This requires a practical understanding of your own reactions. This unified mental and physical process can be brought to your conscious awareness during activity.

As part of the reeducation process, you can respond from your conscious awareness at any time and make choices to change your use, your behavior, and more. But what about overwhelm and the implicit memory—and the accompanying patterns that reside in your musculature? The memory that told the amoeba it could not move and that sometimes runs the show? The question is: How to get to that? How do you do self-improvement techniques when your implicit self does not allow it?

Keep in mind that your intention is linked to your implicit memory and partly influenced by it. You are moving through life with behaviors, emotions, and thoughts that your implicit memories, imprinted in your lower brain, are telling you are true—even if they are not. *You cannot think or talk your way out with your higher brain.*

Remember that sensation is the language of the lower brain. The journey *is* the process of observing the sensations that lead to implicit memories, your movements, and your emotional patterns. Any tension pattern is intimately related to how you move, think, and feel; it is not independent or random. It is not a mystery. Or if so, it is a solvable mystery when you consider the unity. You want to look into the bodily sensations, hidden impulses, movement patterns, and protective intent for the unsolved pieces of the puzzle of yourself. Pleasure is there. The nervous system can then change from fixity to flow. And it is this flow that you now bring to conscious awareness and choose as your use.

I want to recap here because this is so important:

> When you get overwhelmed (something awful happened and nobody was there to help you), your body shifts into a fight, flight, or freeze response. Then the lower brain where the autonomic nervous system (ANS) and survival instinct both are based takes control. Even though the upper, cognitive brain and personality keep going, the functions of the ANS can be dysregulated at this time and may not properly reset. The nervous system can have gaps (missing or misinformed skills) reflected in the fascial weave or the daily bodily functions. Our task is to restore nervous system regulation in the lower brain with sensing and movement to get out of freeze, complete incomplete fight/flight defensive responses (including emotion), and restore rhythm, balance, connection, pleasure, and the ability to be in your body—and observe. The order is important. You need to find a non-manipulative, non-doing, non-alpha way to initiate a spontaneous release ("Be With," Support, etc.). Then make the release conscious. This invites the expanded Self.

Whatever someone says or however someone moves will always give a clue to what is going on. The being seems to broadcast what it needs through the body, a somatic narrative. Following the expressions that are present seems to be key. Then it is easier to frame narratives that are outdated because the use has changed. Be present with your thoughts to see if you really believe them. Heal the parts of you that are adaptive and stuck in a role that is no longer useful. Connect to the unity of the universe and worry less about your own isolated story. (A professor friend in a music department had a group of students with injuries from playing. She took them to a poverty-stricken country to help the local population, and their own injuries healed. Service to others has a strange magical power.)

As you bring the new experiences to consciousness, they can change the real estate in your brain, replacing negative input as well as information passed down through generations.

Many of the methods you are exploring in these pages may help: Can You Do Less, *Humanual* Touch, 50-50 Awareness, Be With, Support, Suspension, and Breath. Do an exploration, then notice settling and regulating. Do another and regulate, and another and regulate, etc. Then the nervous system gets in the pattern of pendulating into down-regulation. Habits are strong, but movement interrupts the cycle, and eventually the old neural pathways are deactivated from lack of use. A page is turned in your life.

> **HUM Journal.**
> **Are you aware of the spark of your conscious awareness?**

4. EMBODYING UNITY/NONDUALITY

There are many modern-day practices—both physical and spiritual—that aim at unity or nonduality. But it is not easy to stay in unity, let alone get there, and navigating can be difficult. Adding to the difficulty, our language barely has the words to convey the idea of the "all-encompassing" and its various nuances.

Head, heart, and hands all meet and grow together in the embryonic state. Years ago, I heard Dr. Brian Freeman speak, an in-utero specialist at the University of Adelaide in Australia. He suggested, "Individual systems do not exist. All systems are one event. This event emerges from a unity."

If someone has many illnesses in different parts of the body, there is a tendency to see them as separate, unrelated problems. A careful examination will reveal them to be related. The problem of seeing the body as separate parts is made worse by today's medical diagnoses: Specialists treat a heart problem separate from a kidney problem, but the organs all connect and communicate to one another. They have the same blood, hormones, or chemicals flowing through them. This is similar to Christmas-tree lights: when seen from a distance, they look individual; but when you look closely, you can see they are all connected, wired together.

Taking this concept a bit further, as you now know, muscles, bones, and connective tissue are part of an intricate lattice or web of support for uprightness. This system does not function optimally without a unified field. The muscles function in service to a larger psychophysical system that operates mostly at the unconscious level. To address this, you must not only restore resilience to the system as a whole, you must also learn to stop performing actions in your old habitual way by becoming kinesthetically aware of the adaptive pattern that created the difficulty to begin with.

EX-PLORATION: CAN YOU DO LESS?

Explore the unity or nonduality of matching your intention, muscular effort, and outcome. Can you stand, sit, or perform any activity with less effort? You can apply the question of "Can I do less?" to any activity; let's take a look. Start texting a message to a friend. Ask yourself, "Can I do less?" Ask again, "Can I do less?" Keep asking until you end up with only the effort necessary to accomplish the task. As you are sitting reading this book, are your shoulders and/or legs tensing? Do you need that tension to read? Are you trying to grasp the ideas? Can you sit with less effort and still read? Sometimes I run into former students, many years after I've worked with them, and they remember and joke with me about "Can I do less?"

> **DO** Whenever you notice that you are using more effort than the task requires.

Modern life is so full of "shoulds" and imperatives that many people are locked in constrictive "doing" patterns. *Humanual* helps people recognize that they have these habitual patterns, charged with unconscious commitment and excess tension. Once these patterns are brought to awareness, deep change can occur on many levels, as the life-force resumes its natural flow. When I work with singers at the Opera Institute, they tell me that when they do less, they are free and sing better. They just sing, which comes from unity, one "me" singing—instead of *trying* to sing, which brings in duality, "me" efforting to be something else. After all, you can only sing as well as you can sing; trying does not help. It only constricts.

5. HOW DOES THE FEELING OF UNITY HAPPEN?

As a teenage seeker, I read about the teachings that said we are all one and unified with everything, but that was not my daily experience. It was years later that I remember actually feeling one with everything.

It was very early morning at an ashram in New York State. We used to go to the hall at 4:00 a.m. Being there early—hours early—ideally meant getting a good seat, close to the Master. I remember this particular morning as cold and dark, and I needed to go to the bathroom. I had to walk through the woods, and I remember the trees and tree roots coming up from the ground. The moonlight was shining at different angles on the ground. As I walked carefully, my body adjusting to the uneven ground, I felt pure exhilaration fueled by the stars, the moonlit sky, the cold, and the soon-arriving dawning light, but also the elation that can come from being in the presence of an enlightened Master.

As all of that ran through me, all of a sudden everything looked like it had something that was the same. That meant that I felt connected to everything, and everything was connected to itself and to me, and to what was around. It was a very specific feeling, impression, and movement. In that moment, I was completely one with the surroundings; there were no separate woods to *walk through*, there was only the unity. The experience was noticeably different from me watching where I was walking and deciding how to navigate through.

In that moment, there was no separation between me and anybody else, and no separation between anything in the environment and everything else in the environment. I noted the experience very clearly as different from my everyday reality.

I wondered if this was a gift I received because I had gotten up at 3:00 a.m. to wait in line to receive meditation guidance, or if it was just an accident. I also wondered if it would ever happen again. Did I slip into another layer of reality because I was too tired to stay present? Did I do it? Or did it happen to me? If so, *how* did it happen to me? And how could I repeat it? Why in that moment? On my very mundane journey, I experienced oneness. How did all those energies converge to allow me that? I wondered.

Finding Oneness at Uluru

In 2015, after my book *The Actor's Secret* came out, I went on a tour around the world, something I had wanted to do since I was a child and saw the movie *Around the World in Eighty Days*. The idea of circumventing the entire globe was thrilling to me. My desire had to do with my search for wholeness. There was something about traveling around and enveloping the planet that seemed part of my earthly journey.

I visited many interesting and lovely places. One of the most incredible sights was Uluru, the sacred home of the indigenous people in Australia. Uluru is a huge red rock in the middle of the desert. I wrote in my journal:

> As I looked at and walked around Uluru, I felt like everything was one. I was seeing everything as one, especially me and Uluru, the large red rock. There was the air, the land, and the sky with no extra space. All was one unit. It was very light with no heavy feelings or parts.

There were stories of people who were able to climb up the steep rocks. That seemed impossible, but I understood that if people felt this lightness, the kind of lightness I was feeling, they could climb up with wings on their feet.

As light as a feather, there was a deep glow of golden sparkle inside me that connected to Uluru. Sometimes there was wind blowing, and I was being pushed along. Other times it seemed like I was still and that Uluru was moving.

One day it was very hot, 130 degrees Fahrenheit. I felt like my insides went through the washing machine. I felt completely empty. I was not really thinking about anything. My hands glowed with golden light. I felt my ears change pressure and my head open. As I looked up at the high rocks, I felt my whole body lift and lose its weight, both physically and mentally. It was kind of like "giving the 'I' away."

130 degrees Fahrenheit at Uluru.

I walked near and upon the massive rock in my oneness bubble. It felt as if I were walking in another level of consciousness, or another world, that the others around me did not seem to care or know about. I wanted to scream to people from the top of Uluru to stop their "idle chatter" and pay attention to this vast, amazing oneness that encompasses everything, that actually *is* everything and nothing at the same time. Then I realized the oneness included all kinds of people, whether they paid attention or not. They too were a part of this oneness. My heart was glowing from inside me and Uluru, "the golden red gift of glow." (I'm quoting from my journal.)

6. ALIVENESS IN LOVE

Traveling around the world, I felt and experienced how things are different in different places. Yet they are all connected. I can sometimes notice the consciousness of the oneness. It surrounds the entire world. I hold it and it holds me, along with everything in it. All connected and all one, though nothing is fixed and everything is fluid, changing rapidly. Universal love is feeling the oneness or the aliveness in everything, both animate and inanimate. Tiny molecules or bubbles flow through all, making everything alive and effervescent. The unified field of love.

When I returned home from Australia and started to teach, I realized that I facilitate people entering into other spaces, spaces unknown. It is a space of wholeness, of oneness, of lightness, a place of freedom from habit. It is a sacred space. With one student, I sensed no connection to the ground; I had her bring attention to her feet, and she started to cry—just from the realization of her connection to the Earth. It was the beauty of this relationship for all beings in each moment that I honored at Uluru.

> *HUM Journal.*
> **Can you experience the unified field of love,**
> **the spark of love of your expanded Self?**

EX-PLORATION: EXPERIENCE THE UNIFIED FIELD™

Smile and then allow your tongue to slide back along the roof of your mouth to your soft palate. Pass the hard surface, and it will turn soft. Keep your tongue on the soft palate.

Notice the effect on your whole body.

Your soft palate is right in front of the top of your spine, where your spine meets your head. It's the point from where your head moves.

Connect to that.

As you touch your soft palate with your tongue, sensing the top of your spine, you stimulate the tubes that go to your ears. Feel the widening in your head, out to your ears from the center. If you can't feel it, imagine and/or visualize it, as your eyes come on board.

Then from the ear tubes, connect down to your suspended larynx, and your voice.

Your larynx connects to your shoulders and out to your fingertips to free your arms to reach for connection and move into life.

As your shoulders open, your breathing rhythm begins its sacred tune.

Your breath then travels down your torso, caressing all your internal organs before it drops down and invites your pelvis to unlock and join the movement.

As your pelvis undulates very slightly back and forth, your legs are awakened to their role as connecting you to the ground, to your support. Recognize that it is this connection that will move you forward into the life you want.

As you receive your support...

Your whole system springs, bounces back up to the top of your spine, your head, and your soft palate. From here, as you inhabit yourself, you look around the room. Now, there is a new moment as you watch the ever-changing universe and realize that you and the universe are one unified field. The space inside you meets the space outside. And perhaps you smile again.

Meeting the unified field.

Exploring the space of the higher unified field
with a partner.

Exploring the space of the lower unified field
with a partner.

7. FREQUENCIES OF ONENESS IN THE EXPANDED SELF

Scientist Rupert Sheldrake developed a hypothesis called *morphic resonance*. Simply put, it says, "Memory is inherent in nature" and that "natural systems, such as pigeons, orchid plants, or molecules, inherit a collective memory from all previous things of their kind."[79] Thus, if a pigeon learned something in one part of the world, this information would be available to offspring of pigeons in other parts of the world, because of this oneness.

I was explaining this theory to my training group one day, and one of the students gave the example that dogs know when their owners are coming home. Two minutes after she said that, the dog downstairs started to bark. We all smiled in awe and thanks for the demonstration.

The oneness also shows up as a vision or angelic presence in the intensity of a life-changing or spiritual experience. If your survival is threatened by a medical intervention or some other trauma and you think you are going to die, then you can have the experience of global electricity down a passageway that leads to or ends up in oneness.

The near-death experience lets you see the oneness of all life. Neurosurgeon and author of *Proof of Heaven*, Dr. Eben Alexander, fell into a meningitis-induced coma and nearly died. During his seven-day ordeal, Dr. Alexander had a near-death experience and an encounter with what we call heaven. He felt he was one with everything in the universe. Life was beautiful, magnificent, and full of light and love.[80] *Humanual* teaches us that this experience is available to all human beings through awareness and training. It is your birthright. And you don't need the extreme of a near-death experience.

Astronauts looking back at Earth saw its oneness. In the images from space, Earth looks like a big balloon with a thin crust upon which we live. The air or gases in that balloon are pushing outward, and we feel that as support. We all get support from the same place—the centrifugal force from the spinning of Earth is the "up" pressure from the ground. We are moved by the same ground no matter where we live.

An older African American jazz dancer (who danced in a musical show when esteemed musician Papa Joe Jones played drums) said that she did not so much listen to the music as feel the floor vibrate as he played the drums; that is the beat she moved to.

The meeting of the forces down from heaven, and up from Earth (support and suspension), that breathe and spiral out to everything is where consciousness, or the "God" principle, exists—call it Source, Self, or Invisible Authority. Something about the exquisite, delicate balance feels so right—a blueprint of innate organization that can hold all life experiences. It must be that oneness that forms the weave of human life—to *everything*, from the mundane event of food shopping to the sublime experiences of listening to beautiful music or climbing Mt. Everest.

You can become aware of the synchronicities, the odd coincidences, the chance meetings that seem to take place in some higher realm of existence. How did I hear the frequencies of the singer at Berklee College of Music in that moment, prior to her actually singing? If we live only in this rarefied aspect of life, we do not have the bottom part of life, the grit, the messiness, or even the connection to the ground. On the other hand, if we only live with and recognize the crude, aggressive, base, and coarse nature of human life, we miss the more etheric, soft-focus, subtle cues.

The *Humanual* way teaches a connection to both: sometimes you need healthy aggression, but sometimes you need acceptance and surrender. You practice through the EX-plorations and EX-ercises: you witness changes in awareness and consciousness, expressive emotions, healing of trauma; and, most of all, you witness your direct experience. With the combination of the built-in order of the universe (your inherent internal organization) and the knowledge of evolution, you can arrive at being one with life and love on your journey to your expanded Self.

Do you now find yourself speaking with just the appropriate words more often? Or moving with only the amount of energy needed to do the task, and not pulled off of your support? Are you more aligned with your genuine dreams and your authentic self? I hope so.

This unity of the expanded Self drives evolution with compassion and love for others. Love is not always easy. Difficult experiences are not eliminated. But they are not the whole picture. They are only part of your experience. As you train yourself to be a large enough container to hold your vast array of emotion and experiences, then being connected with others and everything in the universe can be your experience, sometimes. This love is the training for all human life on the planet. That is true humanness—the teachings of *Humanual*.

Stephen Porges says it this way, "The biological imperative is to survive, and that is to connect with others. If you hurt, humiliate, isolate, bully or marginalize to gain power over someone, you are not connecting. You cannot be human. It violates the biological imperative of what it is to be human: what we evolved to be, a connected species. You are injuring the species. It is neurobiologically not sustainable. A biological imperative that cannot be sustained. Being human is very powerful."[81]

The story I shared in Chapter 2 about the giant sea turtle surfacing through a ring floating in the sea is not merely an amusing little fable. Let it remind you that human life is precious. There are many ways you can appreciate, practice, and celebrate your unique humanness on Earth—why you are here. The expanded Self is yours. The universe is waiting for you to take your higher and more conscious place in it. There will be no thunderous applause, as the journey of human growth and potential is a very private moment. But you can feel the afterglow of your expanded Self, like this young woman did. Here is her moment:

> I was twelve (after a year and a half of playing the cello) when I told my parents that I wanted to play music for life. They laughed and said, "You don't have to decide so soon, as you will probably change your mind." Not wanting to give in, I reasoned, "Everybody seems to be unhappy about going to work; but if I become a musician and earn my living by playing, I would want to go to work every single day!" This episode came to my mind while I was playing in Betsy's class for my final. I had not thought of it in years. It was a very emotional experience, one that I hadn't ever encountered. I kept thinking after class: What was that? Why did my heart pump so vigorously? When I found the answer, my tears were already running down my face. I thought I was enjoying what I am doing every day, and I believe I am, on some levels; but I realized that I had lost my innermost connection with the music—its rawest form—the form that doesn't have to be analyzed. I wanted to sing, with my voice, with my cello.

FINAL THOUGHTS:
THE QUANTUM UNIVERSE

"Open your imagination, suspend past disappointments and take a provocative journey into creative capacities you never knew you had. We have been using a small portion of our magnificent gifts and forget all too often, that we were born to accomplish miracles."[82]

— JEAN HOUSTON, PhD

If we accept the expansive structure of the body and extend it to its smallest version of biotensegrity, then what would stop us from extending it to the largest version—the universe? Can you imagine a universe in which everything is contracting and expanding and connected to everything else, including you? As we explore this unifying thread, we come to a world of quantum ideas—a world in which many levels of reality are possible for explaining the nature and behavior of matter and energy in an atomic and subatomic way. This is the modern study of quantum physics or quantum mechanics.

At the quantum level, the universe births stars. We birth humans. We can be partners in creation, with consciousness as the organizing principle. This is the emerging evolutionary development for humankind. We have evolved from tribal consciousness, before industrialization, and we are moving toward a cosmic consciousness that includes many forms of reality, or consciousness. Wrote William James (who was among the pioneers of this type of thought for laypeople): "Our ordinary waking consciousness is but one form of consciousness. All around us lay infinite worlds, separated only by the thinnest of veils."[83]

Ancient spiritual practices and beliefs are very similar to these quantum ideas. Many ancient people believed that the great universe was all connected, and that our thinking creates the universe and our reality. Shift the story and you shift reality. William James again: "Human beings, by changing the inner attitudes of their minds, can change the outer aspects of their lives."[84]

We looked at mirror neurons for duplicating present action in Chapter 14. There are also mirror neurons for touch. If somebody touches my hand, neurons fire in the somatosensory cortex, in the sensory region of my brain. But the same neurons, in some cases, will fire when I simply watch another person being touched. In essence, I am empathizing with the other person who is being touched. But there is a feedback signal that vetoes the signal of the mirror neuron, preventing me from consciously experiencing that touch. So, I empathize but do not actually feel the physical touch. But . . . !

Neuroscientist Vilayanur Ramachandran explains universal connectedness and outlines the fascinating functions of mirror neurons in his 2009 TEDIndia talk. "If you anesthetize my arm, so you put an injection into my arm, anesthetize the brachial plexus, so the arm is numb, and there is no sensation coming in, if I now watch you being touched, I literally feel it in my hand. In other words, you have dissolved the barrier between you and other human beings," says Ramachandran.

This is not an abstract metaphorical concept. All that is separating you from the other person is your skin. Remove the feeling in the skin, and you experience that person's touch in your mind. Eastern philosophy says that there is no real independent self, apart from other human beings. No barrier. You are connected by your neurons. There is a whole chain of neurons in you "talking to" the neurons in another person. There is no real distinction of your consciousness from somebody else's consciousness. This is not wishful, New Age thinking—it emerges from understanding basic neuroscience. Dr. Daniel Siegel, psychiatrist and educator, coined the term MWE ("Me" + "We") to include myself with others and express this concept.

The universe does not exist separate from our self: we dream up the universe as the universe dreams up us. What we see in our world is simply what the universe is reflecting back to us. But, we are partners in what gets dreamed up. The self has the power in how we view things.

By nature, the Self is unbounded. The vast majority of people have not begun to explore the deepest possibilities of their human creativity. Most are caught up in self-limiting patterns. When we look at the creative discoveries of Leonardo da Vinci, we see that his inventions were hundreds of years ahead of his time. How did his mind enter the union with the great matrix-mind? How did he find these entry points into the larger realms of the universe?

Some say our highest creativity occurs in altered states of consciousness. But because consciousness is changing all the time, all states must be altered states. There is no normal. The universe changes and regenerates every nanosecond.

Quantum reality says time past, future, and present are all one. All events exist concurrently. All points are connected to all others, just like the hologram and tensegrity. Could this account for the odd coincidences, the synchronicities that no one can explain? Like my impulse to buy more avocados when I knew I had two at home?

> *"Time present and time past,*
> *Are both perhaps present in time future,*
> *And time future contained in time past."*
> — T.S. ELIOT, *Four Quartets*

Jean Houston met Albert Einstein when she was in grade school. He came to speak to her class. One young boy asked Einstein, "How can I get to be as intelligent as you?" Einstein answered, "Read fairy tales." His answer to the young boy was meant to stimulate the young boy's imagination. One of Einstein's notable quotes is, "Logic will get you from A to Z; imagination will get you everywhere."

We need evolutionary practices that enhance rather than destroy this planet. We need to go to the source of imaginative creativity itself—sometimes called the great matrix, including male and female, science and spirituality—where all duality connects to oneness, for the benefit of all. Not just a chosen few.

As the astronauts came back toward Earth from outer space, they saw one big beautiful Earth, blue, green, and luminous. As they looked, they realized "what we could be"—the amazing potential of conscious life on our planet. Consciousness is central to the nature of reality and brings us to the highest principles.

What will future life on planet Earth look like? Is it going to be this higher, unified, connected consciousness for humans, or is it going to be robots replacing all human attributes and characteristics?

I vote for HU-man-UAL or HU-wo-man-UAL.

Postscript: I have been writing this book for fifteen years, and *HUMANUAL* emerges just as the global pandemic engulfs the world. Now more than ever, we want to understand what it is to be truly human and embrace our unity.

BIBLIOGRAPHY

Alexander, Eben, III. *Proof of Heaven: A Neurosurgeon's Journey into the Afterlife*. New York: Simon & Schuster, 2012.

Alexander, F. Matthias. *Constructive Conscious Control of the Individual*. New York: E.P. Dutton, 1923.
———. *Man's Supreme Inheritance*. New York: E.P. Dutton, 1910.
———. *The Universal Constant in Living*. New York: E.P. Dutton, 1941.
———. *The Use of Self*. New York: E.P. Dutton, 1932.

Barnes, John F., PT, LMT. "Therapeutic Insight: The Myofascial Release Perspective—A Sea of Information," *Massage Magazine*, April 5, 2011.

Bull, Nina. *Attitude Theory of Emotion*. New York: Johnson reprint, 1951.

Dart, Raymond. *Articles on Skill and Poise and the F.M. Alexander Technique*. London: STAT Books, 1996. From chapter titled "An Anatomist's Tribute."

Felitti, V.J., R.F. Anda, D. Nordenberg, D.F. Williamson, A.M. Spitz, V. Edwards, M.P. Koss, and J.S. Marks. "Relationship of Childhood Abuse and Household Dysfunction to Many of the Leading Causes of Death in Adults: The Adverse Childhood Experiences (ACE) Study." *NIH American Journal of Preventive Medicine*, Vol. 14, No. 4 (May 1998), pp. 245–258.

Fuller, Richard Buckminster. *Synergetics: Explorations in the Geometry of Thinking*. New York: Macmillan Pub. Co., 1982, p. 372.

Garlick, David. Lecture: "The Lost Sixth Sense: A Medical Scientist Looks at the Alexander Technique." Kensington, Australia: University of New South Wales, 1990.

Gershon, Dr. Michael D. *The Second Brain: A Groundbreaking New Understanding of Nervous Disorders of the Stomach and Intestines (Your Gut Has a Mind of Its Own)*. New York: Harper Paperbacks, Harper Perennial edition, 1999.

Glenville, Marilyn, PhD. *Fat Around the Middle*. London: Kyle Cathie Limited, 2006, p. 12.

Gorman, David. *The Body Moveable*. London: self-published, 1981.

Hansen, Rick. *Just One Thing* (series of newsletters), "Be the Body," 2018.

Ingber, Donald. "The Architecture of Life." *Scientific American* magazine, January 1998.

Ingber, Donald. "Cellular Tensegrity: Defining New Rules of Biological Design That Govern the Cytoskeleton." *Journal of Cell Science* 104 (1993), p. 617.

Ingber, Donald, Ning Wang, and Dimitrije Stamenović. "Tensegrity, Cellular Biophysics, and the Mechanics of Living Systems." https://www.ncbi.nlm.nih.gov/pubmed/24695087.

Jones, Frank Pierce. *Body Awareness in Action: A Study of the Alexander Technique*. New York: Schocken Books, 1976. Reprinted as *Freedom to Change*. London: Mouritz, 1997.

Levine, Peter. *In an Unspoken Voice*. Berkeley, CA: North Atlantic Books, 2010.
———. *Waking the Tiger*. Berkeley, CA: North Atlantic Books, 1997.

Levine, Stephen, and Danièle-Claude Martin. "Biotensegrity: The Mechanics of Fascia" in *Fascia: The Tensional Network of the Human Body*, ed. Schleip, Findly, Chaitow, and Huijing. London: Churchill Livingstone, 2012.

Llinas, Rodolfo. *I of the Vortex, From Neurons to Self*. Cambridge, MA: MIT Press, 2001.

Maisel, Edward. *The Resurrection of the Body: The Essential Writings of F. Matthias Alexander*. New York: University Books, 1989. Originally published by Dell, 1969.

Maté, Gabor. *When the Body Says NO: Exploring the Stress-Disease Connection*. Canada: Alfred A. Knopf, 2003.
———. *In the Realm of Hungry Ghosts: Close Encounters with Addiction*. Canada: Alfred A. Knopf, 2008.

Pert, Candace. *Molecules of Emotion: The Science Behind Mind-Body Medicine.* New York: Simon & Schuster, 1997, p. 137.

Porges, Stephen. *The Polyvagal Theory: Neurophysiological Foundations of Emotions, Attachment, Communication, and Self-Regulation.* New York: W. W. Norton, 2011.

Sarno, John. Quoting *New England Journal of Medicine,* July 14, 1994. Dr. Sarno methodology lecture, YouTube.

Sherrington, Sir Charles. *The Integrative Action of the Nervous System.* New Haven, CT: Yale University Press, 1961.

Stern, Jack, neuroscientist. Lecture presented to the International Congress of Alexander Technique, Ireland, 2015.

Stough, Carl. *Breathing: The Source of Life.* DVD video. New York: Stough Institute, 1996.
———. *Dr. Breath.* New York: Stough Institute, 1970.

Talbot, Michael. *The Holographic Universe.* New York: HarperPerennial, 1992.

Tinbergen, Nicolas. "Ethology and Stress Disease." Science 185 (1974).

van der Kolk, Bessel. *The Body Keeps the Score.* New York: Penguin Books, 2015.

Wiesel, T. "Postnatal development of the visual cortex and the influence of environment," *Nature,* Vol. 299, No. 5884 (1982), pp. 583–591. Bibcode:1982Natur.299..583W. doi:10.1038/299583a0. PMID 6811951.

ENDNOTES

1   Bessel van der Kolk, *The Body Keeps the Score* (New York: Penguin Books, 2015), p. 58.

2   Donald Hoffman, cognitive scientist. Lecture, "Can AI Feel Real Love?" Science and Nonduality Conference 2019. San Jose, CA.

3   F. Matthias Alexander, *Constructive Conscious Control of the Individual* (New York: E.P. Dutton, 1923).

4   A biofield is the field of energy and information that surrounds and interpenetrates the human body, biofieldtuning.com.

5   *The Guardian,* "Study of Holocaust Survivor Finds Trauma Passed on to Children's Genes," Helen Thompson, August 2015.

6   Baby center.com/brain.

7   Canadian physician and addiction specialist Gabor Maté tells the story of this experiment in his YouTube video "When the Body Says NO."

8   Relationship Alive podcast.

9   T. Wiesel, "Postnatal development of the visual cortex and the influence of environment," *Nature,* Vol. 299, No. 5884 (1982), pp. 583–591. doi:10.1038/299583a0. PMID 6811951.

10 Gabor Maté, "When the Body Says NO," YouTube video, 2012.

11 D.W. Winnicott, *Collected Papers: Through Paediatrics to Psycho-Analysis* (London: The Hogarth Press, 1958/1982).

12 Lisbeth Marcher and colleagues, Bodynamic Analysis, bodynamicusa.com.

13 Temma Ehrenfeld, "Does Botox blunt emotions?" *Psychology Today* magazine (February 2013).

14 Kelly McGonigal, "Incites at the Edge" Series. Boulder, CO: Sounds True, 2018.

15 Neuroscientist Dr. Stephen Porges is "Distinguished University Scientist" at the Kinsey Institute of Indiana University, and professor in the department of psychiatry at the University of North Carolina in Chapel Hill. His theory of the vagus nerve was first published in 1995 in the journal *Psychophysiology* and later in 2011 as a book (see bibliography): Stephen Porges, "Orienting in a Defensive World: Mammalian Modifications of our Evolutionary Heritage. A Polyvagal Theory," *Psychophysiology,* Vol. 32 (1995), pp. 301–318.

16 Lecture. Psychotherapy Networker Conference, 2017, Washington DC.

17 This researcher was Ruth Lanius, MD, PhD, professor of psychiatry and director of the PTSD research unit at the University of Western Ontario.

18 Cape Cod Institute, August 2016. "Social connectedness as a biological imperative – understanding trauma through the lens of polyvagal theory."

19 Dan Siegal, Psychotherapy Networker Conference, 2017, Washington, DC.

20 See, for example, Peter A. Levine, *In an Unspoken Voice* (Berkeley, CA: North Atlantic Books, 2010) and *Waking the Tiger* (Berkeley, CA: North Atlantic Books, 1997).

21 Rick Hansen, *Just One Thing* (series of newsletters), "Be the Body" (he continues to publish the newsletter).

22 V.J. Felitti, R.F. Anda, D. Nordenberg, D.F. Williamson, A.M. Spitz, V. Edwards, M.P. Koss, and J.S. Marks, "Relationship of Childhood Abuse and Household Dysfunction to Many of the Leading Causes of Death in Adults: The Adverse Childhood Experiences (ACE) Study." *NIH American Journal of Preventive Medicine,* Vol. 14, No. 4 (May 1998), pp. 245–258. The study at Kaiser Permanente was headed by Dr. Vincent J. Felitti, renowned physician and researcher, and one of the world's foremost experts on childhood trauma.

23 Hans Selye, *Stress, Shock, and Adaptation in the Twentieth Century* (Rochester, NY: University of Rochester Press, 2014). See also Mark Jackson, "Evaluating the Role of Hans Selye," Chapter 1 in *The Modern History of Stress.*

24 Gabor Maté, "In the Realm of Hungry Ghosts," YouTube video, 2011.

25 Mayo Clinic website, "Chronic Stress Puts Your Health at Risk" (corroborating Gabor Maté's info), 2016.

26 Marilyn Glenville, PhD, *Fat Around the Middle* (London: Kyle Cathie Limited, 2006), p. 12.

27 I highly recommend Somatic Experiencing® Therapy (traumahealing.org) or Internal Family Systems (https://www.selfleadership.org/).

28 Bessel van der Kolk, Psychotherapy Networker Conference, Washington, DC, 2017.

29 Daniel J. Lewis, MPH, MA. "Nina Bull: The Work, Life and Legacy of a Somatic Pioneer," dissertation. Accepted September 2012.

30 F. Matthias Alexander, *The Universal Constant in Living* (New York: E.P. Dutton, 1941), p. 53.

31 F.M. Alexander quoted in Frank Pierce Jones, *Body Awareness in Action: A Study of the Alexander Technique* (New York: Schocken Books, 1976). Reprinted as *Freedom to Change* (London: Mouritz, 1997), p. 3.

32 F. Matthias Alexander, *The Universal Constant in Living* (New York: E.P. Dutton, 1941), p. 110.

33 Sigmund Freud quoted by Dr. Peter Levine in many master classes, 2010–2018.

34 Inspired by the writings of David Gorman.

35 Sir Charles Sherrington, *The Integrative Action of the Nervous System* (New Haven, CT: Yale University Press, 1961), pp. 299–302.

36 Lecture by Jack Stern, neuroscientist, at the International Congress of Alexander Technique, Ireland, 2015.

37 David Garlick, lecture, "The Lost Sixth Sense: A Medical Scientist Looks at the Alexander Technique" (Kensington, Australia: University of New South Wales, 1990).

38 Raymond Dart, *Articles on Skill and Poise and the F.M. Alexander Technique* (London: STAT Books, 1996), from chapter titled "An Anatomist's Tribute" (xeroxed pages with no numbers).

39 NASA IMAGE satellite, "Ask the Space Scientist" Archive, https://image.gsfc.nasa.gov/poetry/ask/a11511.html.

40 Donald Ingber and Misia Landau, "Tensegrity at Work," *Scholarpedia*, Vol. 7, No. 2 (2012), p. 8344.

41 This is not a direct quote. I'm paraphrasing from Donald Ingber, Ning Wang, and Dimitrije Stamenovi, "Tensegrity, Cellular Biophysics, and the Mechanics of Living Systems," journal article (see bibliography).

42 Candace Pert, *Molecules of Emotion: The Science Behind Mind-Body Medicine* (New York: Simon & Schuster, 1997), p. 137.

43 Donald Ingber, Dartmouth Medical School, class lecture, June 13, 2009, "Tales of Discovery From a Life Without Borders."

44 Stephen Levin, biotensegrity.com/about.

45 Stephen Levin, biotensegrity.com/about.

46 Frank Pierce Jones, *Body Awareness in Action: A Study of the Alexander Technique* (New York: Schocken Books, 1976). Reprinted as *Freedom to Change* (London: Mouritz, 1997), p. 63.

47 F.M. Alexander, *Articles and Lectures* (London: Mouritz, 1995), p. 194.

48 Stephen M. Levin and Danièle-Claude Martin, "Biotensegrity: The Mechanics of Fascia" in *Fascia: The Tensional Network of the Human Body*, ed. Schleip, Findly, Chaitow, and Huijing (London: Churchill Livingstone, 2012), pp. 137–142.

49 Raymond Dart, *Articles on Skill and Poise and the F.M. Alexander Technique* (London: STAT Books, 1996), from chapter titled "An Anatomist's Tribute" (xeroxed pages with no numbers).

50 Dr. Jordan Peterson, "Twelve Rules for Life: An Antidote to Chaos," YouTube video, 2018.

51 Rodolfo Llinas, *I of the Vortex, From Neurons to Self* (Cambridge, MA: MIT Press, 2001), p. 216.

52 Carl Stough, *Dr. Breath* (New York: Stough Institute, 1970), p. 210.

53 Sarno, *New England Journal of Medicine*, July 14, 1994. Dr. Sarno methodology lecture, YouTube. 23 minutes.

54 Lecture, Cape Cod Institute, August 2016. "Social Connectedness as a Biological Imperative: Understanding Trauma through the Lens of Polyvagal Theory."

55 Jaak Panksepp, "Behavioural Brain Research" in *Affective Neuroscience: The Foundations of Human and Animal Emotions* (New York: Oxford University Press, 2004).

56 F.M. Alexander, *Man's Supreme Inheritance* (London: Mouritz, 1996), p. 158.

57 Vilayanur Ramachandran, "The Neurons That Shaped Civilization," TED TALK, January 7, 2010.

58 Richard Rohr, *Simplicity* (New York: Crossroad, 1992), p. 23.

59 Meister Eckhart, Institute for Mystical Experience, Research and Education (IMERE) website, 2015.

60 Carl Gustav Jung, from his essay "The Philosophical Tree," paragraph 335 (originally published 1945) in *Alchemical Studies, Collected Works, Vol. 13,* translated by R.F.C. Hull (Princeton, NJ: Princeton University Press, 1967), p. 265.

61 Thomas Huber, lecture, Cambridge, MA, 2015.

62 Sir Charles Sherrington, *The Integrative Action of the Nervous System,* 2nd edition (New Haven, CT: Yale University Press, 1961), p. xvi.

63 Meister Eckhart quoted at meditation retreat, Center for Action and Contemplation, 1995.

64 Nisargadatta Maharaj, *I Am That* (Mumbai, India: Chetana Publications, 1973), p. 242.

65 Nisargadatta Maharaj, *I Am That* (Mumbai, India: Chetana Publications, 1973), p. 93.

66 More detailed benefits include: an increase in the neuronal cell bodies and synapses in the:

   1. Insula—which handles interoception, the sense of your own body and general self-awareness.

   2. Hippocampus—which plays a key role in personal recollections, visual-spatial memory, and the establishment of context of events.

   3. Prefrontal cortex—which supports the executive functions, knowledge, self-control, and guided attention.

   Meditation can also calm down the amygdala and reduce production of stress hormones such as cortisol. Regular meditation has been found to:

   4. Increase activation in the left prefrontal cortex, which lifts mood.

   5. Increase the power and reach of very fast, gamma-range brainwaves, which promote learning and, perhaps, a sense of integration in awareness.

   6. In a three-month retreat, meditation was found to preserve the length of telomeres, the caps at the ends of DNA molecules; longer telomeres are associated with fewer age-related diseases.

   7. Reduce cortical thinning due to aging in the insula. (1–7 from Media.rickhanson.net).

67 William James on "Attention and the Road to Mastery," enPSYBLOG 1879–1899 writings.

68 https://www.selfleadership.org/.

69 Carl Gustav Jung quoted in Murray Stein, *Jung on Christianity* (Princeton, NJ: Princeton University Press, 1999), p. 184.

70 Stephen M. Levin and Danièle-Claude Martin, "Biotensegrity: The Mechanics of Fascia" in *Fascia: The Tensional Network of the Human Body,* eds. Schleip, Findly, Chaitow, and Huijing (London: Churchill Livingstone, 2012), pp. 137–142.

71 Rolef Ben-Shahar, "Jung & Douglas, 1931–35," *Somatic Psychotherapy Today,* September 9, 2016.

72 Rodolfo Llinas, *I of the Vortex: From Neurons to Self* (Cambridge, MA: MIT Press, 2001), reprint edition, p. 35.

73 Llinas, p. 31.

74 Coleman Barks, *The Essential Rumi,* used with permission.

75 Sheila Weller, *Next Tribe—Age Boldly,* online magazine.

76 F.M. Alexander, *Man's Supreme Inheritance* (New York: E.P. Dutton, 1910), p. 1.

77 Emilie Conrad, in *New Dimensions in Psychotherapy,* ed. Nick Totton (England: Open University Press, 2005), p. 143.

78 John F. Barnes, PT, LMT, "Therapeutic Insight: The Myofascial Release Perspective—A Sea of Information," *Massage Magazine,* April 2011.

79 Rupert Sheldrake, lecture, Boston, 1990.

80 Dr. Eben Alexander, III. *Proof of Heaven: A Neurosurgeon's Journey into the Afterlife* (New York: Simon & Schuster, 2012). Oprah Winfrey interview.

81 Dr. Stephen Porges, "The Neuroscience of Polarization," podcast (part 2 of 4), 2019.

82 Jean Houston, lecture, 2017, Milton Erickson Conference, Anaheim, CA.

83 William James quoted in Rockey Robbins, PhD, and Ji Y. Hong, PhD, "Building Bridges between Spirituality and Psychology: An Indigenous Healer's Teachings about Befriending the Self," *The Journal of Transpersonal Psychology,* Vol. 45, No. 2 (2013), pp. 172–198.

84 Ibid.

ACKNOWLEDGMENTS

Thank you to:

Nina Ryan and Toni Burbank for initial guidance, and Lynn Komlenic for early editing and clarifying. Kathy Glass for trimming, editing, and helping me in many ways to shape the manuscript. Chris Ouellette for the accurate and exquisite drawings. Andrew Brilliant for capturing the wonderful moments in all the stunning studio photos. Chia Messina for the striking author photo. Models Harry Hobbs, Seth Hill, Desiré Graham, Siobhan Carrol, Brant Carter, and Subaiou Zhang. And the little ones: Horace, Axel, and Vaughn. *Waterside Productions:* Bill Gladstone for taking me on; Josh Freel, editor and publishing coordinator; Jill Kramer for her astute proofreading; and Christy Salinas for elegantly designing the book and its beautiful cover.

Humanual is a collection of ideas and information from many fields of study that have long fascinated me. The material is drawn from varied sources and includes many concepts that I put together in my own unique way. Those who have influenced my body, mind, and spirit include the following:

To Dr. Peter A. Levine for his creation of a healing trauma model; and for his role as my teacher, mentor, and colleague for twenty years. Dr. Stephen Porges for his Polyvagal Theory and for living his teachings. Dr. Gabor Maté for his deep commonsense brilliance. Carl Stough for his spot-on discoveries around breath. F. M. Alexander for connecting the unity of body and mind back in 1890. Dr. Richard Schwartz for his wonderful creation of the Internal Family Systems model. Dr. Bessel van der Kolk for his unending research on trauma. Rika Cohen for training me into my body. Frances Cott for teaching me how we move. Tommy Thompson for giving me a direct experience of human lightness. Gisela Rohmert for letting me hear the depth of the human voice. David Gorman for understanding the human body like nobody else.

To my many meditation teachers, and spiritual and ancestral guides, who gift me with down-to-earth practices, otherworldly dreams, and intuitions that grace my path.

To my friends, family, and colleagues for support and encouragement, especially Melissa Stager and Christina Morrow; my wonderful, inquisitive students and clients; and the devoted acting/music students and faculty over the last twenty years at Boston University, College of Fine Arts.

And always, the biggest gratitude to Daria and Ruby, my amazing, wonderful daughters, for the gift of closeness and unending love. And to my most captive audience, Axel and Vaughn, my precious grandsons.

ABOUT
THE AUTHOR

An internationally recognized breathing and movement specialist, Betsy Polatin, MFA, SEP, has been teaching for more than forty years and is currently a master lecturer at Boston University's College of Fine Arts. Her background includes forty-five years of movement education and performance, as well as training in music, dance, yoga, meditation, trauma resolution, and the broader healing arts. Her teaching experience includes Berklee College of Music, Touch and Movement in Trauma Therapy, Muscular Therapy Institute, Kripalu, The Embodiment Conference, Tanglewood Music Festival, and Opera Institute of Boston. She has taught Master Classes for the Psychotherapy Networker, Performing Arts Medicine Association, Bessel van der Kolk's International Trauma Conference, International Yoga Conference in Japan, U.S. Association for Body Psychotherapy, Pittsburgh Symphony Orchestra, Spiritual communities, Children's Hospital, Boston Ballet, Sports Medicine clinics, and the Science and Nonduality Conference—in the United States, Europe, Australia, India, Japan, and Korea.

Betsy leads international trainings where she presents her unique and revolutionary fusion of ideas: scientific knowledge combined with ancient wisdom and intuitive human creativity. This work helps people recognize their habitual patterns, which are often charged with unconscious commitment. Once these patterns are brought to awareness, depth of change can happen on many levels, as the life force resumes. Her work is greatly influenced by the teachings of Spiritual and Meditation Masters. Since 2016, she has been co-teaching ongoing traveling workshops, themed "Trauma and the Performing Artist" and "Trauma in the Public Eye," with Peter A. Levine, PhD.

Betsy's previous book, *The Actor's Secret,* was featured on ABC TV and Fox News, received rave reviews, and is now a recommended textbook in many performing-arts schools. As a well-known educator, she has published numerous articles in the *Huffington Post.* She maintains a private practice in Brookline, Massachusetts, and does online sessions internationally.

Please visit: humanual.com and theactorssecretbook.com.

Printed in Great Britain
by Amazon

Seth Stein Architects

First published in 2017 by Lund Humphries
Office 3, Book House
261A City Road
London
EC1V 1JX
UK

www.lundhumphries.com

ISBN 978-1-84822-239-7

A Cataloguing-in-Publication record
for this book is available from the
British Library.

Designed by Zoë Bather
Printed in Slovenia

Kenneth Powell

Seth Stein Architects

LUND HUMPHRIES

Introduction

Response to context is a fundamental feature of the work of Seth Stein, whether the context is a remote beach in the West Indies, a rocky islet off the coast of Finland, a headland in South Africa – or a street in Notting Hill. As much might be said of many contemporary architects who work globally, in Stein's case from a canal-side base at the less fashionable end of London's Ladbroke Grove. But perhaps his ability to capture the mood of a place lies somewhere in his genes – his family roots. Stein, born in 1959, was raised in London, where his parents had moved from New York when he was a schoolboy. His mother and father had met at university in Norman, Oklahoma, where one of their teachers was the artist Eugene Bavinger (1919–97). Bavinger and his wife, and fellow artist Nancy, were the clients for a sensational house outside the town of Norman, designed by the architect Bruce Goff. (Completed in 1955, the house

was tragically demolished in 2016 after falling into dereliction.) The Steins may have been amongst the group of students enlisted to assist with the construction of this gloriously impractical 'house without walls'.

Moving to London from New York in the 1960s, the Steins sent young Seth to school firstly in Marylebone, where even as a child he was impressed by the consistency and elegance of Georgian London. He went on to a typical London comprehensive in Hampstead, where he decided that his future lay in the field of architecture. He chose to study at the University of Manchester – Norman Foster was an alumnus of the school, which retained a relatively traditional approach to teaching but gave its students a vital grounding in the technical aspects of building. Alongside training to become an architect, Stein discovered the local music scene – with the Factory and Hacienda clubs and groups

Archipelago House,
Finland. South elevation
viewed from ravine

Bavinger House, Norman,
Oklahoma (Bruce Goff 1955)

such as Joy Division and the Smiths laying the foundations
of 'Madchester'. From Manchester, Stein moved on to the
very different ethos of the Architectural Association in
London, then headed by the legendary Alvin Boyarsky,
which was as Stein says, 'something of a drama school
for architects'. Boyarsky had recruited an extraordinary
group of tutors including Nigel Coates, Bernard Tschumi,
Peter Cook, Léon Krier, Ron Herron, Jan Kaplicky and
Zaha Hadid. The latter interviewed Stein who was thrown
into the extraordinary world of Boyarsky's AA.

For all its glamour and focus on the experimental
and innovative, and in contrast to the more conventional
approach of the Manchester school, the AA was a
demanding place – 'crits' could be severe. Between
Manchester and the AA, Stein had done a stint in the
offices of the renowned design studio Pentagram, where
Alan Fletcher and Theo Crosby were leading lights.
Working there was, he says, 'heaven'. It was, perhaps, a
model for the studio which he himself was later to run –
relaxed and non-hierarchical. The same ethos pervaded
the office of Richard Rogers, who admired some of
Stein's projects at the AA and subsequently offered him a
job. Richard Rogers Partnership was emerging as a world
leader, with the Lloyd's building in the City of London
under construction. The office was a nursery of talent
from where many leading British practices emerged, and
Stein spent a happy three years there.

Alongside Rogers, Norman Foster was already
established as a leading figure on the world scene,
with the Hong Kong and Shanghai Banking Corporation
headquarters recently completed, and it was to the
Foster office that Stein moved next. He worked initially
on the Esprit flagship store on Sloane Street, completed
in 1988. The office was awash with projects and Stein
worked with a number of teams on the ITN Building and
the Barcelona communications tower. When the Foster
office announced a move from Marylebone to Battersea,
however, he decided that the time had come to leave and
launch out on his own. He recalls,

> I'd had seven or eight years in the world of "High-
> tech", and the influence of Rogers and Foster was
> to remain with me. Buildings such as the Inmos
> factory, the Renault distribution depot and the
> Sainsbury Centre were inspirations. But the time
> had come to make a fresh start.

**Fountain pools set into
the Tuscan olive terraces**

In 1990, Stein set up his own studio in Leather Lane, off Holborn, which was a spartan space with recycled aircraft seats a feature. It was not a propitious time, with the economy in recession and building projects being cancelled or put on ice. Relatively small scale projects for film companies in Soho and Fitzrovia provided a lifeline – Ridley Scott's production company, RSA, was one client. A project for the production company CiBy (an offshoot of French conglomerate Bouygues) featured a large fish tank. There was also a West End gallery, Interim Art, for collector and dealer Maureen Paley and a fit-out of the foyer of the Screen on the Hill cinema in Hampstead. An early excursion into working in the landscape was the pool garden near Camaiore in Tuscany (1990). There was an existing derelict farmhouse on the site, La Madonnina, restored as a holiday home by Stein's stepmother, Danielle Barr, but the focus of the project was the pool set into a steep site within an olive grove, with a smaller pool for children growing out of the side of the house. The pool's distinctive green lining was inspired by the famous pool at the Hotel Colombe d'Or in Saint-Paul-de-Vence. Another strand in Stein's work – that of adapting existing buildings – found expression in the penthouse

created on top of a 1920s commercial block on Pall Mall, externally the work of Edwin Lutyens. The penthouse had been fitted out in the 1960s to a tame Classical design. All was stripped out and the bones of the steel-framed building revealed, creating a two-room penthouse with a 60ft long main living space and a suspended staircase connecting to an upper level. It had echoes of that High-tech icon and particular inspiration for Richard Rogers (and indeed for Stein), the Maison de Verre.

Richard Rogers had advised Stein 'to get that first house out of your system' – for Rogers, building the house at Creek Vean in Cornwall for his parents-in-law had been a landmark in his development as an architect. For Seth Stein, the house at Kelso Place in Kensington, designed for his own occupation and incorporating a design studio, was equally a career landmark; a project in which he was 'getting Rogers and Foster out of my system', working towards an architectural language of his own beyond High-tech. Lawyer John Eldridge (1950–2007), an enthusiast for architecture and design who had already employed Stein for a series of loft conversions and was to remain a client and a close friend until his untimely death in a road accident, helped to resolve complicated legal issues that had

**Pall Mall penthouse.
Suspended steel stairs
relate to the original
arched window**

prevented any previous development on the site. The site at Kelso Place was not an obvious location for a domestic project. Originally stables, then a builder's yard, narrow and enclosed and sitting directly above the Circle Line, it contained a series of derelict structures within what resembled a cul-de-sac. Stein's approach was to insert a new structure halfway along the open yard thereby creating a courtyard as the centerpiece of the house plan. The central courtyard has been a feature of many of Stein's urban house projects. He argues that the courtyard, as the focus of a house, offers a new dimension to urban living. 'Its like having a back garden, but one into which all the principal living spaces can have a view.' The relationship between internal and external space is a recurring theme in his work. At Kelso Place, the courtyard was just 4.5m wide, but the prospect from within, with a line of tall grass swaying in the breeze, brings nature into the heart of the city. The idea of the central courtyard is familiar from traditional Japanese architecture and extends back, of course, to the classic Roman villa. But Stein has reinvented it for the 21st century. It reflects one of the central themes in his work: creating tranquility and calm.

Where possible, the existing structure of the former workshops at Kelso Place was retained. The language of the house still owed something to High-tech but the use of exposed concrete and bold colour reflected wider modernist influences – the Villa Savoye alongside Southern California. The house, completed in 1995, was well received and featured widely in the architectural and mainstream press.

If Kelso Place represented a virtuoso exercise in creating memorable spaces in a constricted site, the house at Cheval Place, off Knightsbridge, completed in 1997, was, the *AR* commented, 'a skilful exercise in urban evolution'. The site at Cheval Place was just 5m wide and 8m deep, located at the end of a typical London mews and might have been seen as ideal to house a garage. In many respects what was created was a garage – a pied-a-terre for a couple with space for two cars. By digging out a basement level and installing a hydraulic lift with two car decks – the decks doubling as living spaces when not required to accommodate cars – and making optimum use of natural light, Stein created a dwelling which (the *AR* commented) was 'miraculously open to light and greenery in congested central London'.

By the mid-1990s Seth Stein was emerging as a significant presence on the British architectural scene and forging his own distinctive identity as a designer. British architecture was still largely dominated by the High-tech school of Rogers and Foster, the Post-modernist fad of the 1980s having faded, but there was a new expressionist spirit in the air, evidenced by the rise of Zaha Hadid, while a more restrained, minimalist approach was evident in the work of David Chipperfield, himself schooled in the High-tech tradition. Already some critics were describing Stein as a minimalist, a label he firmly rejects. 'All good design is purist', he insists. 'I'm not sure what minimalism really means.' Fundamental to Stein's philosophy of design is a rejection of the irrational and the over-expressive – 'buildings should be legible and comfortable, not overwhelming', he argues. Architecture,

A night view of the Kelso Place courtyard with the illuminated gallery running alongside a narrow planter of tall grasses. The wide stone steps lead to the roof terrace gazebo

Cheval Place. The acrylic car deck allows daylight to penetrate to the lift pit – transformed into a living space

for Stein, is about creating agreeable spaces for people. Wells Coates' building for the Lawn Road flats is, for him, a model example dating from the heroic days of the Modern Movement. It is not, Stein insists, 'about creating status symbols'. He has been fortunate to work with a series of enlightened clients – 'I like to develop a project with clients, working up the original brief in line with their needs'. This kind of empathy is only possible with relatively small projects which, perhaps, explains why Stein has not, so far, worked on large commercial schemes. A series of commissions to fit out fashion stores for the Whistles chain was something of a mould-breaker – though the clients were later to commission a private house from Stein. Using a limited palette of steel, glass and timber, with strong colour, Stein gave the Whistles label a new architectural identity.

Stein's passionate interest in the visual arts made him a natural choice to design the temporary pavilion erected at the Serpentine Gallery in London's Hyde Park when the Gallery reopened after a major refurbishment in 1998. Stein's pavilion, followed by a commission for a second temporary structure a year later, designed by Zaha Hadid, marked the beginning of the Serpentine's acclaimed programme of commissioning a pavilion from a series of architects each summer. Interim Art was an early venture for Stein into gallery design. A more substantial project, won in competition, was the conversion of a robust 1900s industrial building in Geneva into a gallery and offices for the renowned dealer and curator Marc Blondeau. The building, formerly used as a factory for making nail polish, had been much altered. Stein stripped back the structure, exposing the

Whistles, King Street, Manchester. Changing room

Serpentine Gallery party tent for the reopening of the gallery following its restoration in 1998

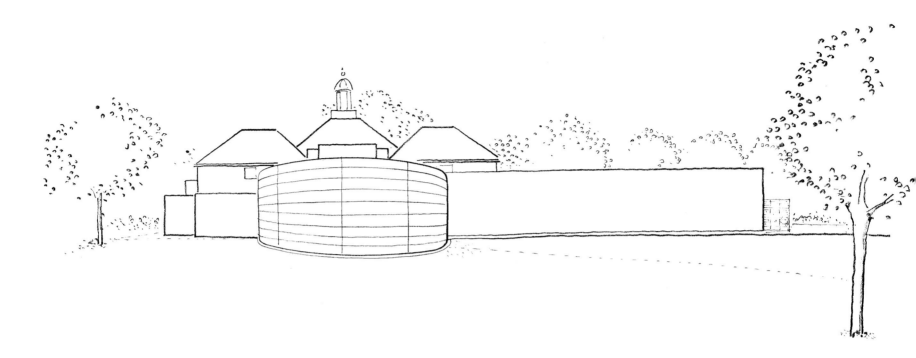

steel frame. Crittall windows, imported from the Essex manufacturer, gave it an appropriately authentic external look. Although firmly rooted in London, Stein was increasingly looking beyond Britain for commissions. Given his admiration for the work of Palladio, working on the restoration of a house in the *Centro Storico* of Vicenza as a family home was a commission to be cherished, not least for the opportunity it provided to work with some exceptional local craftsmen. The house presented a narrow (4m) frontage to the via Contra Porti but extended back some 28m. The client had been impressed by Kelso Place but there were constraints in historic Vicenza (a World Heritage Site) which had not existed in a backwater of Kensington. A key objective was to channel more natural light into the house – the existing stair was extended upwards through

the building using glass treads. The main living space featured motorised screens made of steel and strips of willow to allow for flexibility. The massive bath, made from a solid block of limestone and with something of the dignity of a Roman sarcophagus, was a classic example of Stein's ability to elevate a commonplace domestic object into something monumental and beautiful.

The second half of the 1990s saw Stein working on a number of loft projects – the loft had become a London phenomenon, in no small part due to the work of Harry Handelsman at Manhattan Loft Corporation, whose architectural collaborators included John Pawson and Piers Gough of CZWG. The location for one of the most notable of Stein's projects was Handelsman's Bankside Lofts, exquisite in terms of its materiality and ingeniously planned, with the kitchen in a central core

**Townhouse in Vicenza
Centro Storico**

**Blondeau Fine Art Gallery,
Geneva**

A small window in the shower enclosure at Bankside loft perfectly frames a view of St Paul's cathedral across the Thames

and blinds used to provide a flexible division of space. A small window set within the shower room framed a dramatic view of St Paul's Cathedral across the Thames. The booming London development scene saw London's South Bank transformed. The Baltic Restaurant on Blackfriars Road was one product of that transformation. The client was the Polish restaurateur Jan Woroniecki and the restaurant, completed in 2001, specialised in the cuisine of central Europe – it has become a highly popular South Bank venue. The raw material resembled that at Kelso Place: a former coach-building works, now totally derelict, squeezed in behind a listed Georgian terrace opposite Southwark's new Jubilee Line station. And, as at Kelso Place, the key to the project (completed in 2002) was the expert creation of a sequence of spaces extending from the inconspicuous entrance through a narrow, quite low, bar area into the main restaurant, lofty, top-lit and retaining its original open timber roof. Exposed brickwork and polished concrete floors were key elements in an industrial aesthetic combining austerity with comfort. The use of amber, imported from Poland, to create a striking light fitting in the bar, was a special feature of the fit-out. Stein recalls the pleasure of working with such a precious and sensual material.

Woroniecki was the client too for a project, modest in scale, which Stein found highly satisfying. U-Turn in Bethnal Green was a centre for women seeking a refuge from the problems of drugs, mental health and prostitution. Counselling rooms, bathrooms and recreational spaces were provided within the confines of a church property. The budget was far from extravagant but, as Woroniecki commented, "the beauty of the design and of the finishes gave respect to the women and the workers and helped them have a pride in and a respect for their environment".

A decade or more into independent practice, Seth Stein was busy with London projects – stylish apartment refurbishments and house extensions. Developer Mike Spink was the client for the house in Portland Road, Holland Park (2006), a 'secret house', hidden from the street. A house in Pitt Street, Campden Hill, completed in 2009, replacing a mundane post-war dwelling but set in an extensive garden, made no concessions to its largely Victorian context but has been applauded as a positive element in the Kensington Conservation Area. The client here was again Mike Spink, who set out to build an ideal family house. 'Seth managed to produce a stunning design on a site fraught with planning restrictions', Spink

Aerial view of the courtyard at Portland Road

recalls. 'The design, which was brilliantly penned in one weekend, remained virtually unchanged through the whole tough planning process.'

The practice had also, however, begun to work far beyond London. The house Stein completed in 2000 on a tiny (12-acre) wooded island in the Baltic, west of the Finnish capital of Helsinki, was the first of a series of projects located in remote places. The house, commissioned by a London banker, was designed as a summer residence – the client was later to write of it as 'a spiritual and beautiful home … a very special place where my soul is one with the sea and sky'. It was placed on the highest point of the island, so as to take advantage of 360-degree views across the sea. All the materials had to be hauled by hand up from the landing stage, necessitating a construction strategy that made use of prefabricated materials – the basic component was glulam timber. A form of system building made sense in the context of the site. Sheltered under an enclosing curved roof, the house was equally an exercise in self-sufficiency. The lessons learned in this project were to be applied elsewhere in similarly exotic locations. Capturing spectacular views and working in tune with the landscape were imperatives at Plettenberg

Bay in the Western Cape Province of South Africa. The project, 'the culmination of a long journey' in more senses than one, was one where Stein's approach to design had achieved maturity. The house is set high above the bay, with fine views. Influenced by the Japanese principle of borrowed views, it frames views as seen from within. This is a house full of surprises – bedrooms cantilevered over the main living space and approached along a terrace screened by a mesh of locally sourced eucalyptus poles held in place by copper wire; a shower set on the roof; a linen cupboard formed from a salvaged boat sail stretched like canvas over a frame. By night, it became a lantern of diffused light. With its use of materials found locally – copper wire, for example, is used by local people to make jewellery and toys, commonly sold by the roadside – the house could be seen as an attempt to emulate the local vernacular, but here, as elsewhere, the exact nature of the vernacular is not easy to define.

Though hardly as remote as a Baltic island, the site for the house at Pencalenick (completed in 2006) was scarcely less dramatic – a creek tucked away opposite the Cornish town of Fowey. The house is set close to the water (the easiest approach is by boat) and slotted into

Family House, Pitt Street, Kensington

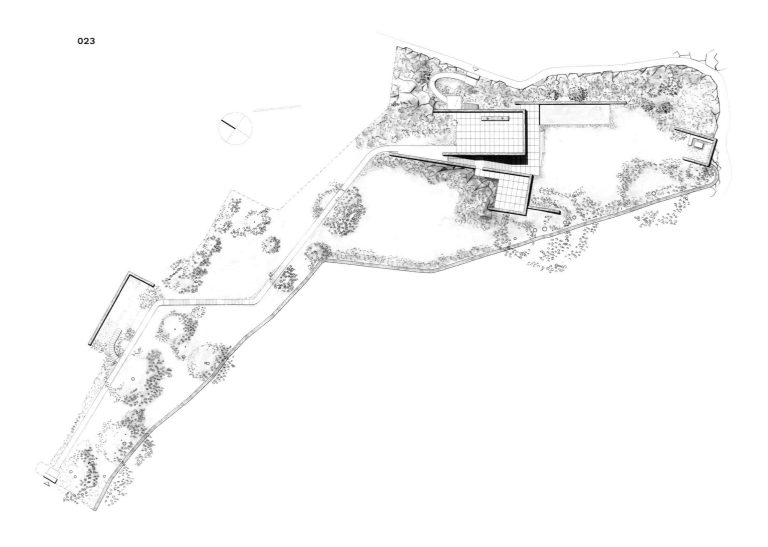

Site plan (above) and
model for cliff top house
in Polperro, Cornwall
(unbuilt)

the steep hillside as a linear block, one room deep and constructed using local slate and timber. The modular diagram of the building is simple: the aim was to open the interior to the views of sea and sky, an aim achieved without any element of display so that it appears to grow naturally from its site. (In 2012, Stein completed designs for a house at Polperro in Cornwall, making similar use of local materials on a rocky headland site, approachable only on foot – he compares it to Adalberto Libera's Malaparte house on the island of Capri – but the project was subsequently abandoned. A project for a house at Pengegon, on the Fowey estuary, similarly remains unrealized.) Stein insists that the success of a project like Pencalenick is dependent on a good relationship with the client. 'I like connecting the technical aspects of a project with the site', he says. 'But to achieve real success you need to work with people – to be a good listener.' With his practice well established, he has clients who have returned to him more than once. Typically, he says, his clients are 'people who have reached a certain stage in their lives and are looking to make their mark with projects that enhance their own lives but hopefully have lasting value'. Most of the clients for the new houses which have formed the backbone

of Stein's workload over quarter of a century came to him through personal recommendation or because they sought him out having seen other projects.

One-off houses for affluent clients have come to form the core of Seth Stein's workload, perhaps more by accident than design, although Stein has largely eschewed the architectural competitions linked to major public projects. A commission to refurbish the Grade II* listed stable block at Harewood House, the great Georgian mansion of the Lascelles family outside Leeds, came through personal acquaintance with David Lascelles – a film-maker by profession – and his artist wife Diane, whose London home was near Kelso Place. Later accretions were stripped away and enhanced visitor and venue facilities, including a cafe and shop, together with offices, which were created with a minimal approach that does not impact on the Georgian fabric. A commission to fit out the offices for the law firm S.J. Berwin came about as a result of Stein's previous collaborations with John Eldridge, a partner in the company. Its 1980s office building close to Southwark Bridge was radically remodelled by John Robertson Architects but the interiors were assigned to Stein, working in collaboration with commercial heavyweight

Illuminated stair box for a city law firm's reception

VIEW FROM TOP OF SITE LOOKING TOWARDS PONT PILL

23 APRIL 2020   SETH STEIN RIBA

Pengegon, Fowey, Cornwall. Concept for a new build house

Spiral bench using salvaged harbour piling timber – located on a roof garden overlooking the Thames

Ordinance Survey scale 1:1250. Sand cast aluminium River Thames memorial. Relocated to Kew Gardens

practice HOK International. 'We designed everything down to the in-trays', he says. The firm wanted offices with a strong sense of identity – artist Michael Craig-Martin advised on the palette of colours used. Within a year of the offices being completed, Eldridge had died and the rooftop garden, which was a key feature of the project, conceived as a series of outside 'rooms', with a striking spiraling bench, became the site for a sculpture as a memorial to him. With views across the Thames to Tate Modern, the garden is a much-used amenity for the staff working in the building.

A starting point for every scheme that comes through the Stein studio is a series of sketches in which Stein sets out his initial ideas and uses them as part of a creative dialogue with clients – 'I do a lot of listening', he says. This process is fundamental to his approach to design. A visit to the site for the project provides an opportunity to experience it. 'I need to see it in morning and evening light, to have a total view of the context', Stein says. 'You cannot read a site from a map.' Sometimes the optimum outlook for a building is at odds with the sun path or prevailing winds. The nature of the local infrastructure also has to be understood before a sustainable design strategy can be developed. The availability of local materials and craft skills also has to be considered. Indigenous materials may be combined with imported components. Local contractors may provide valuable feedback and in some cases projects are developed in collaboration with locally-based architects. From the initial sketches the key diagram for the proposed building emerges; the

basis for further dialogue with the client – 'you need to take the client with you on a process of exploration and investigation', Stein insists. The diagram should be easily legible – 'the worlds' greatest buildings can, in the end, be reduced to a few lines'. Stein has no time for the contorted, self-indulgent presentations typical of a certain school of contemporary architectural design. Nor is he given to opaque theoretical expositions of his work: he is pragmatist at heart, intent on producing beautiful buildings which are enjoyed by those who inhabit or work in them. 'The end result of our design process is always a sense of calm, orientation, and a connection with the natural realm', he says. The aim is to create buildings where the various zones flow seamlessly together, allowing for the flexibility which is fundamental to modern living.

Many clients come to Stein through personal connections. Others through reading of his work in the media, as in the case of the house he designed for a site on a beach in the Turks and Caicos Islands, beautiful but barren and lacking all services, including a supply of fresh water – harvesting rainwater was the only solution. The aim was to make a tiny holiday settlement where family and friends could enjoy a version of the simple life. As in the case of the Finnish project, prefabricated components form the basic structure of the timber-built cabins, which have no glazing – louvred screens (reinforced with mesh to exclude insects) provide privacy. Bathrooms open to views of the landscape. The experience of staying here, says Stein, 'is like being inside a large piece of furniture'. Perhaps the

Side view of beach house, North Caicos

Walled garden pool, Provence. The stainless steel lightweight canopy is clad in reeds casting a striated shadow below

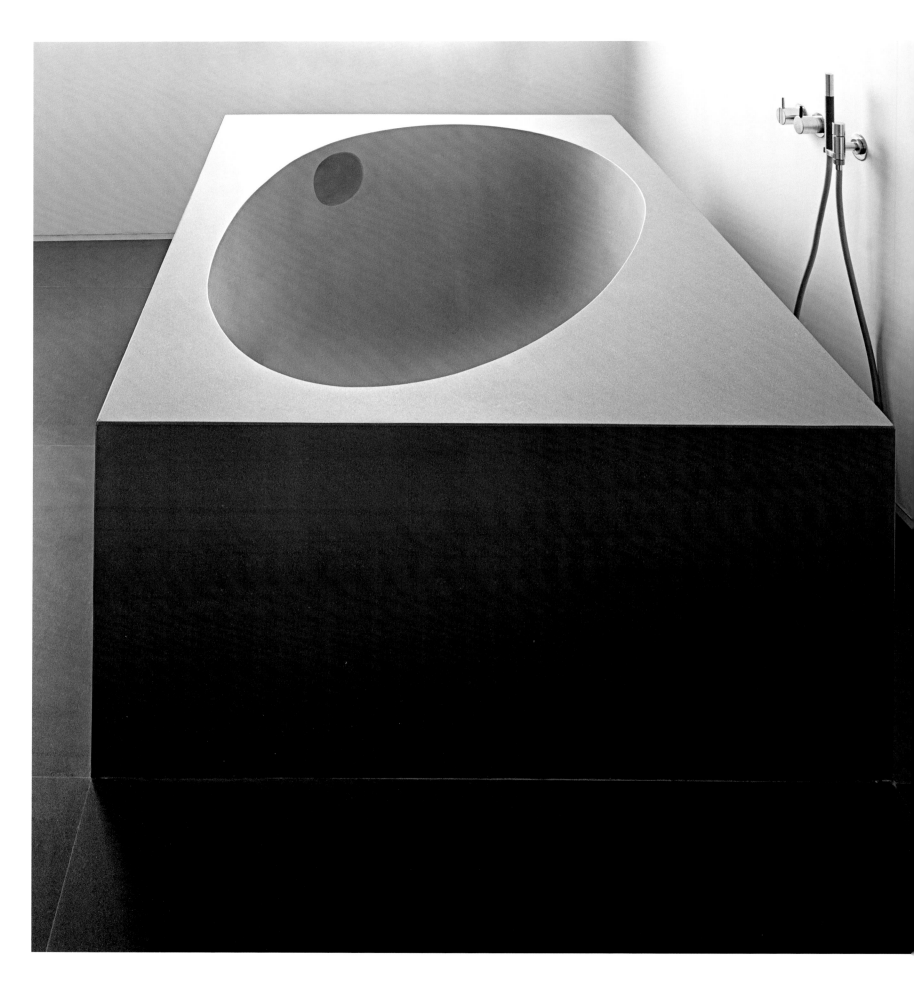

need to experience a spartan existence away from home comforts is something which particularly drives the affluent?

It is the calm and undemonstrative character of Stein's work which allows it to relate to a great variety of contexts. The clients for the Pool House in Provence – close to the magnificent ruined Cistercian abbey of Le Thoronet, itself an inspiration to many architects – wanted a new pavilion serving a swimming pool in the grounds of their house. The site was a walled garden – the new pavilion was conceived as an 'inhabited wall', built of local materials, both sophisticated and utterly straightforward, a clear response to a brief. The pool itself is a stone *bassin* sunk into the land, with a limestone paved surround. The scheme was a good example of Stein's confident response to context and equally of his love of materials, whether they be the local stone used here, Cornish slate, or South African eucalyptus wood, the 'latte' traditionally used to delineate boundaries in South Africa but adapted by Stein for a very different function. Using a great boulder found on site to fashion a wash-basin in the house on Turks and Caicos, a sensible use of a 'found' object, or local limestone for a monumental bath in Vicenza gives

the daily routine of washing and bathing an almost ritual quality. Then there is his sure touch with more everyday materials: concrete, exposed brick or the acrylic (sourced in Colorado) used for a stair in the house at Portland Road, Holland Park. Choice of materials reflects a stress on appropriateness and practicality but also an unashamed enjoyment of their sensual appeal. Collaborating with craftsmen, whether in Italy, where traditional crafts still thrive, or in more exotic locations, is, for Stein, one of the most satisfying aspects of a building project. 'Each project', he says, 'has elements that can only be realized in collaboration with those who actually make the buildings.'

Stein's architecture is rooted in his feeling for materials, but equally characteristic is his ability to manipulate space. The house he completed in Toronto in 2001 is a good example of that skill. Toronto is a metropolis in the classic North American mould. There was no obvious local vernacular to which to respond. The site was essentially suburban, an avenue of expensive but undistinguished villas. To the rear, however, it backed on to a deep wooded ravine. To the street, an element of decorum was necessary in the face of opposition from neighbours to any overtly "modern"

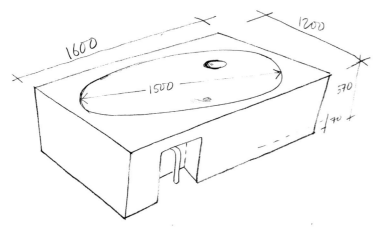

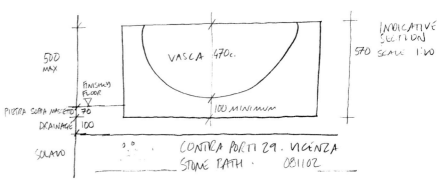

Vicenza townhouse – stone bath – sketch details

design. To the rear, there was the opportunity to be more bold. The brief was to design a practical family home to replace a routine house dating from the 1950s. As at Kelso Place, Stein gave the entrance to the house a sense of anticipation: a circular cloakroom (another feature previewed at Kelso Place) provides a baffle as the visitor enters, then a staircase wall screens the main living space, which has something of the character of a great hall and is top-lit, with *brise-soleil* baffling sunlight – a 'light box' as Stein describes it. Bedrooms look into this dramatic space. Solid and urbane to the street, the house opens up to the rear, with extensive glazing to take maximum advantage of the views.

The run of exquisite house projects has continued. A new house near the historic city of Bath was completed in 2013. The undistinguished old house which stood on the site was demolished but an adjacent barn was retained and restored as a music room, an 'anchor' on the scenic – and highly sensitive – Green Belt site. Local stone from the demolished house was reused, each piece reworked by a locally-based mason. Working with the contours of the hillside site, Stein created a house which makes no attempt to be 'vernacular' in character yet seems at ease in its surroundings. (Local

objections were overruled by a local authority keen to encourage outstanding modern design in this city where 'heritage' is dominant and weak pastiche has been too common in the past.) The house wraps along the site, its plan designed to take optimum advantage of views. A central courtyard is a feature familiar from other Stein projects, here forming a tranquil focus to domestic life. 'We live in a house of calm and peace and even the walls are a thing of beauty', the client commented. The project benefited, as have so many of those undertaken by Stein, from the involvement of an enthusiastic and enlightened client. In particular, the architect's commitment to sustainable design was given full rein. While the former house on the site had been heated by an oil fired boiler, its replacement is hugely energy-efficient. Energy supplied by solar panels and a wind turbine is stored and distributed around the house. Triple glazing baffles solar gain in summer and prevents heat loss in winter. Rainwater is harvested. And all these environmentally benign devices are seamlessly integrated into the architecture of the building.

Back in London, Seth Stein again addressed the challenge of a highly constricted site at Hillgate Street, off Notting Hill Gate. With a narrow street frontage,

Country House, Somerset. The central courtyard providing a southerly aspect to the living room

The balustrade is a single panel of cast acrylic, 6cm thick, and sandblasted to create an icy translucent effect

the site extended back some 28m. Stein created a spacious and dramatic family house to replace a post-war house which had been reworked by an architect couple. The 'period' frontage to the street (its retention was insisted on by Kensington & Chelsea planners) conceals a new house in which Stein brought to bear all his skills of spatial organization. A lightwell extending down through the house is a fundamental element in the spatial strategy, channelling daylight into the heart of the building and opening up the new basement level to the sky. The second key ingredient in the scheme is the stair, which extends in a continuous diagonal axis up the entire height of the house in a top-lit slot. As usual in Stein's architecture there is the element of surprise: one enters a narrow hallway which opens out to a light-filled terrace and courtyard. The use of gold leaf as a wall covering is an opulent touch but has a practical application in bouncing light into the basement. For all the constraints of the site, living spaces are generous. And the ecological credentials of the project are impeccable, with solar panels providing a significant contribution to the demands of heating, plenty of insulation, and rainwater recycled.

Permanently in demand for one-off house projects, Seth Stein is far from reluctant to diversify into other spheres of work. Regrettably, housing projects for a site in Montenegro (where Stein was asked to advise on its potential for a hotel and residential development), and a house in Hampshire have remained unbuilt, as has a proposed chapel in Dublin's Glasnevin Cemetery – planned to commemorate the 1916 Easter Rising. One non-domestic project of which Stein is particularly proud is the restoration of the Novo Cemetery off London's Mile End Road. The cemetery was developed from the 1730s onwards as a burial ground for Sephardic Jews who came to England in the 1650s. Increasingly little used as the Jewish community migrated to the suburbs, the cemetery was eventually surrounded by the ever-expanding campus of London University's Queen Mary College. The older section was cleared in the 1970s and the dead reinterred elsewhere but the eastern section remained, marooned amongst new college buildings, its neglected state something of an embarrassment. Stein's project – run by his longstanding associate Andrew Abdulezer – transformed it into a valued heritage asset, a source of pride to Queen Mary College. In 2014, two

**Glasnevin chapel, Dublin.
Interior view**

CLIFF HOUSES
ZUKOVI PENINSULA
MONTENEGRO
Sebastian Aug 07

Montenegro. Cliff houses

**Section through a
proposed riverside house
in Hampshire**

years after the restoration project was completed, the cemetery was added to Historic England's register of historic parks and gardens.

A sense of place and an instinctive feeling for the appropriate use of materials are key elements in Seth Stein's approach to designing buildings. They combine to spectacular effect in the equestrian centre (2014) on the Mornington Peninsula, south of the Australian city of Melbourne. Working in association with Melbourne-based architect Rob Watson (another former member of the Foster office) Stein created a building which combines dynamism – exemplified by the sweeping arc of the zinc-clad roof – with a response to the Australian vernacular seen in the use of Tasmanian oak for the structural frame, gum tree wood and corrugated metal. A wall formed of rammed earth, rather than concrete, encloses the crescent-shaped structure, a good example of Stein's ability to work with local materials and building techniques. The building is at home amongst the fields and vineyards which form its context.

Working far from the modish London quarters where he cut his teeth as an independent practitioner, Stein has confronted the issue of local vernacular ways of building. Fusing modernity with respect for local tradition is a challenge that has been addressed by architects such as Glenn Murcutt and Sean Godsell in Australia and John and Patricia Patkau and Brian Mackay-Lyons in Canada. Stein's strategy has been to work with local materials used in a contemporary way with no overt vernacular references. The result is a series of buildings that seem to address the issue of the vernacular quite effortlessly by being direct, undogmatic, and relaxed, never seeking to be merely fashionable. These are key characteristics of Stein's work, whatever its context. 'I'm a practical person, not a philosopher – I love making things', Stein says. His buildings are highly practical, but also joyful, sensuous, tactile. These are qualities which architecture badly needs to rediscover.

The Equestrian Centre horse pool and termination of the rammed earth wall

Kelso Place, London
1995

The house in Kelso Place, Kensington, which became the home for Seth Stein and his family, was a seminal project for his youthful practice – a classic 'first house' in which he moved away from the High-tech manner of Rogers and Foster. Finding a site for a substantial new house in a fashionable area of London and then securing planning consent for a building that was frankly contemporary, with no concessions to its context of stucco-clad Victorian terraces, was in itself an achievement.

The long, narrow site (somewhat hemmed in by a hefty apartment block) was a former stable yard, dating from the 1880s, with an entrance opening from the street to the south. The London Underground's Circle Line rumbled below. The two-storey, L-shaped stable block remained, in a derelict condition, as part of a now abandoned builder's yard. A later industrial shed occupied the western flank of the site, equally decrepit but with potential for reuse. The retention and radical conversion of both buildings formed the basis of the new house project. The site was sufficiently large to allow for a spacious low-rise house (with an area of 465 sq.m.) focused on a central courtyard – its diagram, that of the classic Roman dwelling, disposed around an open atrium, equally owed something to the traditional Japanese house. (Stein had travelled extensively in Japan, and its architecture was to remain a potent influence on his work.) The factory building was refashioned to contain a very large, wood floored kitchen/family room, its centre-piece a great table fashioned out of recycled Victorian floorboards, with a dining room and study beyond on the ground floor of the stable block. The dining room, in the former tack room, was given a dramatic backcloth with the retention of an intact wall of Victorian ceramic tiling. The upper level of the stable block was colonised to form a total of five bedrooms, the master bedroom distinguished by the handsome exposed timber roof structure. Elsewhere, original features were largely retained. But this project was about much more than reuse and restoration: it was about the injection of dynamic new design into a mundane setting.

Original view from the street (above) and house entrance and roof terrace gazebo (left)

Fundamental to the scheme was the creation of a sequence of spaces extending through the site, flowing into one another without the barrier created by doors, capitalising on its constraints to produce a sense of dramatic movement which has since become a fundamental element in Stein's architecture. The open entrance to the site from the street was reconfigured to create a preface to the house which ensures privacy but is equally inviting, with a tranquil forecourt, glimpsed through open metal gates and beyond, a wall of white plaster and translucent glazing which gives no hint of what lies outside. Above the entrance screen a concrete cylinder, split in two, rises – there is a memory here of the Villa Savoye although the significance of the feature, beyond forming a gazebo in a small rooftop garden, is not immediately obvious. (By night, it is illuminated to form a beacon to the outside world.) Its function becomes clear when one enters the house: at ground level the cylinder forms a cloakroom, a matter-of-fact facility given monumental form. The cylinder is a component in an exercise in architectural compression of almost Baroque character. The visitor is pushed into the house, as it were, with an angled wall, painted a vivid pink, leading into the kitchen and controlling views into the remainder of the house. Straight ahead a 33m-long gallery, enclosed by frameless glazing, extends along the side of the open courtyard and leads to an all-white living space, entirely glazed, which looks back to the courtyard garden, accessed via a sliding glass door framed in orange – another of the discreet touches of strong colour used throughout the house, offset by polished concrete, timber and glass. A flight of steps, terminating the gallery, provides access to the bedrooms on the upper floor.

The Kelso Place house is, on one level, a highly practical reworking of found material, reusing existing structures. At the same time, it represents an exercise in what Stein calls 'the luxury of openness', a place for open-plan living with only bedrooms and bathrooms as enclosed spaces. There are many references in this house – Le Corbusier, California, Japan, Luis Barragán – which reflect the workings of an acute architectural intelligence confronting a succession of influences and arriving at a remarkably mature statement of intent for the future.

The derelict Victorian builder's yard courtyard provides a focal point for the house with its glass gallery on the left

Guest cloakroom, the
light switch activates
the water spout
(eliminating the need
for a conventional tap).
Carrara marble basin
supported on a steel
bracket

Entrance hall, concrete
cylinder cloakroom and,
right, wall leading to (but
not revealing) the kitchen

A remnant of the tack
room of the original
Victorian stables retains
the box numbering on
the ceramic wall tiles.
The dining table, built to
Stein's design, consists
of old oak floor boards
mounted over a square
tube steel frame

Section looking East

1   Forecourt
2   Brise soleil
3   Entrance
4   Steps up to roof terrace
5   Courtyard
6   Living & stairs

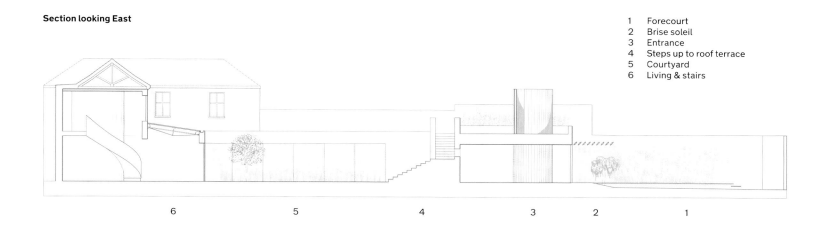

6   5   4   3   2   1

Ground floor plan

1   Forecourt
2   Entry
3   Courtyard
4   Living
5   Study
6   Dining
7   Kitchen

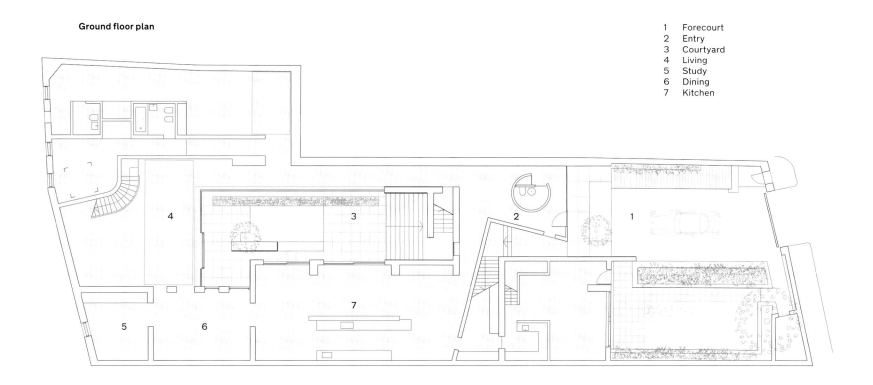

0   5   10

Cheval Place, London
1997

The tiny house at Cheval Place, close to fashionable Knightsbridge, was designed as 'a bachelor pad with space for cars'. On a less valuable site, in fact, it might have contained a garage and nothing more but Stein's client (a collector of classic cars who married while the project was in gestation) wanted a comfortable *pied-a-terre* with accommodation for two cars. It was a challenging brief for a mews site just 5m wide and 8m deep, enclosed by other buildings, which had, not surprisingly, never been built on. Moreover the cars (fortunately small models, including a classic Fiat *Cinquecento*) were not just to be accommodated but equally displayed and celebrated. Planning constraints limited the height of the new house to that of adjacent properties. Its exterior to the mews is entirely conventional, even nondescript; its interior anything but.

Providing the spaces required for cars and humans meant digging down, excavating a hole to house a two-level pit containing a hydraulic lift with two car decks. The upper deck was floored in green limestone, as used elsewhere in the house, the lower in translucent acrylic panels 30mm thick capable of bearing a 2 ton weight. Empty of cars and in a raised position, the lift provides a ground-floor room with a translucent floor opening off an entrance hall, with the limestone floor skied and a basement living space with a translucent ceiling admitting natural light. When lowered, the upper room is floored in limestone, the lower in acrylic – a 2m gap at the base of the pit allows furniture to remain in place. Both spaces can be used for parking; or for living in. This house is about shared space. With two cars stored, space for people is admittedly limited: a living/dining room, plus narrow kitchen and cloakroom in the basement and a bedroom and bathroom on the first floor. Skylights in a tiny rear courtyard channel daylight into the basement living area: the whole interior of the house is suffused with controlled light. A continuous stair, 12m long and with glass treads connects all levels. To the rear, the house, so anonymous to the street, emerges as an expressive work of architecture with a façade clad in zinc panels. Stein comments on the project: 'technology can be a virtue, producing flexibility as space becomes more valuable.' Moveable rooms smack of Archigram and High-tech – Rogers and Piano's initial proposals for the Centre Georges Pompidou proposed moving floors – but Cheval Place is about more than technical virtuosity. A deceptively spacious, light-filled house in a sliver of land in the heart of London, it exemplifies Stein's masterful approach to managing space and creating interiors full of movement and drama.

Car lift 'down'
Car lift 'up'

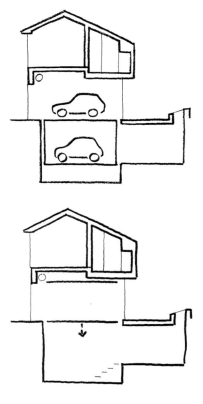

Rear elevation – the planning authority permitted a contemporary architectural scheme unseen from the street

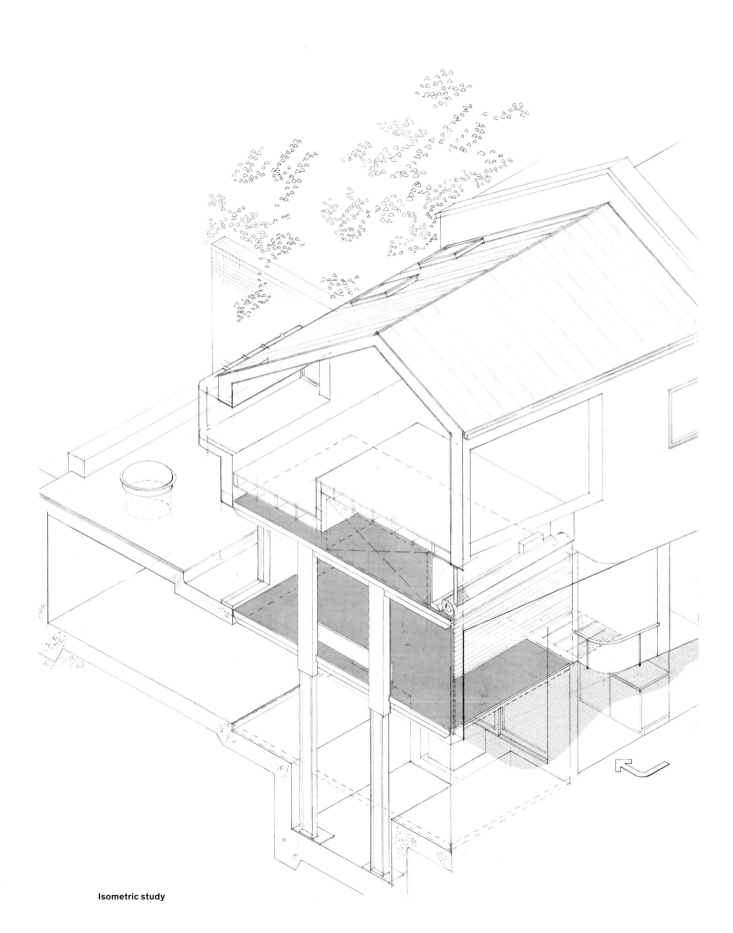

**The lift pit becomes
transformed into extra
living space when
the car deck is raised**

Isometric study

Section through stairs

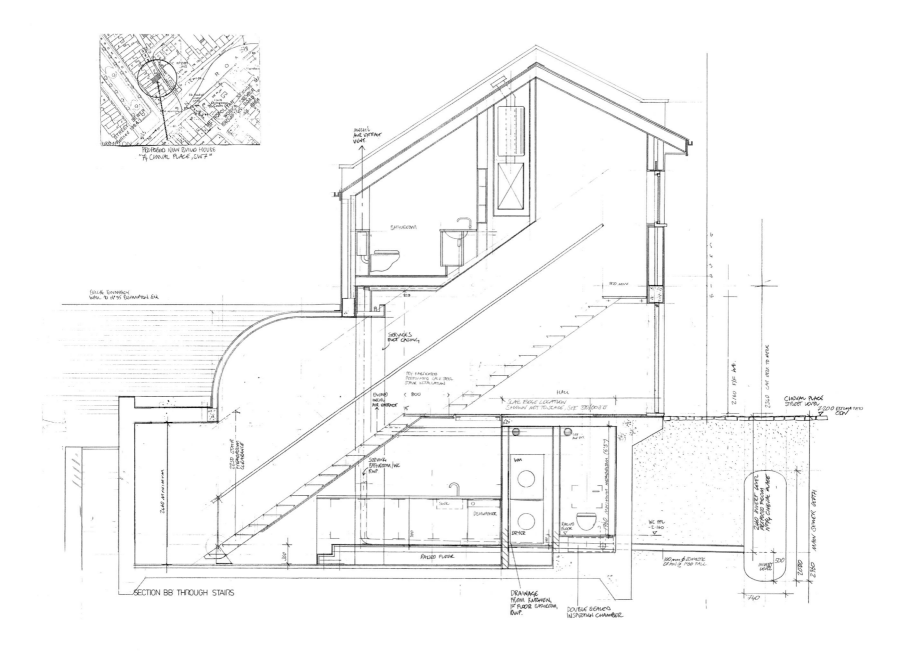

The lower car deck
descends to basement
level but is replaced with
another stone floor above

Archipelago House, Finland
2000

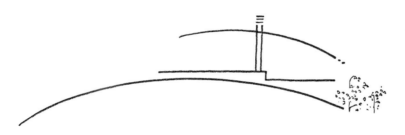

The commission to design a new house for a site on the small island of Skorvon, one of many in the Baltic archipelago west of Helsinki, came from a Finnish-born, London-based banker who wanted to create a simple but tranquil summer retreat far from the City. For Seth Stein, the challenges the project posed were very different from those he had faced when building on left-over sites in London. The island was devoid of buildings, except for an old sauna cabin close to the water; a rocky outcrop in the sea, heavily wooded. There was a clear responsibility to build in tune with the form and ecology of the site. A house close to the shore would provide easy access and not compromise views of the island from the sea – such houses, equipped with saunas, were common in Finland. However, the client wanted to take advantage of the 360-degree views possible by locating the house on the high point at the centre of the island. Planning consent was obtained on the basis that the new home would be below the outline of the trees when viewed from the coast.

There was also the practical challenge of building on a site where all materials would have to be brought in by boat and then carried up to the summit of the island by hand.

The design strategy for the house – just 110 sq.m. in area – addressed these issues head-on. In terms of materials, there was the desire to pay some regard to the Finnish vernacular tradition but to do so in a straightforward and unsentimental way. By using prefabricated materials, including glulam beams and stone from the site, the house was assembled on site by local contractors. Its form, sheltering under an arched timber roof, was both elegant and highly practical; it had to carry twelve solar panels as the only source of power, each designed to sit flush against the roof edge when not in use and angle out to catch the long hours of summer sun. (The building grid was based on the dimensions of a standard photovoltaic panel.) A central fireplace provided supplementary heating but equally acted as a social hub for the house in the best Nordic tradition. Water is drawn from a well and from the sea, with a composting toilet in a place far from sewers. Pine and larch decking, used externally and internally, creates a warm and welcoming atmosphere; the interior of the house is split into two levels, following the contours of the site. Triple glazing was installed in the full height windows providing the spectacular views which were a key element in the project brief. The use of a boulder found on site, fashioned into a wash basin, was a typical example of Stein's feeling for natural materials and his ability to make an art object out of a functional necessity.

The project was the first of a series in which Stein addressed a site far from the city, confronting landscape and nature. Using natural materials, some found on site, he created a house which refers gently to the Finnish modernist tradition.

The summer house is located at the high point (15m) of the 12-acre island and faces the Baltic Sea

Early concept study

Main living space looking south

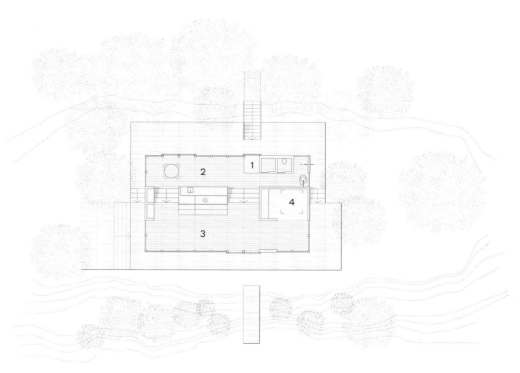

Floor plan

1   Arrival from jetty
2   Kitchen
3   Living
4   Sleeping

Site plan

0 10   100

South façade facing
the sea

A single granite rock, found on the island's coast nearby, provides a wash basin when placed on a steel tube

The central core contains the fireplace and open kitchen

House at dusk

Blondeau
Fine Art Gallery,
Geneva
2001

The commission from gallery owner, curator and art adviser Marc Blondeau, a major figure on the world art scene, to convert a former factory building in Geneva into a gallery and offices added a new dimension to Seth Stein's portfolio. Stein was no newcomer to the art world: he had completed a gallery in London's West End for leading dealer Maureen Paley and in 1998 designed a temporary pavilion for the Serpentine Gallery's reopening after its major reconstruction. Blondeau, who had previously headed up Sotheby's in France, moved to Geneva from Paris in 2000. An invited competition was staged to select an architect for his new Swiss base, to be housed in a 1900s industrial building in the rue de la Muse, originally a nail polish factory.

The building was a typically tough steel-framed structure with few architectural adornments – ideal raw material to house galleries, offices and a reference library of over 16,000 books. Working in association with Geneva architect Antoine Ris, Stein carried out a sensitive conversion, retaining the bones of the building including an impressive staircase. The functional spaces within offered ample scope to create galleries; moveable partitions ensured maximum flexibility for displaying paintings and sculpture. A whole floor was given over to the library, one of the most extensive reference collections on art from 1900 to the present in existence. The industrial character of the building was reinforced externally by the introduction of steel-framed Crittall windows (manufactured in Essex) at first- and second-floor level.

**Street view of restored
nail polish factory**

Reception

**Hinged walls in the
main gallery enable the
reconfiguration of space**

**Alessandro Twombly,
'Parallel landscapes'
exhibition view
at Blondeau & Cie,
Geneva, 2013**

Library design studies

The extensive art book library is used to delineate the office floor

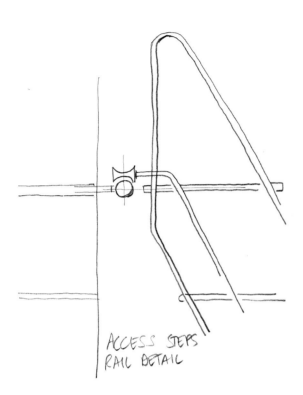

ACCESS STEPS
RAIL DETAIL

42cm

1 metre = 25 BOOKS

400 LINEAR METRES ON 7 N° SHELVES = 57 METRES
= 10,000 BOOKS

EXTEND TOP STEP
TO PROVIDE SOMEWHERE
TO PUT BOOKS WHILE
USING STEPS

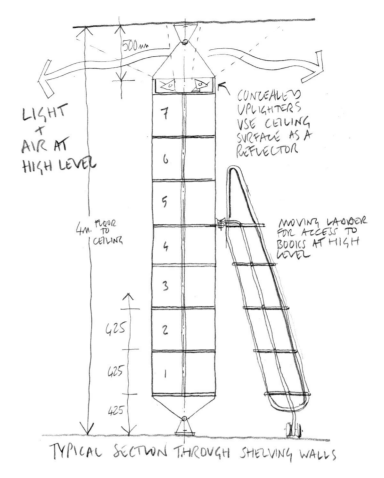

500mm

LIGHT + AIR AT HIGH LEVEL

CONCEALED UPLIGHTERS USE CEILING SURFACE AS A REFLECTOR

4m. FLOOR TO CEILING

MOVING LADDER FOR ACCESS TO BOOKS AT HIGH LEVEL

7
6
5
4
3
2
1

425
425
425

TYPICAL SECTION THROUGH SHELVING WALLS

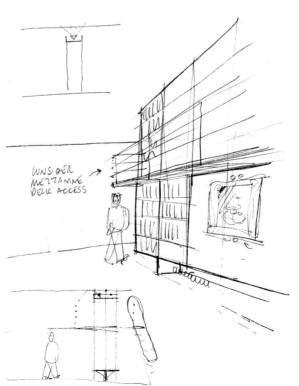

CONSIDER MEZZANINE DECK ACCESS

Baltic Restaurant, London
2001

A significant non-domestic project carried out by Seth Stein's studio, Baltic restaurant was fashioned from raw material akin to that found in Kelso Place: a land-locked site occupied by derelict industrial structures. The location was on London's South Bank, undergoing a rapid wave of regeneration coinciding with the opening of Tate Modern and the Jubilee Line Extension of the Underground. (The new Southwark tube station, designed by Richard MacCormac, was yards away from the site.)

Behind a Georgian terrace on Blackfriars Road, the former coachworks acquired by Stein's client, Jan Woroniecki, was in poor condition but there was obvious potential, as at Kelso Place, to salvage its best elements and create a striking fusion of old and new. The most problematic aspect of the site was its very narrow entrance from the street. Potential customers had to be enticed into a very cramped space as a prelude to the main volume of the restaurant. Stein created spatial drama from the contrast between the long, low bar, dimly lit and the lofty, light-filled restaurant beyond, occupying the former coachworks. Impressive timber roof trusses and exposed brickwork, combined with a polished concrete floor, gave the restaurant a clearly industrial character, combined with an ethos of quiet luxury which has made Baltic restaurant a popular part of the South Bank scene. Fine materials were used to good effect – the bar was dominated by a long counter of blackened steel with chunks of amber brought from the client's native Poland. Fibre optic lighting threaded through the amber produces a spectacular effect – a cascade of golden light.

The main restaurant space retains the original timber roof structure

Fibre optic strands threaded into individual chunks of raw amber create a light installation. The amber was sourced from Kaliningrad on the Baltic coast

**Previous use as a
restoration workshop
dealing only with 1950s
Citroëns (as depicted
in Tin Tin). The main
restaurant space retains
the original timber roof
structure**

Floor plan

1   Entry
2   Bar
3   Fibre optic amber light
4   Main dining

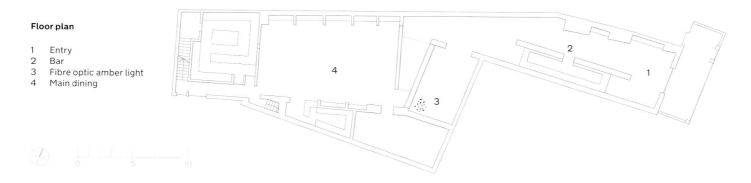

Tabatznik House, Toronto
2001

Seth Stein's first project in North America was the result of a commission from a couple who had previously lived in London and had admired the Kelso Place house. They invited Stein to develop a scheme for a new house to replace the routine villa they owned in an affluent suburb of Toronto. The site fronted on to an avenue of similar dwellings and some respect for established context was necessary. To the rear, however, it looked on to a deep wooded ravine – a touch of the wilderness on the edge of the city.

The client brief was for a family house, with ample accommodation for the couple and their three children and robust, flexible spaces. From the street, the house presents a discreet and rather enigmatic face: two plain white cubes, topped by pitched roofs, separated by a wall of opaque glass and prefaced by a pair of courtyards enclosed by stone walls. There was nothing there to cause offence to the neighbours, nothing radical or especially innovative. Stein described the street elevation as 'almost a child's drawing of a house, simplified as far as you can go'. The magic of the house begins beyond the front door. Entering, the visitor is immediately confronted by a typical Stein device: a cylindrical cloakroom reinforced by a diagonal wall provides a baffle to the route into the house. Beyond, one is in a modern version of the great hall, a full-height space top-lit via a *brise-soleil* roof, with louvres that can be fully open or adjusted to control strong sunlight. This dramatic space, flanked by a family living room to one side and a kitchen/dining room to the other, defines the main axis of the house, which Stein conceived as 'a receptacle for light'; a 'light box'. The culmination of the space is a glazed wall with fine views over the ravine, opening to a terrace and a pool. From the ravine the house, so solid from the street, seems transparent.

Four bedrooms are disposed around the perimeter of the house – externally they can be read as four small houses, linked by a bridge. The master bedroom suite has an elevation of frosted glass to the main living space and a run of clerestory glazing to flood it with light. At basement level there is a large activity room for the children, a steam room (within the lower level of the cloakroom cylinder), and a 78ft-long lap pool. Vivid colours – deep blue and red – are a defining feature of this zone of the house, so fundamental to its identity as a family home. The designs for the house, beginning with Stein's sketches, were developed, as ever, in discussion with the clients. The idea was to create a house able to accommodate the family's lifestyle – a building of subtle quality but one with an element of fun too.

Double-height living space

West-facing high-level window admits late afternoon sunlight into the double-height living space

**View of the house from
the street**

Upper level plan

1   Child bedroom
2   Parent bedroom
3   Linen
4   Void above living (top glazed)

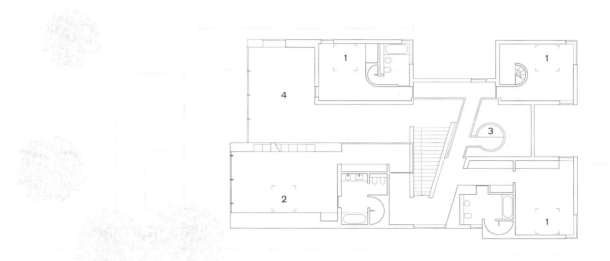

Ground level plan

1   Entry
2   Mud room entry
3   Study
4   Sitting
5   Family kitchen
6   Outdoor pool

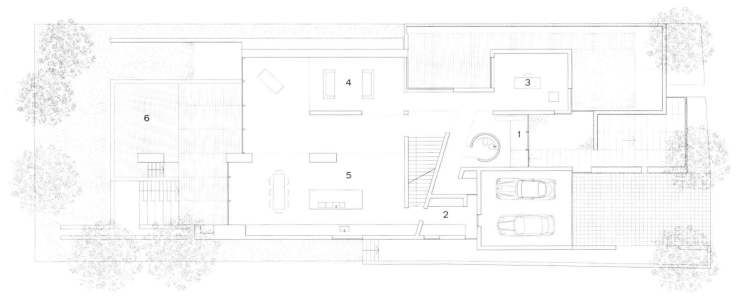

0   5   10

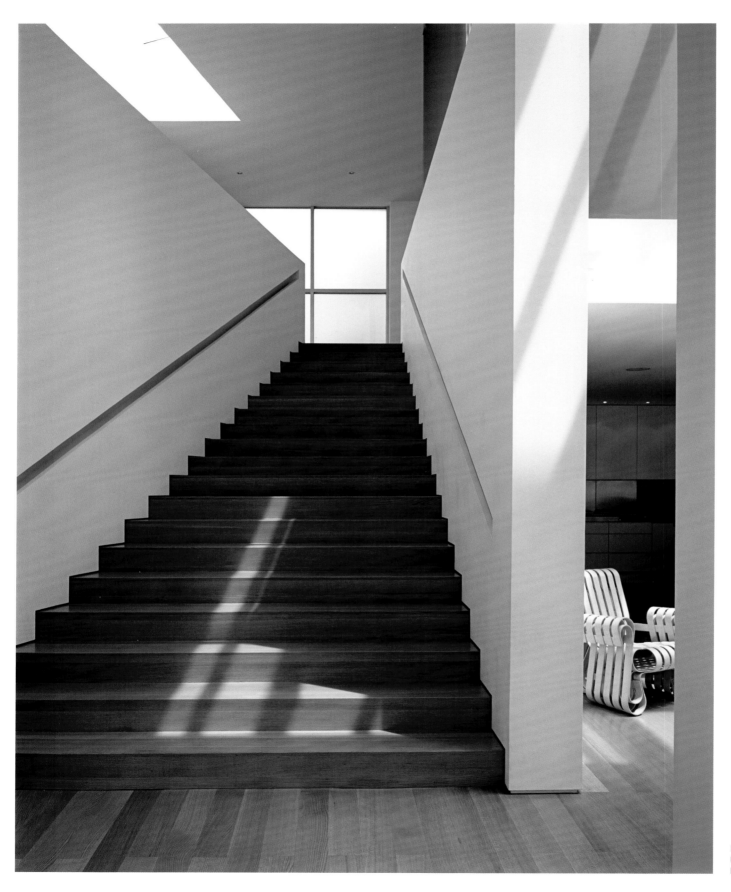

**Double volume
living space seen from
bridge link**

**Design study of
street boundary**

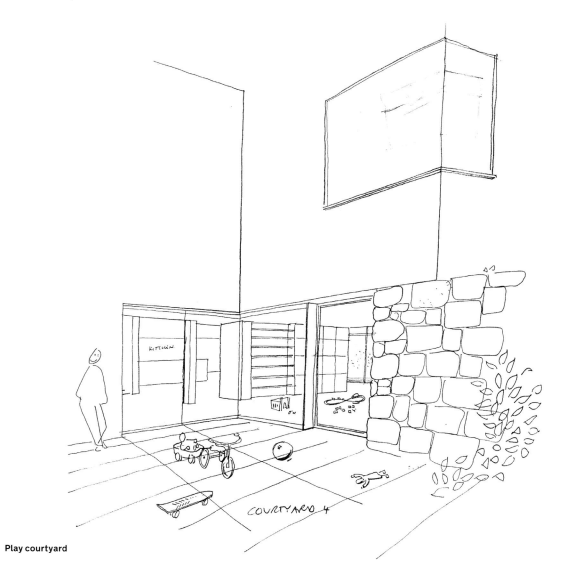

View towards entrance   **Play courtyard**

Rear view of the house
from the forest ravine

Beach House, South Africa
2003

Commissioned by Richard and Lucille Lewin, founders of the Whistles fashion chain – for which Seth Stein had completed around fifteen shop fit-outs – the Plettenberg Bay project continued the dialogue with context and ecology which became a major element in Stein's work. The site was spectacular; high up, overlooking a magnificent prospect of sandy beaches and dunes in the Western Cape, with views across to the Robberg Peninsula, an uninhabited nature reserve.

Plettenberg Bay is a favoured site for expensive holiday homes, not all of them especially distinguished but both the clients and their architect were anxious to create a house that was at home in its setting and which drew on local materials and building methods. (It made practical sense to take advantage of local craft traditions.) The dunes extend virtually to the walls of the house, which is a short walk from the beach. Trees, including a remarkable milk tree, estimated to be up to 330 years old, were carefully retained. The strategy was to design a house opening up to the natural landscape and the views whilst turning its back on the approach road, from which the house reads as a classic exercise in white modernist minimalism. The entrance sequence is deliberately low key but an element of drama is provided by the way in which a 'box' at first-floor level, containing four bedrooms, bursts through the façade. Internally, the 'box' seems to float above the main living area. The bedrooms are accessed from a long corridor enclosed by a screen formed of thin poles of timber. Known as latte and made of locally gathered eucalyptus wood, it extends across the entire 23m-long façade of the house facing the sea, the timber held in place with thin copper wire. The screen provides shading but also allows fresh breezes to permeate the house – there is no air conditioning, a feature of many new houses in the area. Eucalyptus wood is hard and resistant to the effects of sea air and weathers beautifully to a silvery grey. Bedrooms have opening sections to take advantage of the views across to the Robberg Peninsula. By night, the seaward frontage of the house appears as a lantern, with light piercing the timber panels. By day, the bedrooms are filled by subtly striated bands of light.

The contrast between modern and traditional materials – concrete versus local timber – is fundamental to the aesthetic of the house, extending to the terraces which spread out from the ground floor, focused on a pool but with canopies and seating of timber. Only a small area of the ground floor is fully enclosed; everything in this house is about living with the landscape. A rooftop terrace, complete with open-air shower, provides the finest of all the views across sea and land. Stein describes the house as 'a balance between pure form and natural materials. It's really quite textured and, although it's very pure, it's not uncomfortable'. Purity and practicality, enclosure and openness combine to create a house worthy of its site.

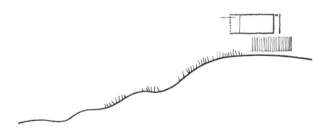

Curved boundary terminates as a water spout into the lap pool

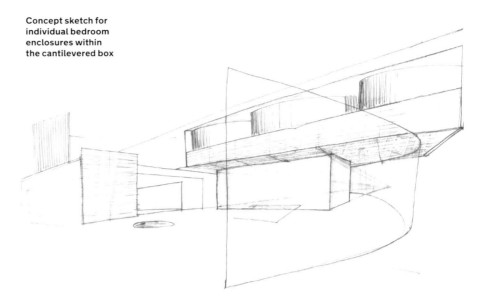

Concept sketch for individual bedroom enclosures within the cantilevered box

The upper-level bedrooms are set back behind a continuous series of timber pivot panels that open up to the sea view from within

View of the house from the feinbos sand dunes

The cantilevered upper
level seen from the street

Ground floor plan

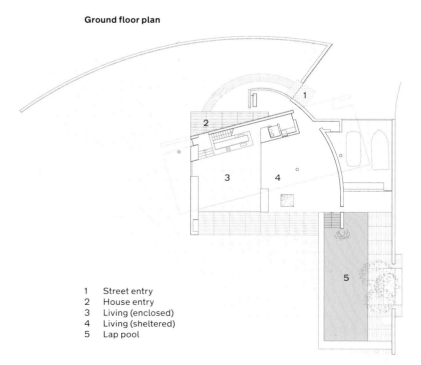

First floor plan

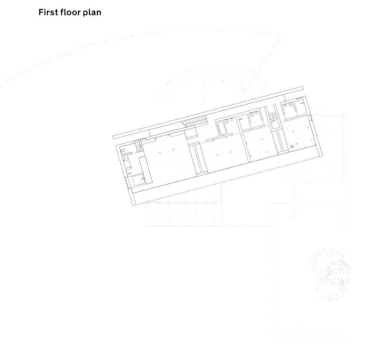

1   Street entry
2   House entry
3   Living (enclosed)
4   Living (sheltered)
5   Lap pool

Sea view from the side
rear of the beach house

Roof plan

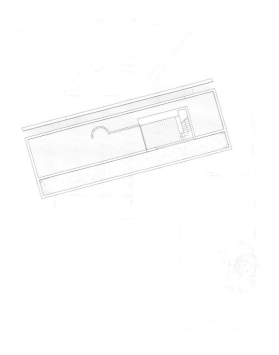

The position of the main
living room was established
by framing the principal
view of the ocean and
nature reserve beyond

Rear view of the house

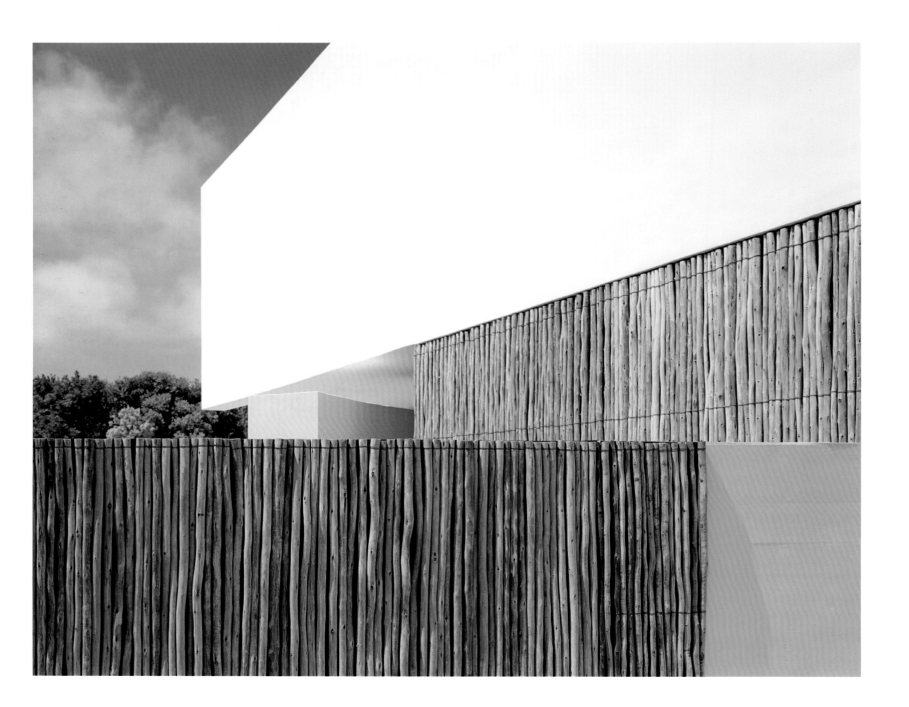

With sunlight shining
through the eucalyptus
screen – a strong pattern
of shadow and light falls
on the surfaces of the
main circulation spine
of the upper level

Ocean elevation with
eucalyptus screens
and cladding

Beach House, North Caicos
2006

The site for this house in the Turks and Caicos Islands was a barren but beautiful deserted beach, bordered by vegetation in the form of tropical dwarf dry forest and with no natural water supply. The client had seen the house designed by Stein in Finland and wanted a simple beach house in the same vein, albeit adapted to very different climatic conditions but with accommodation for guests. As in Finland, one issue was that of transporting all the materials for the house a considerable distance, so that a timber-framed module system, using prefabricated components was used, with overhanging curved roofs. The design strategy, developed in association with structural engineers Atelier One and local architect Rolf Rothermel, was straightforward but entirely appropriate to the location.

The 'house' consists of four separate elements: a central pavilion with kitchen, living and dining spaces and three detached cabins, each containing a bedroom and bathroom/dressing room. The buildings, connected by a raised timber walkway, are designed for the simple, even spartan, life in a warm climate with screened and open terraces extending towards the sea. Bathrooms can be entirely opened to the surrounding landscape. The decision was made to eschew entirely the use of glazing, so that the façades are formed with mesh screens (to exclude insects) or louvres within sliding or fixed panels. There are few extravagant touches, although the use of a boulder as a sculptural hand basin is a gesture typical of the architect. Providing a water supply was obviously a key issue. The only source of water was rain – which occurs in the form of intermittent heavy downpours. An elegant metal hopper channels rainwater into a storage tank, a memorable feature as well as a functional necessity.

Rear view of beach houses

**The cluster of structures
is set back from the beach
line and linked by a raised
elliptical pathway**

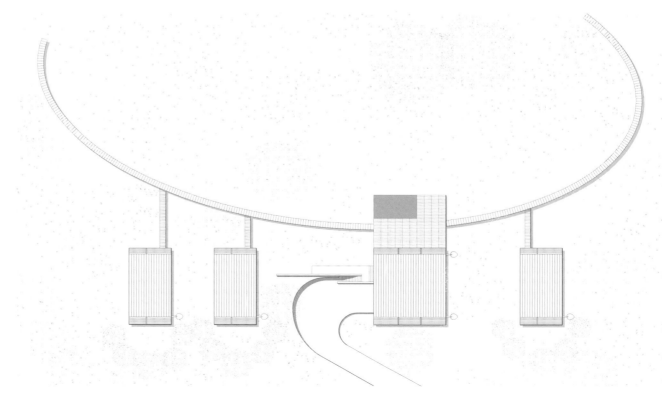

Site plan

0   10   20

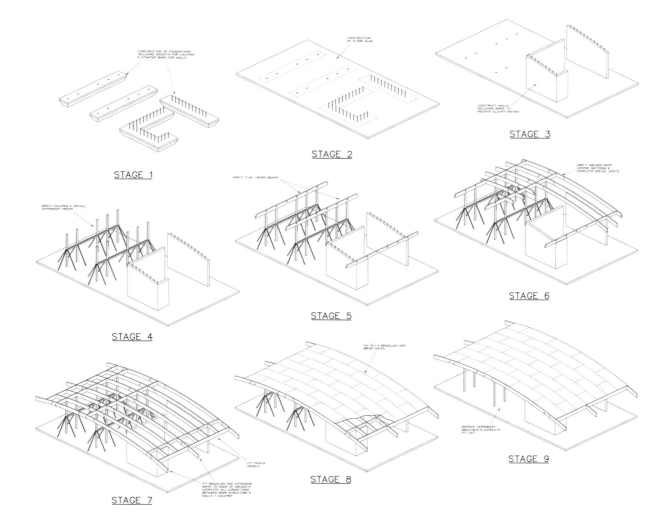

STAGE 1

STAGE 2

STAGE 3

STAGE 4

STAGE 5

STAGE 6

STAGE 7

STAGE 8

STAGE 9

Cabin plan

1 Deck
2 Verandah
3 Bedroom
4 Shower
5 Shower garden

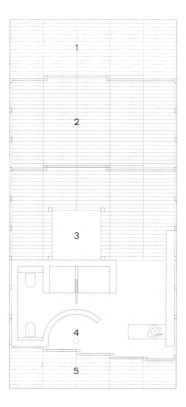

Bedrooms are enclosed
by jalousie panels and
bug screens

Sketch detail study

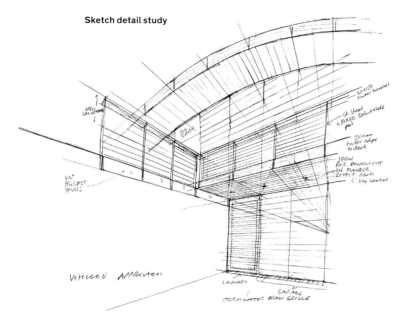

Main pavilion approach

**View from the main
pavilion looking towards
the pool and sea beyond**

In the absence of glazing, the jalousie and bug screens transform the beach houses into two lanterns in the evening

Enclosure/layers studies

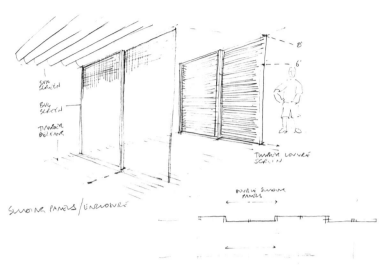

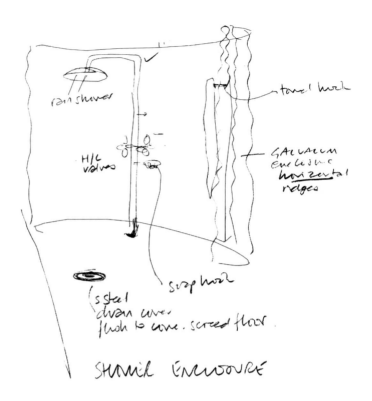

Shower rooms located
at the rear of the beach
houses facing a small
clearing in the jungle

Bathroom basin of local
stone positioned on
cantilevered concrete slab,
facing jungle clearing

Rainwater hopper design

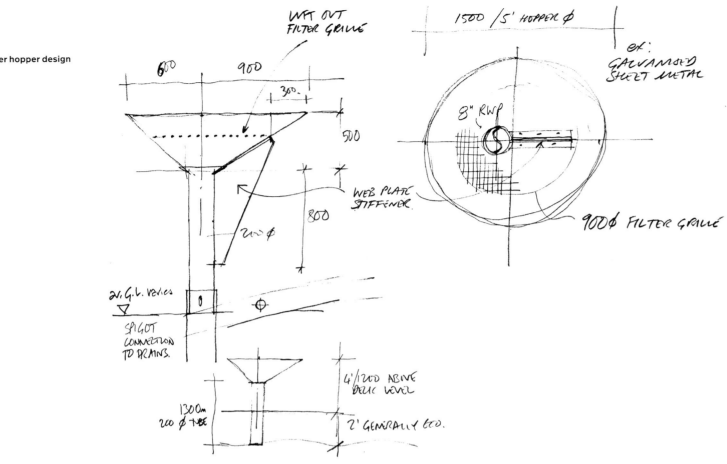

**Free standing hoppers
collect rainwater**

Pencalenick House, Cornwall
2006

The 4-acre site for the house designed by Seth Stein at Pencalenick, near Fowey, 'a creek off a creek', had resonances of Richard Rogers' Creek Vean project that Stein has always admired. Steep and mostly covered in dense woodland, it had previously been occupied by an isolation hospital for patients in quarantine (already demolished when the site was acquired by Stein's client, Johnny Sandelson). The approach by land, along narrow lanes, is circuitous – the house is more appropriately accessed by boat by a causeway and steep path.

The brief was for a family holiday home which would capitalise on the site's proximity to the water and the fine views out to Fowey Creek, with its ever-changing prospect of small boats, sea and sky. The house should be comfortable but not luxurious, spacious (seven quite modest bedrooms) but not extravagant. It occupies a narrow strip of land immediately adjacent to the creek. Low-lying, respecting the character of the site, it is a modular structure constructed of laminated timber and prefabricated off-site, with a solid concrete retaining wall to the rear. The house is one room deep, with all rooms given views from the gently curved elevation looking on to the creek. A narrow, top-lit circulation zone extends along its rear, behind the retaining wall. Timber and locally quarried stone are used extensively as cladding.

The heart of the house is a double-height living and dining space, adjacent to an open kitchen, with slate walling extending from outside providing a distinctive feature and enclosing the fireplace. A freestanding slate wall, continuing the external diagonal axis of the stone jetty, dominates the double-volume space and partially conceals stairs leading to a glass gallery at the bedroom level above. The bedrooms are accessed by a top-glazed passage that follows the sinuous line of the rear wall. The main elevation of the house is clad in a mix of fixed and sliding glazing and louvred panels made of red cedar that can be opened to provide natural ventilation. Stein aimed to create 'a calm place from which to contemplate the world'; the house amply fulfills that vision.

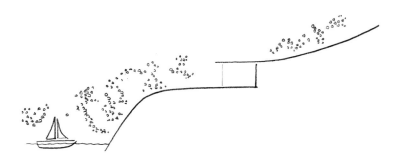

Pencalenick House seen from the Fowey estuary

Site section

1   Double volume living
2   Glass gallery
3   Grass roof
4   Vehicle approach
5   River Fowey

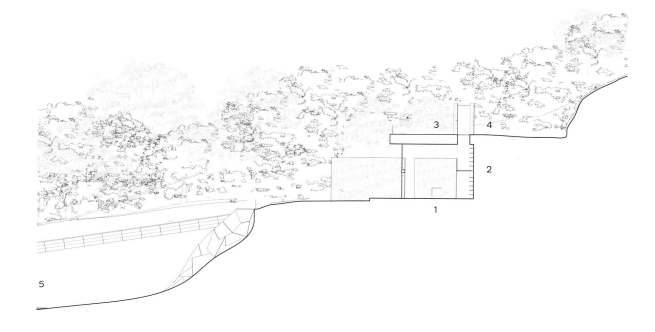

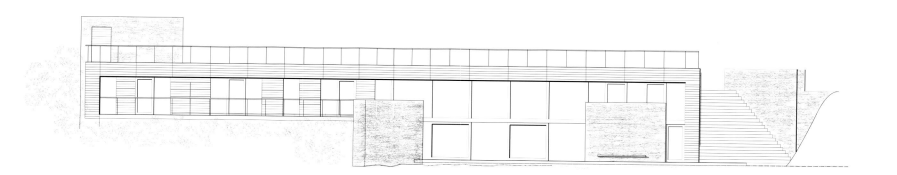

Elevation

**To the north, the house
is glimpsed through
the ancient oak forest**

**Approaching the house
on foot**

Roof plan

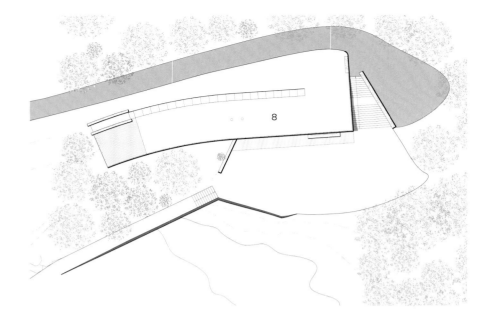

The roof glazing and corridor form the spine of the house plan. The glazed gallery allows maximum daylight to the rear of the main living space

Upper level plan

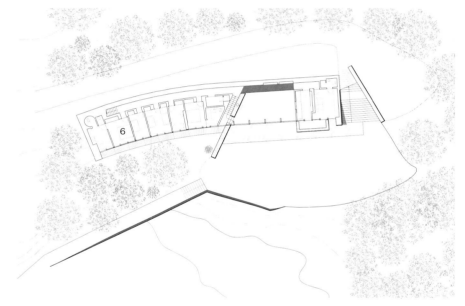

Ground floor plan

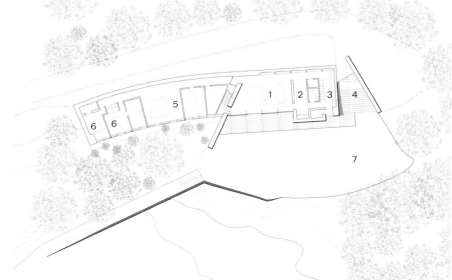

1 Living
2 Kitchen
3 Mud room
4 Stairs up to parking
5 Rainy day room
6 Bedroom & bathroom
7 Cliff-top lawn
8 Grass roof

0   5   10

Main living space
overlooking Fowey
estuary

All rooms, including the bathrooms, overlook the water/estuary

Timber pivot panels animate the main elevation

Approach by boat at high tide

House in Notting Hill, London
2010

Section through house showing stepped terraces

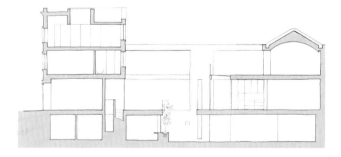

Far away from exotic locations, the house in Hillgate Street, off London's Notting Hill Gate, represented a return to what might be seen as Seth Stein's home territory. The house replaced an existing property, built behind a matter-of-fact post-war façade by an architect couple. There was scope to make more effective use of the site, narrow to the street but extending back some 28m. With consent secured to create a new basement level, the principal planning constraint was the requirement to give the house a period frontage, matching that of other nearby properties, so that the new house makes no impact on the street of modest Victorian residences. But the strength of Stein's design is immediately apparent internally.

The house, designed for family living, is entered from the street via a narrow slot adjoining a garage from which the entry route doglegs into a dramatically day-lit space formed by a light-well extending down into a lower-ground-level courtyard to channel air and light into the heart of the house. To one side a 'ski slope' stair, a larger version of that seen in the Cheval Place house, contained in a narrow top-lit slot, provides access, in one continuous run, to all levels of the house. The experience of moving from darkness and confinement to light and space is memorable. The use of gold leaf as a wall covering, combined with polished concrete floors, bounces light into the basement. The plan of the house is L-shaped, with a large living/dining space to the rear in a three-storey wing, with bedrooms and a study above and below. Two further bedrooms are placed to the front of the house, one at second-floor level, at the summit of the staircase, and another in the basement, looking on to the courtyard. The house offers a remarkable variety of spatial experiences, skillfully accommodated within the constraints of the site. It is a place of surprises, a remarkably ingenious exercise in creating diversity within a narrow slot in the townscape.

A further significant element in the project is its application of low-energy technology, with solar panels providing heating and hot water. The strategy had featured in earlier projects by Seth Stein – for example, in the island house in Finland – but it remains pioneering for a house in the city.

Central lightwell with stepped back terraces

**Entrance hall with
aluminium roller wall**

**Entrance hall and
garage combined**

Study

Concrete plunge pool
with palladium leaf
mosaic wall creating a
shimmering light effect

Serge Mouille wall light
in vaulted bedroom
and stairwell light slot

Bedroom panelled in
sandblasted ash and
sandstone bathroom

Novo Cemetery, London
2012

Aerial images showing the extent of the burial ground pre/post 1970

The Novo Cemetery project was, by any standard, an unusual commission but one which Stein's studio found particularly rewarding, effectively revealing part of London's hidden heritage. The cemetery is located off London's Mile End Road, a main artery of the East End. Its history is inextricably linked to that of the capital's Jewish community. Expelled under King Edward I in 1290, Sephardic Jews won the right to live in England under the Protectorate of Oliver Cromwell. A synagogue was completed in the City in 1701, with a burial ground outside the City to the east. When this was filled, a further 'new' – or Novo – cemetery was brought into use in the 1730s and later much extended. It became the resting place of a number of notable members of the community but was closed in 1936. By the 1970s it was becoming enclosed by the growing campus of London University's Queen Mary College (now Queen Mary, University of London). The older section was cleared, with remains reinterred elsewhere. The more recent section of the cemetery, developed from 1865, remained, enclosed by a tall hedge, with new college buildings rising around it. A long-term strategy for its maintenance as a sacred space was needed.

Working with Queen Mary and with representatives of the Spanish and Portuguese Jews' Congregation, Seth Stein Architects developed an approach designed to conserve the cemetery and make it accessible to visitors as a valued cultural asset. A major constraint was the imperative to avoid excavation and any disturbance of burials, while opening up the cemetery as a focus of the campus rather than a forgotten backwater. On the southern edge of the site a very narrow route linked a number of faculty buildings with a new humanities block under construction. A new open space here, linked to an expanded pedestrian route, would provide a view across the cemetery for visitors and a place where information on its history could be displayed. To protect burials from disturbance the new path was cantilevered out as a bridge with no structural supports within the cemetery, with a metal stair providing access to the graves, which are still visited and maintained by the Jewish community. Jewish law dictated the degree to which the structure should clear the ground and the gravestones. A bowl for ablutions maintains the sacred identity of the space, enclosed by Corten steel panels and intended to invite contemplation. Elsewhere the perimeter of the burial ground was enclosed by low in-situ concrete walls, replacing the forbidding hedge.

Openings within the Corten balustrade panels indicate the original extent of the 18th-century burial ground

Site plan

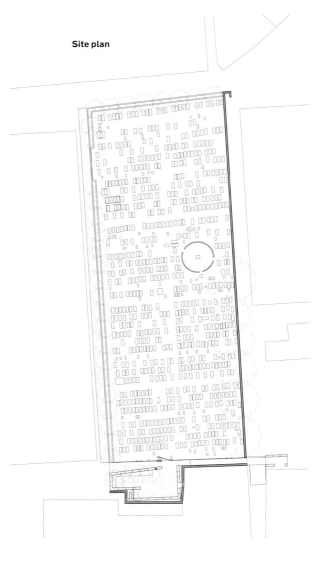

Novo Cemetery. The path is cantilevered over the burial ground in order to minimise impact on the original terrain/surface

Piazza plan

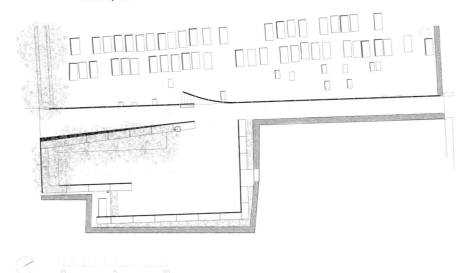

0   5   10

**Analysis of previous
arrangement**

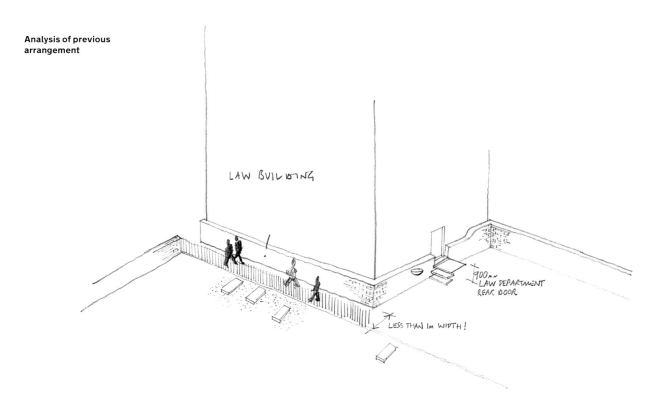

LAW BUILDING

900mm
LAW DEPARTMENT
REAR DOOR

LESS THAN 1m WIDTH !

DESIGN PROPOSALS:

• A BRIDGE GENTLY RISING TO THRESHOLD
  LEVEL OF LAW DEPARTMENT REAR ENTRANCE

• TO PROVIDE A PUBLIC SPACE THAT ADDRESSES
  THE HISTORIC BURIAL GROUND

• TO FRAME, AS WELL AS PROTECT, THE HISTORIC
  AND SACRED GROUND

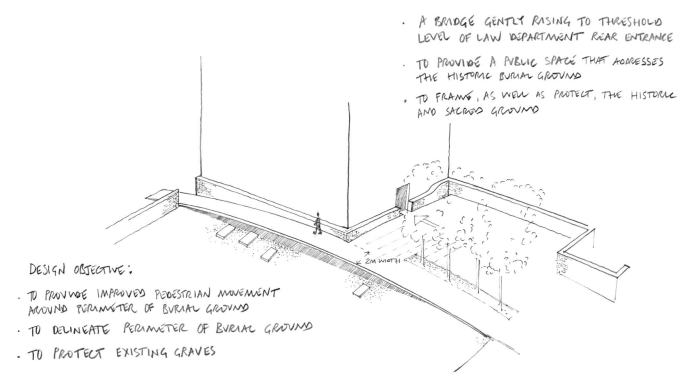

2M WIDTH

DESIGN OBJECTIVE:

• TO PROVIDE IMPROVED PEDESTRIAN MOVEMENT
  AROUND PERIMETER OF BURIAL GROUND

• TO DELINEATE PERIMETER OF BURIAL GROUND

• TO PROTECT EXISTING GRAVES

Design objectives

Victorian graves in
Novo Cemetery

Waterjet-cut weathering
steel balustrading and
signage

The lower edge of the
balustrade panelling
separated by the width
of a hand above a
Victorian child grave

The Corten panels prior
to weathering

Corten steel stairs
suspended above the
burial ground level

Country House, Somerset
2013

This house, close to the historic city of Bath, replaced an existing dwelling – a former farm house, of some age, but no special architectural interest and internally a maze of small rooms. The site was on a north-facing hillside, with fine views, on which the existing house turned its back. In proposing to demolish and replace the old house, located in the Green Belt and within an Area of Outstanding Natural Beauty, Seth Stein's client faced some local opposition. The project finally won approval from a local planning authority keen to encourage outstanding new design which respected its context: a challenge to which Stein responded with customary panache.

In contrast to its predecessor, the house opens up to the view, hugging the hillside. The plan is deliberately fragmented, with spaces disposed around a central courtyard, the interior opening up to terraces for al fresco living. A long 'tube' at first-floor level contains bedrooms and is clad in timber. The use of local stone, recycled from the demolished farm house, connects the house to the landscape. An old barn was retained and converted to use as a music room – it helps to anchor the new house to the site. A small guest house is located discreetly in a walled garden.

With its comfortable mix of materials, timber, stone and glass and undemonstrative but uncompromising modernity, this house makes a positive statement about the potential for contemporary design in the countryside.

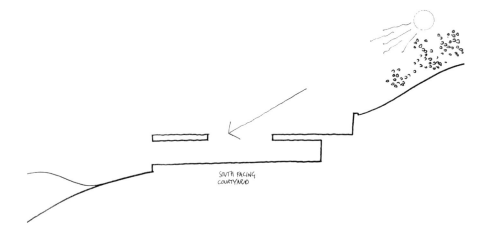

SOUTH FACING COURTYARD

The house facing the valley

**North elevation facing
the valley**

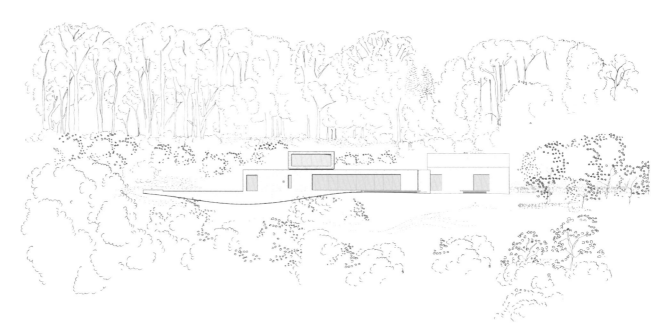

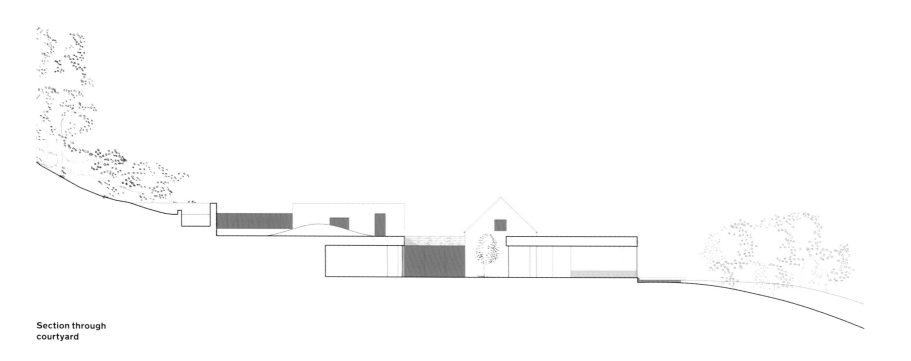

**Section through
courtyard**

**Indoor pool with
opening (on right) leading
to outdoor lap pool**

Upper level plan

1   Walled garden
2   Principal bedroom
3   Family bedroom
4   Guest bedroom

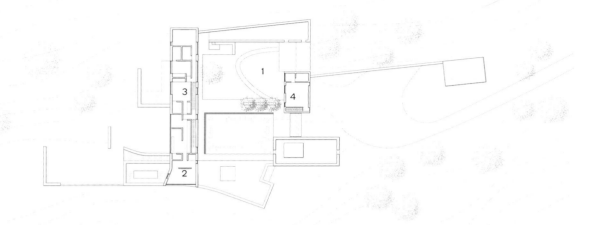

Ground level plan

1   Arrival
2   Hall
3   Sun trap courtyard
4   Music room
5   Book box
6   Living
7   Kitchen
8   Study
9   Changing room / Spa
10 Inner pool
11 Outer pool

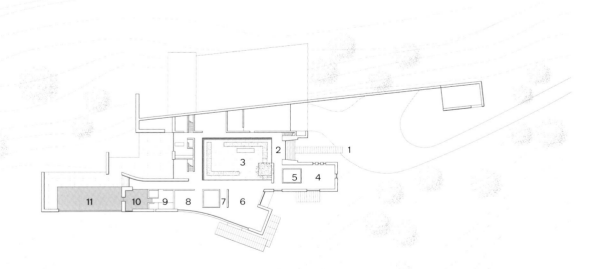

0   5   25

Entrance

Entrance view

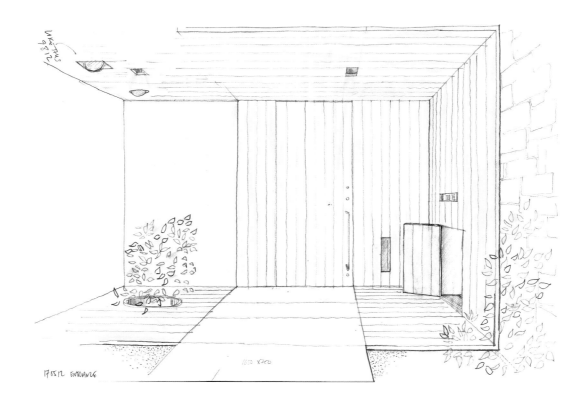

The central courtyard and
perimeter galleries incorporate
the original barn, now used as
a music room

Courtyard (inset planter)

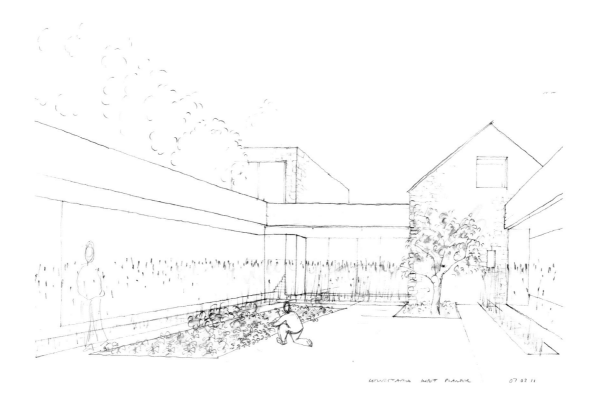

Courtyard (raised planter)

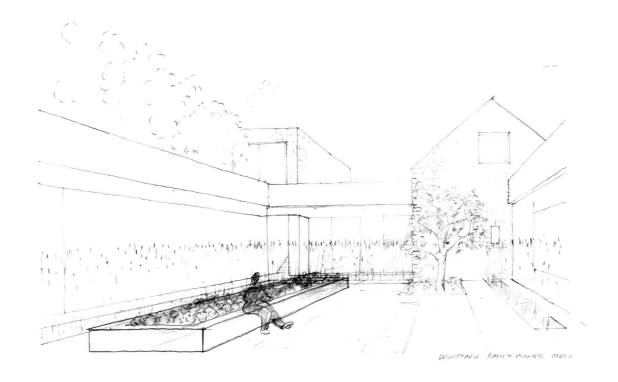

'Book box' in music room.
The top contains a reading
nook overlooking the
music room

**Open kitchen overlooking
the valley**

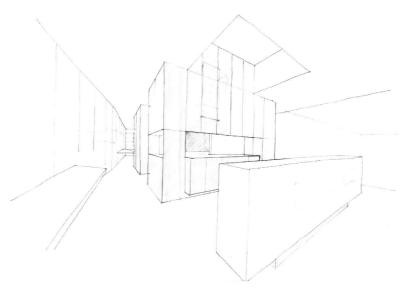

Kitchen view

The music room 'book box'

**View from book box
towards music room**

The principal bedroom
with panoramic views
across the open country

Living-room fireplace
with blackened steel
hearth

The house seen across
the valley

Equestrian Centre, Australia
2014

Designed for a London-based client with family links to Australia, this development is located in an area of remarkable natural beauty, with rolling farmland, wineries and stunning beaches, close to the ocean but little more than an hour's drive from Melbourne. Working with locally-based architect Rob Watson – a former colleague from the office of Norman Foster – Stein created a habitat for horses to rival some of the exceptional modern houses constructed in the area in recent years.

Sustainability was a prime consideration in the development of the project, since water is in short supply in the peninsula. There was also a clear imperative to work with the context and climate and use local materials in a practical and straightforward way – Tasmanian oak for the structural frame; Gum tree wood for the cladding panels, designed to fade to a silver hue. The stables, housing six horses, are contained within a berm formed of rammed earth (a method of construction common in the region), insulating them from the hot sun and rooting them in the landscape. Stables and ancillary facilities, tack room, laundry, workshop and office, curve around a central paddock, with a pool for washing horses supplied from a small reservoir lake created as part of extensive landscaping works. The sweeping roof is of zinc, almost High-tech in its dramatic form, sheltering and enclosing, providing shade and natural ventilation and used to harvest rainwater, employing large hoppers made of corrugated metal in the best Australian vernacular tradition. Underground tanks provide further storage for rainwater, a precious commodity in this extreme climate. A barn wing provides storage for straw and hay and parking for vehicles. A house is planned as a second phase of development on the estate.

Rear wall in rammed earth

Elevation to the menage

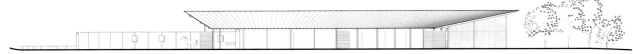

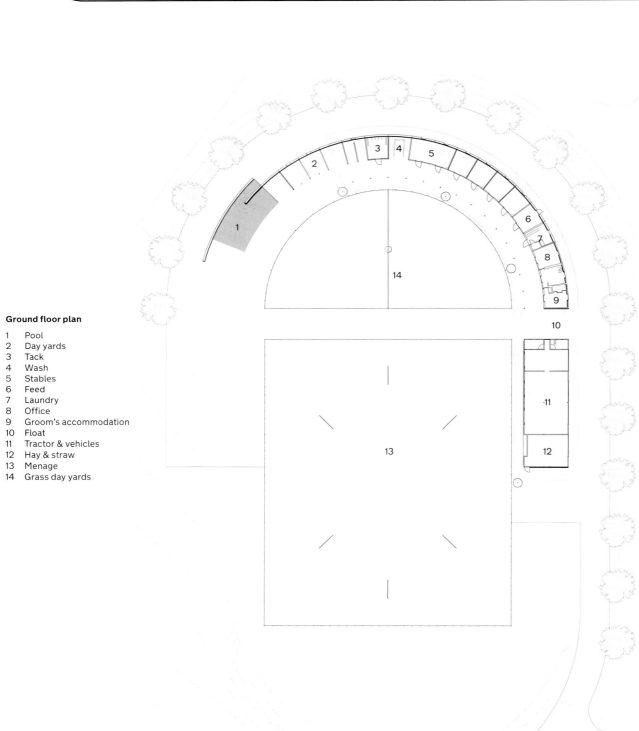

Ground floor plan

1   Pool
2   Day yards
3   Tack
4   Wash
5   Stables
6   Feed
7   Laundry
8   Office
9   Groom's accommodation
10   Float
11   Tractor & vehicles
12   Hay & straw
13   Menage
14   Grass day yards

0   5   10

**Crescent stables
overlooking the paddock**

Horse pool

Roof plan

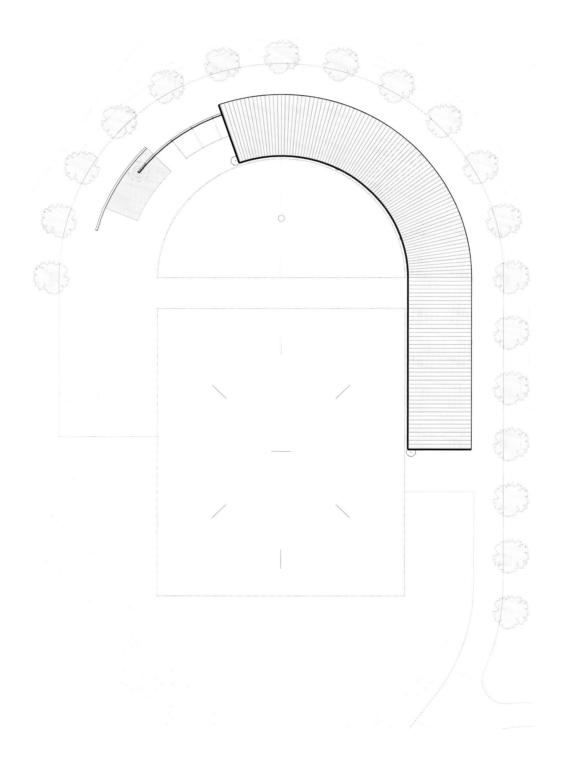

0   5   10

**Rear of stables crescent
facing south**

Menage for eventing,
dressage and show jumping

The horse pool and
water spout

Stables kitchen in
stainless steel and
plywood panels

Horse feed

Individual stables within
the crescent plan

Tack room

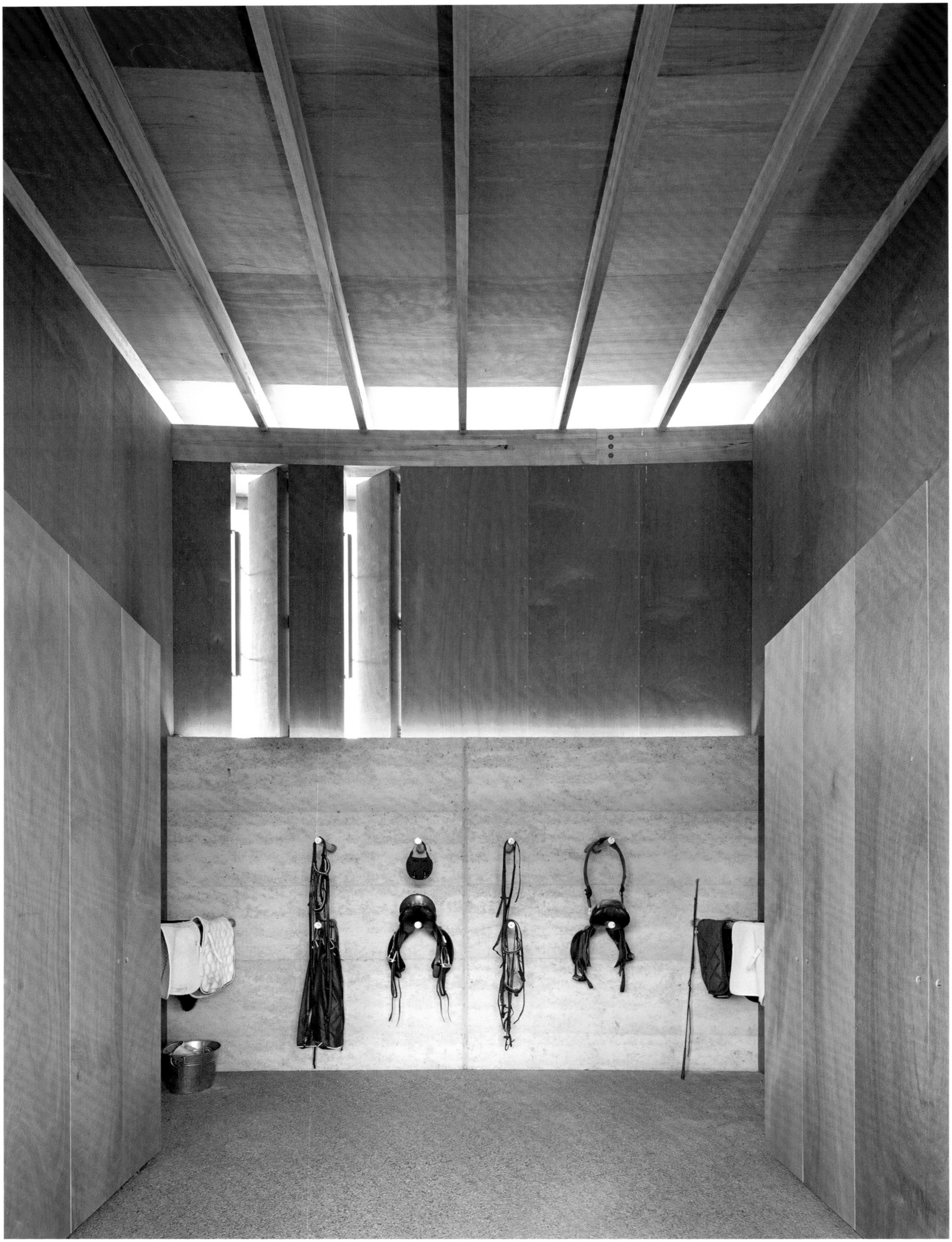

Converted School House, London
2017

Occupying a space with a small footprint but a 14ft (4.3m) ceiling, the bathroom enclosure is located above the bedroom

The third domestic project (including a beach house in South Africa) for clients who had first commissioned Seth Stein in the 1990s, this house exemplifies Stein's sensitive approach to the adaptation of existing buildings. The house is a dramatic conversion of a former school building dating from 1859, a good example of Victorian Tudor Gothic. The elevation to the street, executed in characteristic diapered brickwork, was virtually unaltered but the subsequent history of the building, most recently shared between an evangelical library and fashion showrooms, had generated a series of alterations. A particularly damaging change was the crude brick infilling of the arcade, formed of cast iron columns, fronting the internal courtyard – formerly the school playground. Internally, the basic structure of the building was intact, somewhat compromised by partitions although a number of original features such as doors and chimneypieces survived.

The design strategy for the conversion of the building to residential use was to express the bones of the original structure, to retain features of interest and to expose and celebrate the range of materials, brick, stone, timber and iron, used in its construction. Externally, the most significant move was the reopening of the courtyard arcade, with the original iron columns retained and a screen of frameless glazing, 4m high, set back behind them. Internally, the ground floor of the building was reopened as a single living space, some 21m long. Bedrooms, a further living room and study were inserted at first-floor level. New work is clearly contemporary in manner, with refined modern materials, frameless glazing and Carrara marble, offset against salvaged floorboards, iron columns and sandblasted Victorian brickwork. Original stairs were retained with no attempt to soften their look. The project balanced modern amenities with a clear concern for authenticity.

Movement flow between
the internal living area and
the courtyard forming a
unified space when open

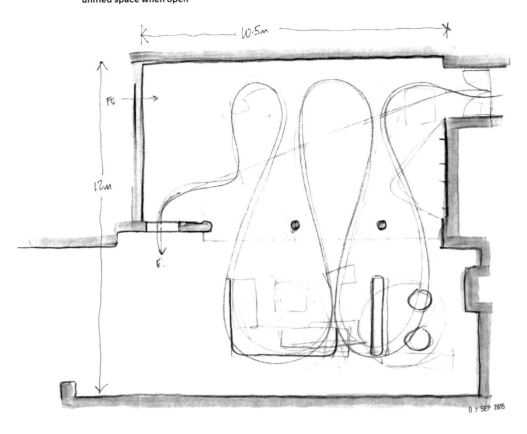

Living room overlooking the
courtyard that was originally
the school play yard

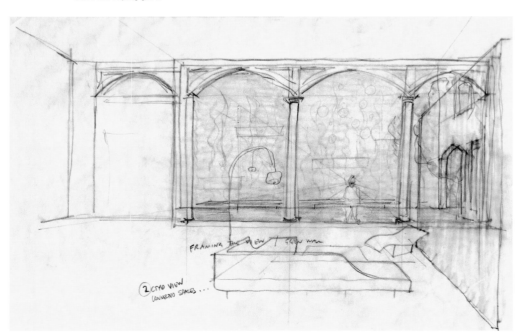

The main living space
extends 21m and retains
the original structural
fabric – cast-iron beams
and columns – providing
the shell for loft living

1   Platform lift
2   Old school stairs
3   Bed
4   Bathroom
5   Study
6   Ceramics studio
7   Up to mezzanine

First floor plan

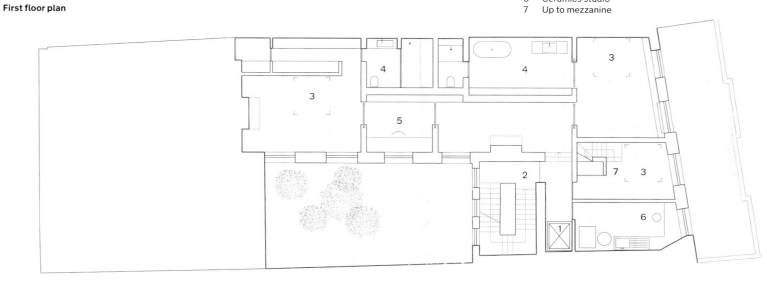

1   Entrance passage from street
2   Courtyard garden
3   Entrance
4   Living
5   Eating
6   Kitchen
7   Paved garden

Ground floor plan

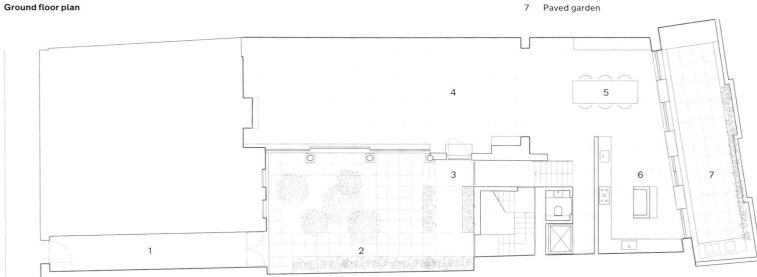

0   5   10

**Guest cloakroom combining
sandblasted surfaces and
Carrara marble**

Carrara marble steam room

The original Victorian school stairs connect the two main floors. Surfaces are sandblasted to reveal the original fabric of the building

Acknowledgements

Architectural projects typically overlap leaving little opportunity to pause for reflection before starting a new commission. I am grateful to Lund Humphries for suggesting this monograph that has given us the chance to review our architecture as a body of work spanning 25 years. In particular our author, Kenneth Powell, who has described it in a cohesive narrative, as well as Susie Newbigging, our studio manager, who has kept a steady watch over the creation of this book.

The process of making a building is complex, protracted and hugely satisfying. Without our clients we would not progress beyond the drawing board and I am grateful to all of them for placing their trust in me.

I would like to express my gratitude to all the members of my studio with whom I have worked over 25 years, in particular my associates Andrew Abdulezer, Evelyn Hayes and Paddy Gallagher.

As a collaborative process the contribution made by our consultants, builders and craftsmen has enriched the realization of these projects.

Finally, my love and thanks to Susannah Pollen. She has lived through almost all of these projects with me and given me the support and sense of balance so often needed.

Seth Stein Architects

Names in bold indicate current staff members.

Hanan Abdulamir
Andrew Abdulezer
Samina Choudhry
Phoebe Dakin
Adam Draper
Flora Fairbairn
Annaleen Feindt
Kirsten Flemming
Cordula Friedlander
Max Friedlander
Patrick Gallagher
Chris Godfrey
Louis Hall
James Hamilton
Alex Haw
Evelyn Hayes
Fiona Henderson
Sarah Homes
Lisa Howard
Carla James
Jamie Keats
Andy Lavelle
Christine Milne
Chris McHale
Gianluca Nencini
Susie Newbigging
Vanda Oliveira
Joanna Pencakowski
Heloise Perignon
Anna Pipilis
Jason Pritchard
Kate Rankin
David Russell
Silvia Scarpat
Seth Stein
Josh Stevenson
Richard Vint
Emma Wales
Paul Wallace
Nico Warr
Alice Weir
Wing Kei Wong

Photography

Number refer to pages.
t = top, m = middle,
b = bottom, l = left,
r = right, tl = top left,
tr = top right,
bl = bottom left,
br = bottom right

Giovanni Alfieri: 18, 30
Nick Bentley: 26(b)
Richard Bryant/ Arcaidimages.com: 14, 20, 40, 42, 043(l), 43(r), 46, 49, 51(t), 51(m), 51(b), 70, 71, 72, 74, 75, 76, 78, 85, 87, 112, 114(t), 114(b), 115, 116, 117(tl), 117(br)
Alix Carmichael: 89
Richard Davis: 6, 13, 16, 17, 23, 27, 33, 44, 52, 54, 56, 58(t), 58(b), 59, 60, 61, 65, 66, 67, 69, 92, 94, 96, 97(t), 97(b), 98, 99, 100, 101, 103, 104, 107(b), 111 (tl), 111 (tr), 118, 121, 123 (tl), 123 (tr), 124, 125, 126, 128, 130(l), 130(r), 132, 136, 137(t), 137(b), 138(t), 138(b), 139, 152, 153, 155, 156, 158(l), 158(r), 159
Lisbeth Grosmann: 37, 140, 143(t), 145, 146, 148, 149(tl), 149(tr), 149(b), 150, 151
Historic England: 119(t), 119(b)
Didier Jordan: 19, 62(t), 62(b), 63
James Mitchell/Spink Property: 21, 32
Kim Sayer: 109, 110, 111(b)
Justin Smallman: 143(b)
Andy Spain: 25
David Spero: 10, 11, 39, 41
Seth Stein: 7, 26(t), 28, 57, 80, 83, 86, 90, 91, 102, 107(t), 117(tr), 117(bl), 123(b), 135
Edmund Sumner: 22, 38
Jonathan de Villiers: 82, 84, 88
Richard Waite: 9